Re-Boot Britain by ch minds on Europe and Brexit

To Dave

Strategies, skills and stories to change ingrained folklore, fables and fantasies about Brexit populism

with my best wishes & thanks

A Better Britain in a Better Europe
for a Better World

APR 2022

Peter Cook
www.brexitrage.com

Contents

Introduction

PART I – New beginnings

PART II – Strategies for Brexorcism

PART III – Tales of Brexorcism

Part IV – Defence against the dark Brexit arts

Dedication

To my two sons, Thomas and James. May you live to see the end of Brexit and peace in the world. Having excelled at learning you are equipped to ride the storm whatever happens. Wishing you every happiness for a more enlightened world.

To Alison, who has put up with nearly six wasted years of Brexit nonsense from our government with patience, grace and support, all my love.

To my mother-in-law Eileen, who always put her grandchildren first and who passed away a couple of years ago. Unlike many older people, she voted to Remain in the EU, so that her grandchildren could enjoy the freedoms afforded by our membership of the European Union. May you rest in peace in the knowledge that you left the world a better place for your presence.

To my mum and dad, Doris and Tom, for whom I was a surprise arrival at 45 and 67 years respectively. Doris claimed I was a virgin birth. I am told that they said I was different and was left to be myself. I'm glad they had the wisdom to let me find out who I am. I have nearly done so finally.

To all at Re-Boot Britain, who join me every Monday to create campaigns in small or larger ways to build a better Britain in a better Europe for a better world, you are the true patriots in this peculiar adventure.

Grateful thanks to Judith Spencer, Helen Gibbons, Susanna Leissle and Irina Fridman for being a constant source of inspiration towards the writing of this book. Paul Cawthorne provided the 350 ++ EU freedoms at the end. I will wait 350 years for the benefits of Brexit to reveal themselves ...

Introduction

Why we still need this book

I was in my late 50s when Brexit began. I am now over 60 and Boris' Brexit came out of the microwave, 'gas mark four', burned to a crisp. Brexit will come undone in the coming months and years, due to the inherent contradictions that were 'baked in' Boris' oven, such as Northern Ireland, frictionless friction, Russian influence, job losses and simple economic and business issues. As I write this book, it has been revealed by HM government's public accounts committee that Brexit offers Britain no economic benefits at all. Still a few ardent Brexiteers from the 17.4 million, duped by our snake oil salesmen, cling on to hope, hopelessness, a blue passport and a unicorn, whilst Nigel Farage has been reduced to offering mother's day video messages for his dwindling fan base.

Speaking personally, Brexit will not affect me either positively or negatively, so I don't write this book from a personal interest. Outside my anti-Brexit life, I am an author, business consultant and keynote speaker who has always traded on a worldwide basis. I am fortunate as I don't work in an industry that relies on movement of goods across continents, nor are my margins so thin that they are critically threatened by increased costs of doing business due to Brexit. I am not a fisherman who was promised a great catch, nor a closet racist who thought that my job would be taken by a Pole. I am not a nurse who was promised £350 million every week to properly fund our NHS. In fact, I am pretty sure I'll be in a shallow grave by the time that any of the supposed Brexit benefits materialise.

Even 18th century retro-Latin imperialist adventure capitalist Jacob Rees-Mogg bragged that we will get nothing back from Brexit for 50 years … I am impatient in the age of COVID … not for myself, but for future generations. And the softly-softly approaches used by some of the central Remain organisations have largely assisted us in getting a 'boiled frog Brexit'; so slow that we (the frogs) hardly notice our slow declines and eventual deaths. This makes any approach to undoing Brexit especially difficult, as it requires a large majority of people to have their lived experiences changed by Brexit realities, which will only be visible in slow motion and in small doses.

Setting Brexit and COVID aside for a moment, we are merely responsible landlords of planet earth. If we do well in our lives, our aim should be to leave the planet in a better state that when we arrived. If the nature of our life and work does not allow us to answer that call, we must at least be guided by the principle of 'do no harm'. We owe it to our children, their kids and the planet to do our best and stand up to those who would do harm in pursuit of narrower and more destructive short-term goals.

Whatever you were sold in 2016, it becomes apparent that Brexit is a narrow ambition that continues England's love affair with disaster capitalism, lower standards of environmental stewardship and increased carbon footprints from more global trading. This is all happening at a time when the drive to solve world problems requires greater levels of collaborative leadership and co-dependency. Complex world problems require joined up thinking instead of splendid isolation and 'I am alright Jack and Jill' behaviours.

This diagram illustrates the basic problem of how great leaders see the world versus voters who were brainwashed by our Brexit snake oil salesmen. Boris Johnson won the 2019 election by aligning himself with the concerns and aspirations of this voter but without any intention of delivering on any of the so-called people's priorities. As I write this, it becomes painfully obvious that Johnson's only priority is Johnson.

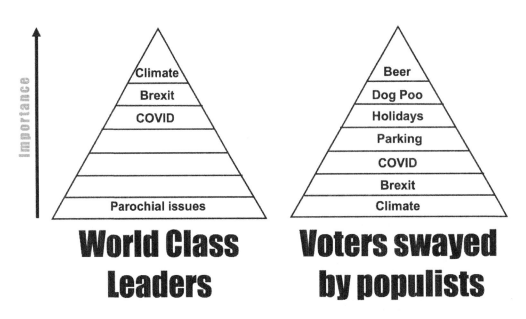

- Although the impact of COVID is in the here and now, it is merely a crisis in the mid-term, whereas Brexit is a long-term disaster affecting Britain. I coined the term

'Britastrophe' to describe the toxic cocktail of COVID x Brexit as a particularly English catastrophe.

- On the world stage, climate change is a much greater global problem than Brexit, but is, for some voters, far away, and thus ignored. We must learn to be responsible custodians of planet earth. Brexit threatens not to insulate Britain but to isolate it in a world that desperately needs more collaboration and co-operation.

- Worse still, Brexit takes Scotland, Northern Ireland and some parts of Wales and England down with it. To what purpose? I am still waiting for answers as I keep the conversation with Leave voters open in all social settings.

We change minds one by one through conversations. Short-term parochial thinking requires us to continue the conversation about Europe and Brexit with people across the entire Leave – Remain – Rejoin spectrum, many of whom now have terminal Brexit apathy. These difficult conversations are made even more difficult if we conduct them using socially distanced means due to COVID restrictions. It is far easier to 'Brexorcise' someone face to face than it is on social media.

This book equips you with strategies, skills and stories to help you have these difficult conversations, be they in person or over social media and the web. Mind shifts require skill, extreme levels of patience, empathy, unconditional positive regard (UPR) for your subject and time, lots of it, sometimes spread out over several separate encounters. Over thousands of hours of fieldwork, it becomes apparent that, sometimes you need several sittings with your chosen subject, client or victim, depending on your viewpoint. This book provides a compendium of support in the areas of skills, patience and UPR. It will also help you use your precious time to greater value and impact. A Brexorcism does not require a master's degree in satanic rituals, nor the use of holy water on your subjects!

You may be asking yourself 'Surely it is too late to end Brexit? A piece of paper was signed on 31 December 2020 so isn't it all done now?' Brexit will end one way or another. However, many of us now suffer from what psychologists call 'learned helplessness'? This is the condition where people believe that there is nothing they **can** do to alter the course of Brexit. Nor **should** they interfere, due to misguided notions of 'democracy', or 'the will of the people'. In other words, 'we can't do anything' and 'we must not do anything'.

My own brother who voted to Remain is part of what the Rt Hon Ken Clarke calls the 'indifferent majority' and has quoted 'the will of the people' as a reason not to get involved in resistance. In truth, he is easy going and it is easier to comply or look away rather than resist. Whilst I completely understand his position and that of others like him, these people are an absolute danger to the resolution of problems. I am quite sure that the vast majority of the good German people did not think that Mr Hitler would do anything awful in 1938. Some looked away. Simply stated, silence is assent.

Learned Helplessness I : The skill of the people

It is untrue that nothing can be done to change things. Some feel that five years of trying is indeed proof that we cannot move the dial on Brexit. There is also intense social pressure to airbrush Brexit out of the lexicon. I humbly suggest that trying something different is more important than to keep trying the same things. High level skills are needed to change minds that are based on people's very soul and identity and we need a cadre of change agents to do this. This book integrates concepts from psychology, social change and therapeutic intervention to arm you with a practical cocktail of strategies, skills and stories to lever changes in even some of most difficult circumstances.

Learned Helplessness II : The will of the people

Should we interfere with the will of the people? Yes. The notion that we should not interfere is a simple matter to debunk. Here are some reasons.

- Democracy is a continuous process and not a one-off project with a finish date. If it were, women would not have a vote, hanging would be legal and so on.

- Democracy informed by gross lies regarding the NHS, a 'tsunami' of immigrants, Turkey's accession to the EU, bent bananas, targeted Facebook ads, overspending on election campaigns are not the high-water marks of democracy.

- Since 2016, the demographics of the 52 : 48 Brexit vote have altered considerably with approximately two million Leave voters having spun off this mortal coil and up to three million young people becoming eligible to vote. Demographics alone create a significant shift in the 'will of the people'.

- As I write this, these demographics are also likely to be disproportionately affected by Boris Johnson's cull of older voters through his careless treatment of vulnerable people during the COVID crisis. 'Generation Greta' understand our connectedness and co-dependency better than what Roger Daltrey called 'My Generation'.

- People will change their minds when they connect the decline of their lived experience to Brexit. The change will happen even faster when the mainstream media they consume tells them so too. Thus far, the slow-motion impacts of Brexit and the parallel experience of COVID make it hard for people to isolate Brexit as a contributory cause of their problems. The COVID umbrella will eventually lift. Therefore we advocate activity in local and national media to change minds as well as 1:1 conversation.

Is it possible to reverse Brexit? We deal with this question in the scenarios we plotted for Brexit in our opening chapter. Reversing Brexit is possible but will not be easy, especially as divergence of standards embeds itself into Britain. But Brexit is a political process. So, if political will could be changed on both sides of the channel, the law would find a way to 'follow the politics'. However, as we have left the EU, several preconditions are needed for a re-entry to be considered :

1. Our Brexit belligerence has been largely informed by decades of the UK 'having its cake and eat it', i.e., getting our own way. The European Union would have to be convinced that our approach is sincere, in so far as it would not be a cynical attempt to continue our 'cakeist' approach to our relationship with Europe. Even some Remainers were telling me that 'the EU need us more than we need them'. English exceptionalism is not only the realm of Leave voters; even some Remainers have told me that 'the EU need us more than we need them'.

2. The EU would also have to be convinced that our re-entry would not be followed by another exit if our political leaders changed. I believe they would need to see that the Brexit ultras had been removed permanently from positions of influence and power. I doubt that they would accept a 'flip-flop' or 'hokey-cokey' Brexit. Whilst there are many viable routes and journeys to recalibrate the 'will of the people',

Brexorcism unplugged

The Brexorcist

Gavin Esler's encounter with the Brexiteer who was confused about having a democratic vote in a system she claimed was undemocratic (*TNE* #150) is typical of street encounters. Generally people want to achieve a change in mindset within minutes and become quite frustrated when it does not happen.

In many cases Brexit thinking is located at the level of beliefs or even wrapped up in peoples' identities. Change at these levels require special skills along the lines of a religious conversion. A Brexorcism takes time, extreme patience and considerable skill.

Peter Cook
Kent

Mindshift requires skill, extreme levels of patience, empathy, unconditional positive regard (UPR) for your subject and time, lots of it, sometimes spread out over time.

You cannot hope to do this whilst shouting at the opposition at a street stall or march. It needs a relationship over time.

if a referendum were to be used, it may need a super-majority to gain acceptance by the people, even though our first Brexit referendum was let through with a simple majority.

3. One could argue that setting a higher bar is itself unfair but it may be required. I explore alternatives under Strategies to join the EU anew. These include a general election with a Rejoin manifesto promise, Unfortunately, the main parties remain tight-lipped on their Brexit stance at the time of writing.

4. I am not convinced that we would of necessity have to accept the Euro currency and Schengen as part of a re-entry deal. Like all things it may be possible to trade these away. But I am quite sure that the EU would require what could be described as a 'no-mischief clause', having had nearly six years of their time, money and energy wasted by our vacillation.

5. The longer we leave any re-entry, the more 'undoing' will be needed in terms of divergence of standards. That said, if we wish to trade in global markets, market forces themself will act as a brake on the promised bonfire of standards. We may find ourselves having to meet EU standards to trade anyway rather than becoming purveyors of 'dodgy' goods and services. In the words of a colleague 'Every extra day with Boris the Clown in charge is an extra year before France agrees to let us back'.

6. The ultimate test is one of trust. Since 2016 and over a much longer time, trust in our politicians has been systematically degraded, through dramatic events such as the illegal prorogation of parliament, and via more mundane but no less harmful thousands of lies. Trust is easy to break but hard to restore. The European Union would be wise to set us some tests for our democracy as a pre-cursor to any re-entry.

Brexit is a gross example of selfishness, greed and avarice by a few disaster capitalists. These people successfully persuaded the masses that Brexit would be good for them, although the mounting body of evidence suggests otherwise. The Dunning-Kruger effect and misplaced nationalistic pride prevent some Leave voters from admitting that Brexit will not deliver any of the supposed benefits we were mis-sold so slickly and compellingly.

Learned helplessness

The condition when people do not believe they **can** or **should** affect the outcome of an event.

They also don't know what they **could** do about it to alter the outcome.

English faux politeness and the 'keep calm and carry on' spirit has assisted us in letting Brexit happen.

This is tantamount to having been sold a Porsche only to find that once the car is delivered it turns out to be an Austin Allegro without a clutch and some holes in the floor. In the case of Brexit, the slick sales patter was played out almost daily via snappy catchphrases such as 'Take back control', 'Brexit means Brexit', 'Pop Brexit in the microwave, gas mark 4', 'Let's get Brexit done', 'Put a tiger in the tank', 'Levelling up', 'Build back better' etc. Feelings overwhelm facts in the tsunami of data that arrived across our TV screens, computers and smartphones.

The information age is also in part responsible for the Brexit vote. Aside from interference in the voting process by Cambridge Analytica and underground targeted Facebook ads, another effect is in play here. Eminent neuroscientist Dr Daniel Levitin [1] established that each of us 'receive' some 34 GB of data daily. This more than the average person received in their entire life in 1800. One response to 'drowning in data' is to shut down from information overload altogether. Nigel Farage understood this well when he asked the nation to vote with their hearts and not their heads in the final week before the 2016 referendum. He knew that people had been numbed senseless by data. I am aware from conversations with both Remain and Leave voters, that some people quite literally tossed a coin to decide.

People tell me that the Brexiteers they have talked with do not listen, so they give up on them. Through thousands of hours of 1 : 1 conversation in cafés and bars I find it essential to listen to people's 'Brexit monologue' before rushing to any meaningful dialogue. You simply cannot expect your target to listen to you until you have invested sufficient time and energy in listening empathetically to their viewpoints, however much you may disagree with them.

Spending time listening also allows you eventually to establish a platform of expertise if they are to listen to you in preference to their own trusted advisor, be it Nigel Farage, Michael Caine or a bloke in the pub. Some level of change can occur by allowing these people to vent their feelings of rage, disappointment, and regret about their lives without intervention. One of the techniques in this book is quite simply what George Michael would have called 'listening without prejudice'.

---

[1] Read more about the information age in Brain Based Enterprises (Routledge).

Mischief not managed

Dominic Cummings said on Twitter : "In 2017, the EU showed its own slides that a Canada-style free trade was the only relationship available to the UK. Now they say that offer is not on the table after all Michel Barnier what has changed?"

Barnier reflects in his book My Secret Brexit Diary : "In reality, nothing at all has changed! And our staircase shows very well that it is possible for a third country to have a more ambitious relationship with the Union than a free trade agreement, for example by being in the internal market like Norway, or in the customs union like Turkey.

It is the UK, with its red lines (regulatory autonomy, no substantial financial contribution to the EU budget, end of the free movement of persons, no jurisdiction for the EU Court of Justice, independent trade policy close brackets that has closed these doors one by one. So, it is the UK that has opted for the kind of free trade agreement that the Union has concluded with South Korea, Canada and Japan.

And when it comes to the UK, there are many particularities to consider. Our geographical proximity, for one : we are 5000 kilometres from Canada, while on the island of Ireland we are zero kilometres from the UK. And then the intensity of our trade : €516 billion with the UK in 2018 as compared with €54 billion with Canada.

Brexiteer politicians have tended to compare 'eggs with onions' when banging the table making demands that are not equivalent".

Occasionally and usually after a longer period of patient listening, it is possible to separate their feelings from the causes of these feelings. We must carefully separate Leave voter frustrations from their biased view that the EU is the root cause of their grievances. Once we achieve this, we have a possibility for a 'Brexorcism', a minor or major shift in their beliefs about the world and about Brexit and the European Union in particular.

This book provides strategies, skills and stories to help you change minds, whilst helping you to look after yourselves in the process. I use the word Brexorcism not because I am expecting you to throw holy water at your subjects! Nor do I expect you to have to deal with people whose heads and viewpoints rotate 360 degrees.

We are generally dealing with quasi-religious beliefs or even identity level change (how they see themselves), where Brexit is intimately linked with people's sense of self, Queen, country, flag and so on.

The Brexit Brain

When we engage with a Leave voter, we are sometimes challenging people's beliefs of who they are or the very why of their being. As I have mentioned already, this requires skill, time, patience and flexibility on your part. As a brexorcist, you need massive supplies of resilience to face your subjects, clients or victims, depending on how you prefer to see them! Below is a slightly belligerent view of the mind of the Brexit voter. Of course, it is generalised, but this is what we face. It requires us to suspend our beliefs about our subjects and take their views on board at face value.

This book is not just about changing minds on Europe and Brexit ghostbusting. Where Brexit leads, Trump, Putin, Lukashenko and others follow. Just as sure as ladies' hemlines rise and fall for no identifiable reason with the whims of fashion every year, populism and the rise of the far right in difficult times are also fashion statements that others follow. So, you will find this book of immense value if you are trying to fight theatres of populism anywhere in the world.

The wonderful work of @AidanGrooville on Twitter

Brexorcism in action

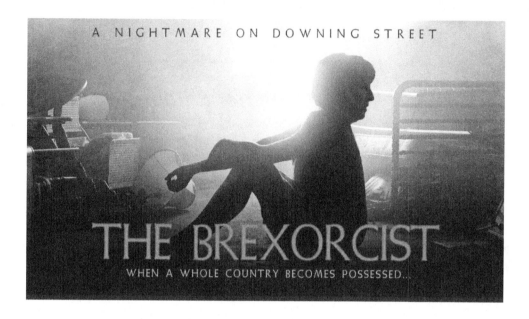

"The argument for Brexit has changed. Once it would be the easiest thing in human history and would create an earthly paradise. That argument has looked ever more dubious for some time. Now Brexit must happen despite all the horrors that it brings because ... the will of the people ... betrayal of democracy ... Brexit is going to be less horrible than World War Two according to Ann Widdecombe. There is a hard core of Leavers who will not admit they are wrong and we should point out their 180-degree changes of argument".

(Don Adamson, Kent Brexorcist

On New Year's Day 2017 I coined the catchphrase 'Break Brexit Before Brexit Breaks Britain' in the shower where I do a lot of my thinking. This was adopted and adapted quite widely. I realised that it needed updating. On New Year's Day 2019 I came up with a new mantra which remains relevant to anyone:

Re-Boot Britain

'We seek a Better Britain

in a Better Europe

for a Better World'

We are all in this together. It is about time we woke up to the fact that we must Re-Boot Britain. We can no longer live in unsplendid isolation in the 4th industrial age. Yes, we need to reform our politics and the very notion of capitalism if we are to survive. But turning our backs on problems and opportunities that we face as a global village is not a sensible response. Therefore, we must continue the conversation about Europe and Brexit.

The whole book on a page

Brexit is a quasi-religious set of beliefs, based on things like Queen, country, imagined notions of Englishness and a faux nostalgia about a lost golden age that never existed.

Five years of seeking the benefits of Brexit have failed to reveal any tangible advantages for most people who wanted to leave, making them the angriest winners on the planet.

Traditional change management approaches cannot be used to remove such stubborn beliefs. We need methods that are used in therapeutic settings at the deep levels of identities, values and beliefs.

To successfully 'Brexorcise' someone requires skill, considerable patience and time. Not everyone has access to such skills, the patience or time.

Whilst protest is a 'push' strategy for change, the 'pull' strategies offered in this book are often more effective, even though they take longer and require more skill. We need to be skilled in all the strategies and tactics to successfully change minds on Brexit

I advocate personal communication strategies in the book (face to face, telephone, online encounters). Social media changes our approach and is less effective.

We can make change happen by writing to MPs, especially those worried about the impact of Brexit. We can also work by gaining credible inputs into national and local media alongside social media amplification.

One of the best ways to change minds is to keep it personal, by meeting or phoning a Leave voting friend or Remainers with Brexit apathy.

Reasons to be cheerful

We have reached 'Brexit oblivion' on both sides of the false binary debate that has atomised our United Kingdom. Brexit voters are rightly tired of Remainiacs, proselytising, cajoling, shouting behind TV reports, singing, meme making and so on. On the other side of the divide, some Remainers have attempted to hug Brexit supporters to death, 'killing them with kindness, understanding and warm fuzzies'. There's nothing wrong with humanistic behaviour and what therapists call 'unconditional positive regard', but these are only part of the palette of strategies needed to transform identity-based paradigms about Brexit. We need to be competent across the full range of skills or work with others who are to achieve the required changes.

Remainers sometimes make the mistake of trying to convert Brexiteers to their viewpoint – a full Brexorcism or a 360-degree conversion. This resembles an approach of a zealous evangelist. In reality, a minimum viable outcome is to take your subject(s) to a point of indifference or a sense of doubt about Brexit.

Some Remain supporters are now paradoxically convinced that we must follow the 'will of the people', especially if that avoids civil unrest or perhaps worse, social disapproval within your circle of friends. As an extreme example, one husband threatened to divorce his wife if she continued to talk about Brexit, even though both voted to Remain. If your friendships are strong enough, they will withstand a difficult conversation or three about Brexit. If you face stresses and strains with friends and family, strengthen the relationships.

"Hanging on in quiet desperation is the English way
The time has come
The song is over
Thought I'd something more to say"

(Pink Floyd – Time)

It's all about the bass

The question that should be troubling people some six years after the referendum is the one that asks the Buzzcocks' Brexit question 'What do I get?'. It's entirely reasonable and relevant to ask what benefits are on offer to our fellow citizens if we are to endure some 50 years of pain to get there. It is a question I have asked tirelessly during thousands of hours of street encounters and the one I still cannot get any sensible answers to from the common man or woman. The best one came from the man I bumped into on the banks of the river Swale underneath the bridge to Sheerness. He wanted to leave the EU so that he could land a 5 lb bass from the Swale in Kent. After an hour's conversation, he realised that laws about fishing were there to protect the species and admitted that his dream was unlikely to be realised by Brexit.

Another man in Kent was willing to throw all the benefits of EU membership away because he thought that garlic was used too much in the local cafés and restaurants. After my probing, he admitted that he was really referring to the fact that he did not like pizza or kebabs. He too began to realise that the EU had not foisted these food outlets upon him. So far, the pizza parlours and kebab joints remain in the high street after Brexit, alongside a lot of café run by foreigners, who serve English breakfasts!

Although these answers seem ludicrous they do illustrate how parochial concerns often overwhelm macro-economics and global questions of trade and justice etc.

in my area of 'Brexit Central', some people even believe we have already 'done Brexit'. Every time I attended events at parliament with stalwart anti-Brexit activist Steve Bray, you can count on a few hands the number of Brexiteers who show up as an angry mob, sometimes dressed as mythical figures such as King Arthur. Once this appears on television in pursuit of 'balanced reporting', it appears that we are still equally divided in half. The truth based on actual 'feet on the street' is quite different. Our government have managed to preserve the illusion of the 'will of the people' equalling 52% despite demographic change and considerable doubt amongst Leave voters who now realise they were conned. This is gradually being reflected in the research on attitudes as they are revealed through various surveys.

This book will help you :

- Change minds on leadership for a complex world. In my real life I am a leadership expert … don't you just hate experts, ha! However, I do know something about the artform and have applied myself to the problem of leadership in a complex world in this book. For a deeper treatment on leadership see my book Leading Innovation, Creativity and Enterprise (Bloomsbury).

- Change minds on informed democracy for the information age, where we receive more data every day than we did in our entire lives in 1800. Instead of drowning in data we must swim with information rather than ignoring the tsunami of stuff that fills our lives daily. For a deeper treatment on the 4th industrial age see Brain Based Enterprises (Routledge).

- Deal with parliamentary paralysis in other words, the stuckness of our political parties to speak out about issues. We have Brexit in part because there has been little effective opposition to it over the last six years, across the board of parliament. All opposition within the Conservative party has been met with the iron fist of mob rule by an increasingly hard-line government. The COVID crisis has exacerbated the problem. It is harder to hold government to account, and we are sleepwalking towards dictatorship in Britain.

- Deal with Brexit apathy; to change minds so we stop the rush into Brexit self-harm. Brexit apathy is exemplified by capitulation to the stock phrase of Boris Johnson /

Dominic Cummings 'Get Brexit Done'. It is always a mistake to make a bad decision just because you are bored with the decision. You would not buy a house if it was unsuitable just because the estate agent had bored you into submission. I submit that Brexit is a much bigger decision than a house purchase and requires more scrutiny.

- Overcome the sheer despair of offering reasoned debate to Leave voters, only to be shouted at with chants and platitudes such as 'Get Over It – We won – 2-Nil – We got are country Back – End Off'. Many of you reading this will be painfully familiar with such responses. The smart move is to realise that 'if what you are doing isn't working, do something different'.

- Cope with verbally and physically aggressive Leave voters in their attempt to silence democracy. Over nearly six years I have had a bottle of cheap wine (disappointing that it was cheap) thrown over me, was threatened and had pictures taken for identification by Tommy Robinson extremists. I was also punched in the face, receiving two black eyes, by seven people who had run out of words to conduct a dialogue. An ex-policeman sent threatening letters to my family about 'democracy' and attacked my property because I have posters in the window of my house. I remain unapologetic about the delusion of Brexit.

- Win the battle for hearts and minds in populist mainstream media. The 2016 referendum resulted in Brexit because much of the population consume their news from just a few sources. Those sources have systematically distorted facts about our relationship with the EU over decades. It is therefore no surprise that biased, distorted and misinformed beliefs have been etched onto some people's minds. To reach into the minds of those people means being, briefer, more direct and punchier, whilst backing up our arguments with quality information for those who wish to dig deeper. Instead of copying the populists, we must better them. Let's 'dumb up' rather than 'dumb down', using headlines to reach people, and quality information to give people the ability to conduct their own critical thinking.

- Heal strained relationships with friends and family after Brexit, at home, on the streets and on social media. Friends and family present a special case and I am aware that many people have made unofficial pacts not to discuss Brexit for fear of ruining relationships. My deepest regret is that my 81-year-old sister continues to believe that she will be invaded by millions of German rapists in Tonbridge, but I did say that a Brexorcism needs huge doses of patience. Paradoxically, the closer you are to your subjects, the harder this can become.

- Ride the roller coaster of personal emotions that Brexit uncertainty has thrown at us – what J.K. Rowling calls 'Defence against the dark Brexit arts'. Gaslighting by our government has made some people question their sanity. The skills in this book are equally applicable to the healing process that needs to take place in Brexit broken Britain.

- Be more effective on social media in debates about Brexit and other contentious issues. Social media is devoid of the human expression of face-to-face dialogue. This presents specific challenges where much of the nuance of communication is lost. I give this special treatment in Part III.

In Part II and III of this book, I set out strategies, tools and techniques that I and others have used over many years of full-time anti-Brexit activism. They are illustrated with stories giving examples as to how to turn around some of the most closed minds on the subject. This is to offer inspiration, support and practical examples to others. Of course, not everyone's mind can be changed. Our choice of target is very much part of a successful Brexorcism. We are after Leave voters who have, at least, doubts about Brexit realities rather than far-right zealots who have not and will never move.

I have also included some examples of 'glorious failures', so you can find alternative strategies that work. Failure is a better teacher than success. In the end, all such work is highly situation dependent. Just because something does not work in one circumstance does not mean it won't work in a different situation.

These approaches are still needed, despite our exit from the European Union. We cannot rely on what is glibly called 'demographic change', or crudely put, deaths, to change the nation's views on Brexit. This book is also useful against any populism where ideologies take precedent over critical thinking and pragmatism; or you can apply it to climate change and other so-called 'wicked global problems' [2].

Some of the stories that are embedded into this book is sublime, others verge on the ridiculous. I have tried not to be too serious in putting these stories together, as humour oils the imagination. However, I am deadly serious about having fun whilst defending myself against the dark Brexit arts and conducting Brexorcisms'. In other words, undoing embedded quasi-religious beliefs about Brexit, associated myths and legends.

Are you ready to help flush Brexit?

Peter Cook, April 2022

---

[2] The term wicked problems was coined by Rittel and Webber in 1972
https://en.wikipedia.org/wiki/Wicked_problem

Brexorcisms summed up

A Brexorcism needs skill, patience, unconditional positive regard (UPR) and time.

This book arms you with expert knowledge, skills and attitudes of influence and persuasion, drawn from psychology, sociology and therapeutic approaches to change.

Whilst only you can give the time to change minds, the book will improve the value and impact of the time you spend changing minds about Brexit.

PART I

New beginnings

Brexit scenarios 2021 – 2031

In my work as a business consultant, I have used scenario planning as a 'gaming' technique. In particular, to help companies such as Johnson & Johnson and Pfizer anticipate and respond to alternative futures. Scenario Planning [3] was popularised by Royal Dutch Shell who was widely regarded as being ahead of its time in helping others to understand complexity and uncertainty.

A fortuitous meeting with Vince Cable re-ignited my enthusiasm to think about some of the more likely combinations of events that could lead to the death of the Brexit beast. Vince was an ex-Shell employee and fellow scenario planner. He and I agreed that it was probably impossible to game all the possible permutations. However, it was at least possible to consider the end coming, in either one of three directions :

1. Internal combustion, put crudely, 'heat without light', or;
2. From a toxic combination of external shocks;
3. More likely, a combination of both internal and external effects, inner political civil war combined with a tsunami of socio-economic and political events.

We are in disruptive times. Linear planning perspectives no longer apply. Just consider these examples that illustrate the unlikely, unwitting and criminally insane approaches of our government in recent times :

*   How unlikely it was that Theresa May would 'get into bed' with the DUP?
*   Who knew that Boris would expect the taxpayer to fund the cost of stockpiling food, drugs and fuel as a strategy to frighten the country into submission and as a 'game of chicken' with Michel Barnier?
*   Who would have predicted that our government would expect people to exist on a what has euphemistically been called a 'reduced diet' to get us through a No Deal Brexit? Would Johnson also have expected Pease Pudding and Marrowfat Peas to become gentrified as a national favourite dish on Jamie Oliver's TV programme?
*   Who could have foreseen that our government would engage a shipping company with no ships to reassure us about transport of food and medicines, or suggest that

---

[3] Find out more on scenario planning at https://en.wikipedia.org/wiki/Scenario_planning

Ireland should be subjected to famine in order that we can strike a better deal with the EU?

- Who would have thought that Matt Hancock would look away whilst people died in care homes, so he could bring the 'prize of Brexit' home for The Brexit Party?

Brexit will therefore unravel of because of/due to its own contradictions. I believe this will be sooner rather than later from our earlier work on the scenarios which follow. Brexit's implosion will come from either what I call external socio-economic, political, environmental shocks or 'internal combustion', due to the underlying inherent instability of the Tory party and the self-destructive nature of Brexit, which has already claimed two Prime Ministers and cost £66 000 000 000 in waste.

During 2021, I worked with over 100 people of all persuasions across Europe, to develop some plausible scenarios for our eventual re-admission to join the European Union anew. Scenarios are a strategic planning tool that describe 'the history of the future'. Originally developed for long range business planning scenarios are a tool that enables us to 'prepare to be prepared'. A good scenario is not so fantastic that it is discounted as science fiction, nor is it so close to current reality as to be discounted as being 'boring'. The political, economic, social, technological, legal and environmental scenarios we developed are presented here as a series of stories an aid to your own thinking about how we might bring about our re-admission to the EU which we examine later.

I guarantee that they will be both accurate and of course faulty, as we indulge in the dangerous game of making predictions about a disruptive and mercurial situation. The many moving parts in these scenarios may of course interact in different ways. Nonetheless the group considered these to be plausible routes and journeys which will set the tone in terms of responses to external events.

Breadline Britain

By 2031, the impact of The Brexit Hunger Games had been fully felt through civil unrest, the fragmentation of traditional politics and the formation of The People's Progress Party (PPP), formed from the fragments of Labour, Lib Dems, the influence of powerful individuals such as Gina Miller's True and Fair Party, a merger with The Green Party and memoranda of friendship with the independent governments of Scotland, Ireland, Wales and The European Union. Although The PPP could not stop the damage done by Brexit, Brexit carnage had eventually unified the people against the remnants of the

Conservative party, allowing a return of some of the more moderate conservatives to public life. This took place after an attempted takeover by Jacob Rees Mogg and following the worst riots ever seen on the streets of Britain in 2022, after the impact of Brexit on food supplies, gas and electricity supplies, the three-day week, drinking water safety issues and availabilities of goods and services previously taken for granted. One of the earliest acts of the PPP was to prosecute various culture carriers of Brexit, assisted by The Good Law Project. In 2026 a group of these people were jailed for various offences, including Boris Johnson, Mark Francois, Nigel Farage, Lord Bethel, Daniel Hannan and Priti Patel.

The PPP was formed in 2023 in a complete volte face of traditional politics after panic set in with Putin's advances in Europe and the breakdown of the Conservative party. People were selected for office, based on rigorous selection methods and then elected by people's assemblies. Whilst the party had some politicians drawn from the best of the crop, it was formed from people from business, the arts, community leaders, public figures and so on. This was informed by the insight that some celebrities and sportspeople were more skilled and popular than Westminster politicians. However, this was no populist uprising. The PPP insisted on informed democracy, fought the election in 2024 on some old-fashioned ideas about truth, fairness, trust, reforming politics and healing the country. They won most of the votes but lost the election to the Conservatives due to the existing First Past The Post (FPTP) system, which Labour had failed to confront and which eventually led to the breakup of the Labour party. The PPP's meteoric rise was based on some very good campaigning, based on an 'Enough is Enough' message and a promise to make a Better Britain in a Better Europe through Better Politics. This included plans for electoral reform. It had become clear that the European Union felt they were better off without Britain at the table and, although they had left the door open to joining the EU, it would come with some important pre-conditions. The most important one was for a complete removal of the Brexit ultras from power, to avoid a 'Hokey Cokey Brexit', in other words, an in / out / shake it all about approach to EU membership. Other items such as Schengen and Euro membership were negotiable depending on whether they felt that our standards of democracy were acceptable and the degree to which English exceptionalism and cakeism had been removed from the political culture. Some former Brexiteers hid in the shadows rather like people did from 1975 until 2016.

Breadline Britain tipped over in May 2022, when children were seen crying in the aisles of Dudley Tesco, as their parents fought over the last packets of frozen chicken nuggets, Pampers and Haribo, brought about by lorry driver / fuel shortages and lack of carbon dioxide supplies.

Brexit lessons from Michel Barnier

"Jeremy Corbyn is a paradoxical character. He remains ideologically faithful to old, internationalist commitments. This is what led him to approve of Brexit, since he persuaded himself that Europe is only a vehicle for globalisation, and a huge supermarket".

My Secret Brexit Diary – Michel Barnier.

An angry woman was heard to say 'I voted to get my country back, but not for a chicken run and nappies. I was duped'. Once full Brexit food import restrictions kicked in on July 1st 2022, the situation rapidly deteriorated. Shortages were not limited, sporadic and selected. They were continuing, occasionally deep and they touched everyone in strangely different ways. Still one or two Leave voters celebrated the blitz spirit, egged on by Nigel Farage who continued to claim victory over imperial measures, something we have had throughout our EU membership. Laura from Basildon won a prize on 'Come Dine Without Me' and went to No 10 Downing Street. She was reported as saying "I'm actually not that hungry", when having an austerity lunch of pease pudding and faggots with Boris Johnson.

Government plans to mitigate foreign lorry driver shortages due to Brexit backfired badly into 2022. The 2000 army HGV drivers diverted to deal with the 100 000 foreign lorry driver shortage were quickly redirected to deal with the Winter of Discontent, which emerged because of the food and utility shortages and rationing of specific items. Attempts by food retailers to up HGV driver wages to £55 000 were of course welcomed by lorry drivers. However, it quickly became apparent that this would 'drive traffic' around the supply chain of drivers, as some refuse collectors, ambulance drivers, HGV drivers in other sectors etc. decided that they fancied a better wage. It simply created deficits in other areas and more disruptive effects. For example, waste was not collected in certain parts of Britain. The initial reaction of the public to the 'Keep on Trucking for Britain' campaign was positive but turned sour quickly, as people realised impacts on prices, NHS services and rotting food in bin bags.

A tipping point in the Brexit debate was the so-called sporadic 'Pigs in Blankets' famine of December 2022 where frantic parents fought for chipolatas in supermarkets after the supply chain broke down. Preceded by several marches for and wildcat disturbances at food depots in Britain, Jason Matthews (son of Bernard Matthews) was asked to join a government taskforce with Ian Botham and Roger Daltrey on the future of turkeys for Christmas. Botham promptly attempted to blame farmers for the problem and was squewered by Matthews, who was heard to say 'Bootiful'. Meanwhile M&S Chair and former Conservative party MP Archie Norman eventually caved in and said 'This is totally down to Brexit. Nothing to do with COVID and the product of a party I was once proud of, but which has now put Brexit ideology above pragmatism'. For the first time, the underground chasm in the Tory Party was exposed.

How Brexit Ends

Through deliberate or accidental seismic combinations of :

External Events

Internal Obstacles

"Jacob Rees-Mogg seeks an 'erotic spasm' for the hardest possible break from the EU".

Vince Cable

But Britain was not beaten. Boris Johnson, buoyed up by the birth of his third / twelfth son, Winston, whipped up enthusiasm for 'British Bulldog Spirit' and initiated a new scheme called 'Grow for Britain', where house owners were given a £50 grant to convert their gardens to allotments, using Afghans and Ukranians as live-in labour, as part of their cultural conversion under Priti Patel's orders. Johnson appeared on Gardener's World in a project with Monty Don to convert the No 10 rose garden into a cabbage patch after the scandals about 'Partygate'. This was swiftly followed by the delivery of Winston to offset people's thoughts about food shortages. In real life however, the British people found that micro farming celeriac and cabbages was not popular, especially in the middle of winter. They were also too preoccupied with parochial concerns to celebrate 'royal babies'.

Brits, freed from lockdown restrictions and loaded with cash sought to unload their excess financial baggage by holidaying in Europe and beyond in 2022 and 2023. But they faced a new problem. Sterling. In 2022, Sterling had parity with the Euro and in 2023, with the dollar, due to Britain's new standing in the world as a third country. Although some continued with their holidays, Rishi Sunak introduced restrictions limiting the amount of money taken on holidays to curb the Sterling crisis. The Daily Express was unable to blame the problem on 'Johnny Foreigner' and used the headline 'Pounded by Brexit'. Queues at passport control when the EU channel was empty made holiday makers irate, aside from the hassle and £30 per family charge to go into Europe. Meanwhile most staycation holidays in Britain were out of reach financially for many people, as prices were hiked due to supply and demand considerations.

Can't get no

Shortages continued at a deep level for two more years until 2024, but they never actually went away completely, despite the government's attempts to incentivise farmers to grow more crops rather than animal feed. Some items simply disappeared from shelves. Many were unexpected, such as bleach, diagnostic tests, pesto, tonic water, sun dried tomato paste and some medicines for rare critical medical conditions. As with all crises, human ingenuity finds a way. If an out-of-stock item was discovered in a particular town on a given morning, all the stock would be gone by 9 am and then sold on the black market. 'Only Fools and Horses' became the reality in trading scarce goods and every village had a character known as Del Boy. Clandestine banana trading was used as a kind of proxy to preserve community spirit as Del liked to say "Ave a Banana" to keep the customers satisfied when things they wanted were out of stock. Police noted a small rise in looting, not of money or property, but of vegetables from gardens. All the while Boris Johnson refused to accept support from the EU during the UK 'hungry gap'. This is the few weeks, usually in April, May and early June, after the winter crops have ended but before the new season's plantings are ready to harvest. Boris Johnson continued his campaign of deflection into 2023 after he swapped Carrie up for a Russian debutante who was working as a media relations executive at GB News. This followed Carrie's failure to host a fourth child for the Johnson dynasty and Stanley Johnson's unfortunate declaration on GMTV that she was 'barren'.

Little things seem to irritate more than the big-ticket items. Whilst people seemed prepared to shrug at the war in Ukraine, the £37 bn of their taxes wasted on fictional PPE and 150 000 unnecessary COVID deaths, they found queuing at airports almost intolerable whilst EU citizen lanes were empty. Even more humiliating was when it was discovered that the EU's new satellite system Galileo made GPS navigation much more accurate. This had serious implications for driverless cars and HGV's into 2027. Insurance companies started to offer discounts to drivers who had installed Galileo instead of the UK satellite system as the gold standard for driverless vehicles. British citizens were able to access Galileo from the EU on a paid for basis, much to the annoyance of PM Truss who had tried to over-rule access but was thwarted by a class action from the insurance industry supported by The Good Law Project.

Although Boris Johnson attempted to deflect the fact that Britain has systematically degraded its levels of food security over decades, people were more persuaded by the continuing food shortages in 2022 and the so-called 'Andrex Wars'. Strategies to pay lorry drivers extra by commercial companies backfired after it became obvious that these were taking staff away from NHS ambulance drivers and critical services. In any case smart young people who saw the future did not want to take up careers as lorry drivers as they saw the advent of driverless trucks in 2028. Some hauliers upgraded to LHV rather than training new HGV drivers. The trucks were more efficient, with lower GHG emissions per tonne transported. The combined effect of Brexit and the unattractiveness of the jobs meant that Britain's food and goods shortages became normalised. Despite the protestations of the remaining few Brexiteers that 'shortages would make men of us', most real men and women saw a return to WWII supply chains as a backward step for Britain and began to realise just how harmful Brexit had been.

The mainstream media became more fickle as a result of realising that they had backed the wrong horse with Brexit. GB News appointed a Brexit correspondent in 2023, whose sole job was to identify problems caused by Brexit and blame these on the Tory party. In truth it was a desperate move as audience numbers crashed following Nigel Farage's decision to move to Monaco 'for health reasons'. Dominic Cummings gradually continued his journey of attacking the Conservative party to the point where he released a book in 2023 about the critical mistakes from 2017 – 2023 in government Brexit Policy. The book 'My Brexit Mistake' was a revelation, in so far as Cummings openly criticised the implementation of Brexit, saving himself from being the subject of attention, by saying that his vision had been perverted by useless politicians. In 2022, The Daily Mail, Sun and Express began open warfare on Brexit and the government that caused it. They held back at backing Keir Starmer and the Labour party though, preferring to focus on their audience and casting themselves as supporting the people and not the politicians.

After a complete meltdown of the Conservative party in 2027 and the removal of the Brexit ultras from power with some being imprisoned, the PPP finally got elected in 2028 and began the business of joining the EU anew. This was preceded by the so-called 'Zimmer Riots' by pensioners, after free prescriptions were removed in 2026 on the road to privatisation of the NHS. The tipping point occurred after two pensioners glued themselves inside No 10 Downing Street on a visit of a delegation of elderly citizens to a VE Day commemorative dinner on 8th May 2025. This had been preceded by a series of wildcat strikes in the NHS. One or two very memorable protests had been dubbed 'Crapping for Carers' after a series of sporadic E-Coli outbreaks had occurred in hospitals due to water purification problems. An outbreak of legionnaires disease in Medway Maritime Hospital also claimed 735 lives. It seemed that lowering standards had entirely predictable effects which were not obvious to PM Sunak.

Never ready

By 2023, the implications of Britain's decision to leave Europe's internal energy market started to become visible. Initially it was simply steep rises in electricity bills. People were asked to remove additional lightbulbs from their homes by Grant Shapps who had become minister for power in 2023. Restrictions were also imposed on commercial buildings and corporate premises and these were floated on the general ambition of environmental need rather than Brexit induced desperation. Self-appointed wardens sprang up in some areas who were referred to as 'Mr Hodges' with their call 'put that light out' taken from Dad's Army.

The 'Build Back Better' initiative was confounded by hyper-inflation in the building industry and shortages of materials that led to a stop-start building cycle. Builders were initially happy about it as demand for their services increased and they could to some degree name their price. However, it paid back in terms of unaffordable homes and unemployment in the sector. Attempts by Alok Sharma, minister for reconstruction, to slash safety standards, remove listed building status, occupy the greenbelt and increase hours in the industry, were met with mass disapproval. As a result, many new housing developments were 'never ready'.

Bluff, bluster and bust

London made a bid for independence [4] in 2030 as news that the UK economy slipped from No 4 in 2015 to No 11 in 2029. This had been preceded in 2028 after the UK Brexit economy finally tanked. The Mail reported the headline 'England sick as a Brexit dog'.

The rot had started much earlier when Rishi Sunak removed the triple pension lock early in 2023. Although originally stated as a temporary measure, it became a permanent one as the astronomical bills for Brexit mounted up. This produced a generation of pensioners that were effectively living on the breadline, unable to support children and grandchildren, selling off their homes to pay for retirement and private care homes and increasingly privatised healthcare. This was compounded by further lowering of student loan thresholds which would see a generation of young people living below the poverty line, stagflation due to Brexit, as wages levelled off and National Insurance increased. Working people struggled to get well-paid jobs. Brexit economists struggled to find diversions to point the finger for Britain's problems elsewhere but the underlying logic of high structural costs and declining economic activity defined our early years of so-called freedom. Things became so bad in 2024 that some people in UK insisted on being paid in Euros. The Lugano Convention had still not been signed by 2026 but Britain continued to rely upon services to drive its economy, yet Lugano prevented UK from thriving in a post Brexit world. Save for an uptake in food production which happened as a necessity after The Hunger Games in 2022 with 'conscription' of 18-year-olds to work on farms, Britain was broken.

The new EU tax avoidance scheme came into force on January 1st 2022. Brexit supporters started to become angry that it meant that Amazon et al had to pay tax in the countries they operated in within EU countries, whilst Britain became a haven for companies who wished to avoid tax. This meant that people were exploited at work to even greater levels than before as compared with employment practices in more progressive countries in Europe. Thus, the dream of Brexit became ever more distant as the realities of deregulation began to become visible.

---

[4] We already see early signs of Londipendence https://www.londependence.party/

Contributory factors to the decline of Britain as a world economic power began quickly after Brexit, with a vote for Scottish independence in 2023, proposals for Irish unification in 2025 and a decision by Wales to seek independence in 2027. Their economic contributions to the Treasury disappeared too, although Boris Johnson tried to hold back Scottish independence [5] by moving UK public service agencies out of Scotland. However, Scotland had produced a detailed plan to unite the people and take things forward, profiting from having the best of both worlds; a land border to England and a place in a market of 500 million people. This would spawn the development of international travel hubs in Edinburgh, financial centres in Glasgow alongside traditional industries and a properly sustainable community in the highlands and islands of Scotland. Once the contagion began, it was unstoppable, with London seeking to make itself a Crown dependency and Cornwall, Merseyside, The North-East, Birmingham and Greater Manchester asking for Regional parliaments.

In other disruptive and unexpected events, cybercurrency became regulated as the bitcoin economy collapsed in 2025. Jacob Rees-Mogg lost everything in 2024 in the sterling crisis, after overplaying the markets with his financial trading company. The Daily Express headline said 'How the mighty have fallen', whereas The Sun ran with 'Mogged off'. The Brexit illusion of Singapore on Thames came back to bite people where it hurt most. Never more had bluff, bluster and bust made more sense to the blustering blowhards of Brexit.

Rough trade

Meanwhile, Brexit trade deals failed to make up for EU losses. The widely vaunted £39 billion savings paled into insignificance when compared with the costs of doing 'fire sale' deals, to save face in the wake of 'Britastrophe'. 'The Truss' talked confidently of conquering the US, China, The far east and other blocs, but the harsh reality was hard to avoid. The Australian trade deal whose advantages to the UK amount to 0.02% of GDP after 15 years was not noticeable. The tariff cuts gained were worth £1 per UK household per year. For comparison the UK Australia deal was worth £14 billion as compared with £660 billion for the EU. It became obvious that the Australian deal had the side effect of lowering of UK standards for meat and inflicted lasting and increasing damage to the UK beef industry.

---

[5] More on Scottish Independence at www.brexitrage.com/scotland

By 2025, Britain had failed to secure trade deals with US, as it became clearer that Northern Ireland had been sacrificed for 'the greater good' of keeping up appearances.

In 2022, the foreign secretary announced trade deals with Moldova, Saint Vincent and The Grenadines, and The Marshall Islands. Beneath the bluster of the headlines, most of these were 'cut and paste' jobs of existing regarding arrangements with no additional value for Britain and considerable upside for participating nations. The net worth of these trade deals barely registered on UK GDP although they were trumpeted at the Festival of Brexit, now a low-key affair in Bradford comprising a model railway layout of HS2, a few street stalls and some digital food banks.

Boris Johnson dubbed the new era as 'adapting to scale' but it was hard to hide the realities in so far that many of these states wanted market access to UK and freedom of movement as parts of a trade deal. The immigration 'problem', far from being solved, became more pronounced with an ageing British population and a growing demand for social services, care and healthcare.

At the same time, the European Union continued to balkanise its structures, accepting Ukraine into membership in 2024 and then Albania in 2027, setting strict conditions on human rights and democracy for Turkey to join five years from 2028, forging major links with China and playing a major role as a bridge between the US and Eastern empires. They did this whilst maintaining stability amongst the 27 EU partners, against the odds predicted by Nigel Farage et al. The EU began to emerge as one of the few players with sufficient size to face down mega corporation's demands to avoid tax and this improved its image in the eyes of those who had seen it as an 'evil empire'. Rather the European Union became a force for good in the world and some of its much-criticised decision-making processes a little nimbler in the process. It was one of the few things it had to thank Brexit for.

Brexit realities

"Of course, Brexit means that something is wrong in Europe. But Brexit means also that something was wrong in Britain".

Jean Claude Junker

"An Englishman, a Scotsman and an Irishman walk into a bar. The Englishman wanted to go so they all had to leave".

Anon

Back to the future

The Bank of America's 2021 prediction about Britain's financial status was to guide the decade, that the pound was to behave like an emerging-market currency, in terms of volatility. The pound had never been a strong currency. For example, it has fallen against the Swiss franc from Fr. 10 to the £ in 1969 to around Fr. 1.3 in 2021. The fall against the US $ was similar. The decline however was slow and generally passed unnoticed. The chronic deficit in the UK trading balance of payments was the main cause.

COVID masked the effect of Brexit, including its impact on exchange rates. The effect was felt as the EU's economy regained the full impetus generated by the single market whilst the UK's recovery remained shackled by Brexit bureaucracy. This was aggravated by the 'stand on our own feet' policy, enunciated by Grant Shapps, a policy reminiscent to those of communist Albania in the 60s and 70s, and by North Korea to this day. Trade relations centring UK on the other side of the world between the Pacific and Indian oceans did not rectify matters. Sterling fell below the value of the Euro in 2022, and below the dollar and Swiss franc in 2023.

Britain's status as an economic international power as measured in GDP was also affected by sterling's exchange rate. Having been 5th in the world for some time, we fell to 6th in 2021, having been overtaken by India whose higher growth rate ensured its position. France also improved due to Brexit stagnation and Eurozone recovery and meant that Britain reached 7th place in 2022. Italy took over 7th place before 2024 and we eventually fell to 11th place by 2031.

As the exchange rate fell, familiar scenes from the 1960s/70s alike returned. Mounting inflation, particularly on food prices, increases in the cost of living, civil discord and disorder, strikes. Whilst these were not general, they touched everyone's lives in different ways. The government resorted to exchange controls to stem the outflow of currency reserves as in the past which presented a further complication for industry. British holidaymakers, keen to party after COVID, found that they were rationed on the amount of money they were allowed to take abroad.

I fought the law

The 2020s was characterised by a number of removals of freedom in Britain, the very thing that was promised to people in the 2016 referendum. 'Take Back Control' was missing the object of that control i.e., government and not the people. In 2022, the government moved to cripple judicial review, to reduce the power of the law to interfere in its affairs. Additionally, they took further steps to remove power away from MPs by asking them to sign their rights away to object to policy decisions. The collective actions were dubbed as a 'Zombie Government' by Jess Phillips, shadow home secretary in 2023.

Further anti-democratic moves followed in 2022 when Priti Patel introduced a bill that required protestors to apply for licences to protest three months in advance of any actions and required them to pay for policing of any actions. This effectively closed most protests but encouraged others to act spontaneously under cover. In 2024, Voter id was used for the first time to discourage young voters. This was a major factor in allowing the Conservatives to regain power even through general antipathy towards them was at a high point.

Meanwhile the Conservatives continued to give their political cronies lucrative contracts without any scrutiny or competition. In some cases, they were quite unqualified to deliver the contracts and this caused great strain / amusement, depending on which way you look at the issue. For example, new contracts for rail were awarded to a Conservative farmer who had become bankrupt after food shortages had broken his business resilience. Despite his enthusiasm in naming the new TOC "The Broccoli Line", it turned out that competence in planting seeds did not transfer to industrial plant and equipment.

The eye of the Irish tiger

The situation in Northern Ireland and Ireland was reminiscent of the 1920s when the Irish national debt was written off in return for no opposition as to where the land border was drawn in the division of the spoils of war, leading to worse wars for 30 years from 1969 to the turn of the new millennium. The people of Ireland decided to reject a repeat performance. In the end, the Northern Ireland Protocol meant that food and fuel supplies continued to flow on the island of Ireland. Fuel shortages only ever reared their heads mainly in local ASDA branches in two counties, particularly because the Asda fuel supply chain could not differentiate between deliveries to the home counties vs those on the possessed counties. This presented the people of Ireland with stark comparison of EU membership with the Brexit of the mainland and drew Northern Ireland and Ireland closer together. Julian Smith (NI secretary) was more inclined to act than drift and took decisive actions to unify people and politicians. The rise of the Irish tiger was also spurred on by what happened in Scotland.

Scottish independence was a hard-fought battle and was emboldened by the move to celebrate 100 years of British rule in the six counties of Ireland that constitute Northern Ireland back in 2021. It galvanised Northern Ireland and Ireland to consider ways in which the social and economic benefits of unification could mitigate or even overwhelm traditional tensions between unionists and republicans. Scotland gave everyone some surprises about Boris Johnson's assumptions that Britannia could rule the waves. But it became clear that Johnson's notion of having your cake and eat it too could become a reality in Scotland's case, having the benefits of a land border with England and being able to profit from EU membership. The European Union received Scotland's bid for membership sympathetically and assisted by supporting various development programmes around sustainability, e-commerce, fisheries, shipping, infrastructure and business support in cities and remote areas in a digital world. This should have been obvious to anyone who watched the Irish miracle some decades ago as the EU supported improved transport networks and other areas of the Irish economy. However, it was not obvious to the Brexit ultras. As Halloween 2021 approached, a lot of things began happening behind the scenes to try and derail the Northern Ireland Protocol. They failed and eventually Sir David Frost was thrown under a bus by Boris Johnson.

The antipathy towards Brexit outside England escalated rapidly after Liz Truss broke the Irish Protocol in the summer of 2022 under cover of the continuing civil war in Ukraine and, in doing so, broke international law and the remnants of trust with the Biden administration. The US preferentially chose to develop trading and political relationships with the EU, based on size and political similarities. The atmosphere in Northern Ireland was tense for many months alongside movements in Stormont by the DUP.

On the upside, there was a net flow of international companies coming to Northern Ireland and Ireland to set up operations. In 2022 Ryanair pulled out of all Northern Ireland airports. This was followed by a gradual drift of shipping routes to circumvent mainland Britain. Once customs checks were factored in, it turned out that driving through Britain to reach Europe was incredibly tiring and costly on time. Onboard ships drivers could rest and recuperate and, of course the destinations in France offered much better access to Southern European destinations.

The plan 'Best of Both' for Scottish independence was a detailed document and there was a concerted attempt to reach all communities to unite the people. This would pay various dividends later, as people were united and committed to the various losses that would inevitably be taken from Westminster's intervention in areas such as public service jobs. Unlike Brexit, Nicola Sturgeon's approach was honest, direct and showed the people what they would lose but also how they would gain from the proposal. The slogan 'Together but Separate' conveyed the notion of continued collaboration with England but having greater independence in a much larger market. Increasingly, as England declined, it was Scotland that called the shots regarding trade and co-operation and not Westminster.

In particular, Scotland became an attractive place to locate for people wishing to sell services in the wake of the Lugano Convention remaining unsigned in Britain. COVID had finally put an end to the illusion that people had to work in cities and this spurred a desire to return to the country. The Scottish government offered attractive incentives for businesses and individuals to set up service-based businesses in Scotland. This magnetised skilled people away from England.

Although there was a fight between Westminster and Holyrood about national debt and various other pieces of sabre rattling, the EU were helpful in ensuring the Scotland could be given fair treatment as a smaller country, in return for various trade-offs around borders, just as Ireland had done in the 1920s.

Tensions eventually spilled over after PM Truss broke the Irish Protocol several times from 2022 to 2024, to deflect attention from Brexit carnage. This resulted in President Biden and then President Harris refusing to sign a US / UK trade deal.

In the intervening period from 2022 to 2026, trade links between Northern Ireland and Ireland were strengthened to the point that the idea of removing borders became a no-brainer. This was facilitated by improved transportation links between Europe and the island of Ireland and eventually GB became an irrelevance in terms of trade, save for exports from the island of Ireland.

Events in Stormont also eventually moved in favour of accepting the idea of Northern Ireland and Ireland having their cake and eat it too through unification and full alignment with the EU, leaving England and Wales as rule takers.

The empire strikes back

Brexit was predicated on a form of English exceptionalism that expected the Commonwealth to become natural partners in post-Brexit Britain. The reality was rather shocking. In 2028 Cyprus decided to leave the Commonwealth, after some surprising departures by others around the world. It was spurred on by Gibraltar's gradual separation from the UK, initially via its application to join Schengen in 2022, which had not even been noticed by most people.

Further afield, the empire behaved in ways that were perfectly understandable to the people but not to the government. Canada, South Africa, Singapore, Australia and New Zealand left the Commonwealth in 2030 after the Royal Family descended into farce, following the death of Queen Elizabeth II. This would be followed by other nations into the 2030s as the notion of a Commonwealth run by a weakened nation became an increasing national embarrassment. In 2028, a delegation of The African Union offered to send observers to UK General Elections to detect and eliminate corruption.

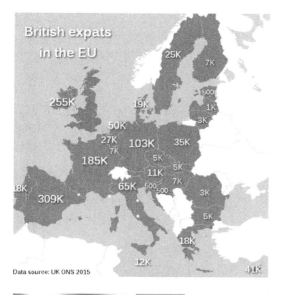

Did you vote to have your UK bank account removed?

Did you vote for US styled private health insurance in Europe?

Did you vote to lose UK job opportunities if you live in Europe?

Let's Re-Boot Britain

www.brexitrage.com

What the politicians won't say

This is the end my friends

It is never a good idea to pursue a strategy in the face of compelling evidence that it will not deliver a better future. All good business leaders know this and so do most serious politicians. The difficulty for Boris Johnson and his government is how to end Brexit **AND** remain electable. Johnson does not want to go down in history as the shortest-lived Prime Minister in history. A change to the 'parliamentary paralysis' that has locked Britain in a state of political entropy can come from a combination of actions on our part. Here's my 'Five A Day'. What are yours?

1. Continue to explain the benefits of being European and EU membership. Debunk items labelled project fear as Brexit reality. Many of the effects branded 'Project Fear' have already come to pass or are now starting to materialise, including David Cameron's prediction of war in Europe due to Brexit after 70 years of relative peace. It is becoming clearer that nobody voted to make themselves poorer or have fewer rights, even if they are unprepared to openly admit it. We do not need to make them admit it. We just need them to change their minds.

2. Challenge misconceptions that continue to occupy the minds of Leave voters, sometimes sensitively, sometimes provocatively, depending on the person / group involved. We will turn to these in subsequent chapters.

3. Keep asking your MP to have courage, in some cases, to begin growing a spine and occasionally, in some cases, to have a spinal implant. Point out gently or otherwise that they are unelectable if they do not stand up for the best interests of the country. This is written into their job description, so we are just asking them to do their job.

4. Keep talking about the state of play and the fact that Brexit can be ended. Speak with friends, family, colleagues, burnt out Remainers, Leavers in regret, Leavers in denial etc. to target the issue of learned helplessness.

5. Protest and get active locally in whatever way you can. Never let a day pass without doing something to 'Break Brexit Before Brexit Breaks Britain'.

This book deals with the slow but steady work of personal influence and persuasion needed to achieve your five a day.

Thinking about Brexorcism

My 'Five a Day'

Element	My applications
1. Continue to explain the benefits of EU membership. Debunk items labelled project fear as Brexit reality.	
2. Challenge misconceptions that continue to occupy the minds of Leave voters, sometimes sensitively, sometimes provocatively, depending on the person / group involved.	
3. Keep asking your MP to have courage, in some cases to begin growing a spine. Point out gently or otherwise that they are unelectable if they do not stand up for the best interests of the country.	
4. Talk about the state of play and the fact that Brexit can be stopped, to friends, family, colleagues, burnt out Remainers, Leavers in regret, Leavers in denial etc.	
5. March and get active locally in whatever way you can. Never let a day pass without doing something to 'Break Brexit Before Brexit Breaks Britain'.	

Strategies to join the EU anew

Some people believe that the only way we could consider joining the EU anew can come from an election or some other democratic process based on 'the will of the people'. Yet, we know that the Brexit referendum was won with only 37% of the UK electorate's approval. This came after considerable psychic distortion of the population's collective consciousness through lies, social media interference and a call by Nigel Farage to vote with your heart and not your head, in other words, not to think. This was an incredibly clever strategy by Farage however deplorable. He effectively asked people to engage their limbic systems aka their crocodile brains to overcome the confusion of the tsunami of information on the conscious mind. Elections are thus only one of several democratic routes to joining the EU anew. Alternatives include :

1. Normal parliamentary business : Shifts in opinion once Brexit carnage becomes widely visible followed by normal parliamentary processes to pass bills to mitigate the effects of Brexit, for example a Single market or customs union application. If supported with the combined weight of opposition parties, who are currently giving the government a free ride on Brexit, this may offer an incremental route back into EU membership. I am however a little cautious on the value of what is called 'logical incrementalism' and I will discuss this in the next section.

2. Via a general election : One could also envisage the levels of Brexit carnage to become so great over time that joining becomes an election issue again. Set against that possibility, people would have to conclude that Brexit was a cause or correlation with their lived experience. This has been difficult so far, due to COVID masking Brexit's effects, but that umbrella is slowly being removed as I write. For this reason, it matters that the word Brexit is not airbrushed out of the political lexicon. Labour have thus far boxed them into a position that makes a U-turn difficult but not impossible, but it seems that they cannot win an election without collaboration. Once again, we are in disruptive times and anything is possible.

3. Another referendum ... sigh : A new referendum could be offered even though I personally don't favour their use in their present form. However, a second referendum might be considered as a 'christening service' once the 'will of the people' had changed sufficiently through lived experience. Despite the first referendum having been conducted on a simple majority, it is likely that a second one would require a super majority of 66% This presents a very high bar and I would

argue that it is fair to use the same system to conduct a second vote i.e., a simple majority. We can debate the rights and wrongs of referenda as instruments of democracy after we have righted the wrongs of Brexit.

4. Things may become so bad that the idea of a government of National Unity (GONU) becomes feasible once again. In August 2019, a GONU seemed feasible until the opposition parties responded to Boris Johnson's temptation of a general election. Considerable social and economic and political disruption would be needed for such a scenario to be possible so I am guessing the probability is low, but nothing can be ruled out in a disruptive political environment. Present scandals with the Tory party and Putin may yet reveal more problems with the status quo.

All these routes are viable even if they have different probabilities and desirability. They are living proof that democracy is not a project with a fixed end but a continuing process, a point which is poorly understood by some Leave voters and ERG extremists.

Then there are what could be politely called the non-constitutional route:

1. Another less palatable alternative is mass rioting on the scale of the poll tax riots or a meltdown of civil society followed by crisis measures. Of course, the English 'do not do' rioting, so this is an improbable development, even in Brexit England's unpleasant land. At the same time, Priti Patel has already installed the means to crackdown on such measures by criminalising peaceful protests. Nadine Dorries, minister for cancel culture, has also acted to demonise heretics, journalists and other people who voice dissent in Brexit Britain. That said, sporadic civil unrest is possible in 2022.

Incrementalism versus all or nothing approaches

There are almost as many views on the routes to join anew as there are protagonists, Get PR Done, progressive alliances, GTTO, customs union, single market etc., and this is a major weakness of the movement. It was not always thus. In August 2019, the Remain movement was relatively united, but the lure of an election destroyed that unity and the movement once again fragmented into party political and other tribes. One of the main protagonists of the incremental approach is Lord Andrew Adonis, Chair of The European Movement, with his "step by step" and "brick by brick" catchphrases. One can see why Adonis' populist catchphrases are alluring, after all the best way to eat an elephant is allegedly slowly and in bite size pieces. The idea is that if we can maybe join the Single market, that takes us a step closer to joining anew is clearly an attractive vision for Remainers / Rejoiners.

English exceptionalism

"After nine months of negotiations, this is the last time I see David Frost, and our final exchange is cold and professional. He knows that I know that up until the last moment he was still trying to bypass me, my opening up a parallel line of negotiation with Ursula von der Leyen's office. And he knows that he did not succeed in doing so".

My Secret Brexit Diary – Michel Barnier.

However, the problems with Logical incrementalism may be summarised :

- Joining the Single market may well be met with the same levels of resistance as joining anew. In essence it is more cakeism on the part of the British, in terms of trying to mitigate UK industry's problems without necessarily offering many reciprocal benefits to the EU.

- If we were to succeed at solving the problems of a single sector e.g., farming, fishing, automotive etc. that community effectively has its needs settled and the desire to join anew dissipates with it. Divide and conquer is a well-known strategy to dissipate resistance.

- The longer we leave the matter, the more UK divergence from EU standards occurs. This simply makes any incremental adjustments we might wish to make more difficult, as we are not aligned on standards. In short, undoing the damage done by Brexit may be more difficult than wielding the damage itself.

- As already mentioned, the EU are enjoying their freedom from UK as I write and I doubt they will welcome a return to English exceptionalism any time soon. The whole psychological contract between Britain and Europe will need to be reset before we can consider a serious approach to join anew. My European sources tell me that the EU enjoy the fact that they no longer must deal with Nigel Farage and that they can now pursue European integration without the veto of a tiny island on the edge of Europe. The first signs of this new-found freedom have been shown in their rapid response to the Ukraine crisis and moves towards the building of an EU army European army. It is possible that such moves would likely have been resisted by Britain, as the continent's 'most violent state'.

So, although the 'all or nothing' approach is possibly 5 – 10 years on the horizon, it may allow for the kinds of adjustments to our democracy and the shifts in power necessary for UK to be listened to and treated seriously by the EU if we applied to join anew.

The political landscape of Brexit is so fluid and our government moves so fast to avoid being trapped that I believe it is a mistake to back any single horse in terms of achieving the needed reforms to put us in a position to join anew. Rather, our campaigning and political leadership needs to be agile, nimble and flexible to seize advantages as they come, whilst maintaining a long-term approach to joining anew. I am most impressed with the work of Gina Miller and her True and Fair Party as the most serious contender to refresh the thinking of traditional politics and politicians towards a better Britain in a united Europe for a better World.

Brexit freedoms

I read the government's 105-page document on Brexit freedoms. Some of my Remainer friends tell me there are no Brexit freedoms. They are not looking hard enough! I have come up with a long list of Brexit freedoms to counterbalance the cost of Brexit (see Part IV for the long list). These freedoms are currently standing at an eye watering **£128 BILLION** and predicted to outweigh the cost of COVID multiple times into the future. Of course, we have also already spent more on Brexit than all our contributions to the club over our 40 + years in the European Union, but hey ho, we got a blue passport. So, doomsayers, prepare for a shock! But here are some of the freedoms outlined in the government report :

Pints

For years I have been compelled to go into English pubs and say in a weakened voice "Can I have 564 ml of Champagne please?" No longer. I can now stride in proud and say "Stout Yeoman, I want a pint of foaming English brown beer in a straight glass". And it has a little crown on the side. As I drink the hoppy infusion, I am reminded of are Queen and Prince Andrew. It just gets better and better … Soon, we'll be able to have English Lions back on our eggs … HM government state that imperial units like pounds and ounces are widely valued in the UK and are a core part of many people's British identity. I don't know anyone of my own age that can count in stones, pounds and ounces. My sense is that this is a LIE.

Helping people to quit smoking. The UK is already recognised as a world leader in tobacco control and has made good progress reducing smoking rates. However, with around six million smokers in England and stark health disparities associated with smoking, more still needs to be done to help people to quit smoking. We have now launched a rapid independent review to identify which policies and regulatory reforms will be most impactful in supporting our 2030 Smokefree ambition, including where it may be beneficial to go further than the EU's Tobacco Products Directive allowed us to. We will set out proposals for our regulatory reforms in a new Tobacco Control Plan due to be published later this year.

Promoting healthy eating and preventing obesity. We are considering potential changes to our food labelling requirements relating to health, and how these can be done at pace. We also plan to launch a consultation on proposals to introduce new regulatory powers on the marketing and labelling of infant food and drinks to more effectively tackle childhood obesity.

Brexit freedoms summed up

Outright lies, provable by simple research. Not caused or correlated with Brexit at all.

Changes which are the result of Brexit but which entail significant downsides.

Vague and woolly policy aspirations with no Brexit causation or correlation.

Ephemeral items, of no real value but high imaginary value in terms of sovereignty.

Fifty pence freedoms

We now have the Brexit fifty pence piece back, although I confess I have not seen one of late. But it signifies the fact that we now have the Pound back as our currency. I did speak with a woman who told me that her dad said that we no longer had the Pound before Brexit. Did you notice that? I also note that Brexit 50 pence pieces are selling on e-bay for £750, although they are not rare. If Brexiteers really want to pay £750 for a 50 pence piece, I am happy to indulge them in this freedom so I have listed one, along with an empty bag of sovereignty.

Freedom to be racists and misogynists

Brexit affords people the freedom to be openly racist and misogynistic. The Metropolitan Police have taken full advantage of this freedom, murdering women, brutally attacking people of colour and, most recently, strip searching teenagers, tampering with tampons. In the words of Prince, "If there ain't no justice, then there ain't no peace".

Brexit freedoms - Filet o' fish

Scottish salmon fishermen report that Europeans still want our salmon, although exports have been hit to EU countries due to Brexit. Since Scottish salmon is a major Scottish export, salmon fishermen can hire entire containers to ship their goods to Europe, reducing the mountain of Brexit paperwork and other costs in their segment of the fishing industry. Sadly, this benefit does not exist for other fish varieties and the predicted decline in fishing continues, as predicted by the Remainiacs. And let's remember this is **Scottish** salmon. Once Scotland have independence, they will take this benefit with them. Scottish salmon and Whisky are major exports from Scotland.

Against the backdrop of the BBC's nationalistic drive to back Brexit on Farming Today, The Food and Drink Federation showed that Scotland's whisky and salmon exports were down by 11% and 6.4% respectively since 2019, with the UK's total exports of food and drink was down by £2.7 billion (-15.9%) in the first three quarters of 2021 – with £2.4bn (-23.7%) directly from a drop in sales to the EU. It's not necessarily true that the salmon are swimming against the tide.

Irish unification

The current troubles with Edwin Poots and the DUP draw Irish unification ever closer. The DUP seek to throw away 30 years of relative peace on the island of Ireland by asking the government to break international law on the Northern Ireland Protocol, a bill which they signed up to. I cannot comprehend the nuclear levels of two-faced stupidity being brought to bear on the people of Ireland by the DUP. It seems that plans are underway for a cross-border administration in the wake of the breakdown of the Stormont government. Meanwhile trade between Ireland and Northern Ireland is **up** after Brexit with trade between Northern Ireland and mainland Britain **down**. Our Brexit scenarios predict that this will continue to a point where most people see the economic advantages of a united Ireland outweigh the religious and political forces that divide the island.

Blue tape freedoms

Brexit is reckoned to **save** £1 BILLION in cutting red tape. It is not specified where this will happen, but we presume it will be in a bonfire on worker protections, food, environmental and other regulations, making our products less safe and returning to Victorian levels of exploitation and climate damage. At the same time, The Financial Times reported that Brexit has **added** £7 BILLION of red tape. We only need ask lorry drivers, farmers, fishermen et al. Taking Back Control never specified who would gain that control and plainly it was the government through moral hazard and a return to Victorian England. In case of doubt for the mathematically challenged, £7 bn is more than £1 bn.

Please see this 'simplified diagram' from HM government that explains the various algorithms for importing and exporting goods to the EU. As Michael Gove might have said "frictionless fiction".

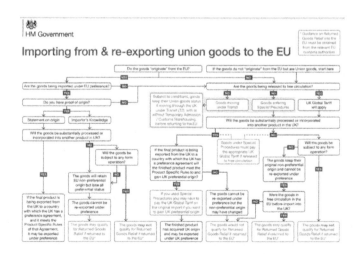

Turns out that EU red tape was in fact 'British Brexit blue tape' ...

Freedom to fire and rehire

P&O Ferries' employees have just had their first taste of Brexit freedoms as I write this book. 800 P&O Ferries' staff have just been fired without notice via Zoom, with their jobs going to overseas workers, in a race to the bottom on wages and employment rights. Natalie Elphicke, MP for Dover, was on the front line with the RMT union, crying crocodile tears for the workers, presumably en-route to visit her husband in prison ... Natalie forgot to mention that she helped to block a potential new law in October 2021, which would have curbed employers' ability fire UK employees without notice or rights, informed by our Brexit bonfire on standards. In case of doubt, P&O Ferries have not been able to adopt the same policies in France and The Netherlands, due to better employment standards in their own countries and, of course, EU directives. Damn that EU – protecting workers rights! So much for Brexit providing British jobs for British workers and so on. MP Chris Grayling recently changed the law which allowed P&O to do this.

Alongside our Natalie, the RMT union are also united in grief about the move when, in fact, they advised their workers to vote for Brexit in 2016. For the avoidance of doubt, here is the statement the RMT put to their membership, to help swing the Brexit vote. The RMT are far from being the only union to have been succoured in by the Brexit illusions, mainly due to a dislike of free market economics, faux sovereignty and nationalism. Here is the RMT's statement in full, from 2016:

TRANSPORT UNION RMT today set out six key reasons why it will be advising members to vote to the leave the EU in the forthcoming referendum:

1. Leave the EU to end attacks on rail workers

New EU rail policies are set to further entrench rail privatisation and fragmentation. That will also mean more attacks or jobs and conditions and EU laws will make it impossible to bring all of rail back into public ownership.

2. Leave the EU to end attacks on seafarers and the offshore workers

The EU has promoted undercutting and social dumping leading to the decimation of UK seafarers. The same is now happening in the offshore sector. EU directives also require the tendering our public ferry services.

3. Leave the EU to end attacks on workers' rights

It's a myth that the EU is in favour of workers. In fact the EU is developing a new policy framework to attack trade union rights, collective bargaining, job protections and wages. This is already being enforced in countries which have received EU "bailouts".

4. Leave the EU to end Austerity

If you join a union you expect members of the union to protect each other in times of trouble. The European Union has done the opposite. It has used the economic crisis to impose austerity and privatization on member states. Instead of protecting jobs and investment EU austerity is driving UK austerity.

5. Leave the EU to stop the attack on our NHS

The Transatlantic Trade and Investment Partnership (TTIP) trade agreement being negotiated between the EU and the United States will promote big business at the expense government protections and organisations including our NHS! Environmental regulations, employment rights, food safety, privacy laws and many other safeguards will also be secondary to the right of corporations to make even bigger profits.

6. Leave the EU to support democracy

The vast majority of the laws that affects our lives are now made in the EU and not the UK. We have no say over those Laws. As the late Tony Benn said in 1991...

"We are discussing whether the British people are to be allowed to elect those who make the laws under which they are governed. The argument is nothing to do with whether we should get more maternity leave from Madame Papandreou [a European Commissioner]."

The RMT find themselves in the rather awkward position of being complicit. So, frankly, are the employees who voted for Brexit and still believe in the sunlit uplands. Still, quite literally, this group now have their freedom ... from jobs and a livelihood. People are calling for the law on fire and rehire to be amended and, of course, it is hard to argue against this as being a good thing. But the root cause of the mess is Brexit and a 'patch up job' misses the underlying malaise. It is always a mistake to treat symptoms and not deal with the causes of problems. We will see many more examples of the 'unintended consequences of Brexit' in the coming months and years.

I do feel sorry for the employees, especially those who voted Remain, next, those who were taken in by the slick Brexit lies and now regret their decision and are prepared to say it out loud. I'm finding it difficult to be concerned about the small hardcore Brexiteer group of P&O employees and trade union ideologues who remain (sic) resolute that Brexit is a good idea, despite losing their jobs. This is an act of self-harm.

We can envisage a new Maslow styled hierarchy of Brexit blame:

Hierarchy of Brexit blame

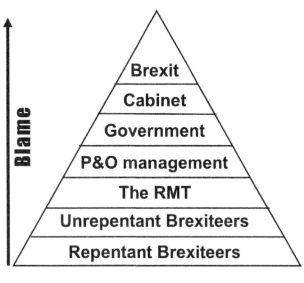

The root cause is Brexit

At the top of the blame hierarchy is Brexit, which consumes all its children. Of course, the Brexit cabinet are next in line, but so frankly are the MPs who failed to oppose Brexit. Silence is assent.

P&O management simply exploited poor UK labour laws, enabled by the Brexit bonfire on standards.

The RMT, of course, are not without blame. They recommended Brexit to members without studying the form. Unrepentant Brexiteers will have plenty of time to reflect on their decision at the Job Centres.

Least to blame are those Brexiteers who have changed their minds on Brexit and who now have the opportunity to brexorcise others.

Vaccination vacillation

Boris Johnson claims that the speed of our vaccination programme was due to Brexit freedoms. Sadly, it is not true. The BBC reported that we were always able to authorise the supply of this vaccine using provisions **under European law**. Johnson simply acted first in a desperate move to buy up the vaccine and starve the rest of the world from supplies, like the little boy in the playground who kept all the sweets and then realised that nobody wanted to play with him. Johnson, almost literally masked Brexit with COVID. By the way, the 'British vaccine' was developed by Turkish and German scientists. I am surprised that Brexiteers want such a 'foreign invasion'. At the time of writing Johnson has weaponised Putin's war on Ukraine to distract people from Brexit realities. In a 1984 twist of propaganda government ministers have said that the port of Dover does not tell government how long hauliers are waiting for 'security' reasons. Do they really think we are that stupid?

Brexit freedoms : Rich pickings

Undoubtedly Brexit has caused an exodus of foreign workers, in part due to red tape and associated costs, but, in the main because, England has once again become a racist country under Brexit. Arguably, we did not need Brexit freedoms to 'take back control' of the fields, lorry parks, bus stations etc. I await the queues of Brexit voting OAPs to pick for Britain, drive for Britain, stack shelves for Britain and so on. So far, we have been underwhelmed with applications from 'Dad's Brexit Army'. Meanwhile illegal migration proceeds, due to our government's attempts to kill people who flee from terror. This has come into sharp focus with the war in Ukraine where our performance on accepting refugees is frankly shameful. Priti Patel acts tough to pray to the altar of Brexit racism, whilst children, women and men die from Putin's Brexit enabled terror.

Sovereignty freedoms

The government claim that the Brexit freedoms of sovereignty are many and various in their 105-page document. I can only find wind. The report specifies no such freedoms and a three-year-old could have done a better job. That's an insult to three-year-olds by the day.

Blue passport freedom

Undoubtedly the showstopper in Brexit freedoms has been the blue passport. We will pay £30 per family and hours of queuing to benefit from this Brexit freedom, but clearly it's worth it. In case of doubt, we were always able to have blue passports, even if they were made in France. This is simply **fake news** :

- **Reintroduced our iconic blue passports.** All new British passports are now blue, a return to their original appearance, with the colour first introduced in 1921, and updated to be the most technologically-advanced and secure British passports ever, with the carbon footprint from their manufacture reduced to net zero.

Funding the NHS and social care

The government document claims that £57 billion is to be given to the NHS. They were promised £18.2 billion **every year** based on £350 million every week promised by Brexit. You do not need a calculator to realise that the £57 billion over several years is smaller than £18.2 billion **every** year. This issue, taken on its own, ought to have been enough to declare the Brexit referendum null and void.

In case you are wondering whether the £13 billions of social care funding had to be paid for by raising national insurance, please see some alternatives :

- Reintroduced our iconic blue passports. All new British passports are now blue, a return to their original appearance, with the colour first introduced in 1921, and updated to be the most technologically-advanced and secure British passports ever, with the carbon footprint from their manufacture reduced to net zero.

- Reviewing the EU ban on imperial markings and sales. This will give businesses and consumers more choice over the measurements they use.

Option 1 – The Brexit Bounce

Robert Dyer coined the phrase 'The Brexit Bounce'. Going back to the £350 million Brexit freedom payment for the NHS from the EU every week, we can of course have paid for the social care funding with the Brexit Bounce, except the money has never materialised.

Option 2 – The COVID corruption fund

Dido Harding spent £37 billion on Test and Trace, much of which was either non-existent or faulty. Let's be generous and suppose that only 20% of the project was fictional or faulty. That's a cool £7.4 billion towards the social care uplift. Then there is the PPE fraud …

Option 3 – The Tory spaffing Fund

Liz Truss took a lonely trip to Australia in the government A321 Airbus at a cost of £500 000. Small beer I hear you say. But these trophy flights could help pay for the NI hike !! What's wrong with Ryanair? Or BA if you wanted to be truly patriotic at a cost of around £4000 to Oz.

Rishi Sunak seems to have cancelled £4.3 billion of fraudulent COVID loans. That would be a nice contribution to the social care fund? Closing tax loopholes would make enough funds to fund good quality services not just care and allow for less taxation on those that can least afford it.

Then there are the small ticket items but 'every little helps' as they say at Tesco. The No 10 wallpaper bill (£840 per roll), Priti Patel's eyelashes, suitcases of wine, the royal yachts at a snip of £250 Million. Everything adds up.

Option 4 – Brexit to the rescue

Brexit has cost £128 billion so far, or £727 per second. Although it would not be straightforward, stopping Brexit would give us access to all the social care by stopping Britain bleeding to death. Here's a helpful chart to show what you can buy with £128 257 825 862 in case you have never thought of 'how to spend it'.

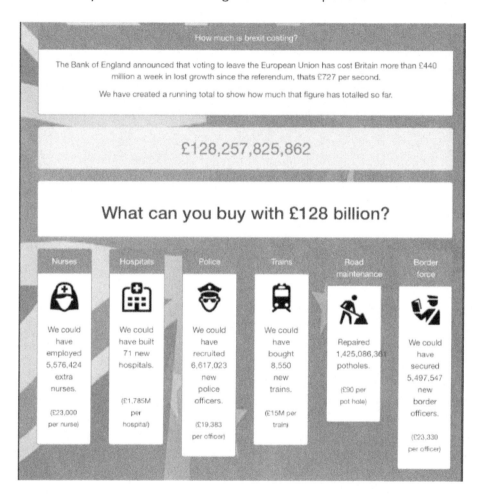

Freedom from state control

France recently decided to make EDF Energy subsidise energy price hikes. So, energy consumers in France will get a 4% price hike whilst UK consumers will experience a 54% price hike. And France is in the EU. How then were France able to do this if they are 'controlled by an EU superstate'?

There is still more to say on the faux sovereignty argument. How, for example, was Viktor Orban able to buy his vaccines from Russia whilst being part of the EU? The EU superstate argument is vacuous.

Tampon freedom

Surely we left the European Union to be free of the Tampon tax? Women may surely rest easy in the knowledge that the VAT man is not taking a percentage of their periodic blood losses. Except that even this is also a **lie**. Let me explain. The trouble with so-called 'tampon freedom' is that this arrangement was made in 2016, whilst we were a member of the EU. We have **not** been prevented from removing tax on tampons by our EU membership.

- **Back in control of our own VAT rates.** We used our control over our own VAT rates to immediately put an end to the tampon tax as soon as we were free from the EU law mandating it, ending VAT on women's sanitary products, helping to end period poverty.

An outright bloody lie

Freedom of EU unity and speed

Now this one is a real Brexit freedom, not mentioned in the report. Since the UK left The European Union, the EU have been able to unite the 27 nations. This has been especially evident in their response to the Ukraine crisis which has outstripped Britain's performance in this area. The EU have been able to speed up decision making in areas such the building of a European military force to face world conflicts, something which Britain would probably have vetoed or obfuscated. It rather looks as if Britain were one of the major obstacles to faster decision making and unity in Europe at this point of writing.

Amidst the other Brexit freedoms that the government paper puts forward that we could not do as members of EU are :

1   Giving up smoking – really?

2   Healthy eating – who knew that the EU were stopping this?

3   Ending the throw away culture – Britain leads the world in throw away culture.

4   Faster HGV licence approval by reducing the difficulty of HGV tests, so more dangerous OAP lorry drivers on the roads.

5   Simpler, better railways – this means not doing the northern leg of HS2.

6   Pints of French champagne.

7   Use of the 105-page document for redecoration of 10 Downing Street when Boris Johnson leaves.

Helping people to quit smoking. The UK is already recognised as a world leader in tobacco control and has made good progress reducing smoking rates. However, with around six million smokers in England and stark health disparities associated with smoking, more still needs to be done to help people to quit smoking. We have now launched a rapid independent review to identify which policies and regulatory reforms will be most impactful in supporting our 2030 Smokefree ambition, including where it may be beneficial to go further than the EU's Tobacco Products Directive allowed us to. We will set out proposals for our regulatory reforms in a new Tobacco Control Plan due to be published later this year.

Promoting healthy eating and preventing obesity. We are considering potential changes to our food labelling requirements relating to health, and how these can be done at pace. We also plan to launch a consultation on proposals to introduce new regulatory powers on the marketing and labelling of infant food and drinks to more effectively tackle childhood obesity.

I mean, yes, the EU **always** stopped Brits from smoking and getting fat …

The 105-page document of Brexit freedoms fall into four categories :

1.   Outright lies, provable by simple research. These are not caused or facilitated by Brexit at all. Examples include blue passports, tampon tax and so on.

2.   Changes which are the result of Brexit but which entail significant downsides. A good example is our so-called 'frictionless trade' which has been shown to be far from frictionless. Many of these freedoms are not costed out so it is impossible to make any sensible comparison of costs and benefits. Some entail significant legal, or practical drawbacks. I have rarely seen such sloppy work.

3.   Vague and woolly policy aspirations which have no causation or correlation with Brexit. Reduction of taxes on alcohol are cited as one such advantage yet we have always been able to do this as part of our own sovereign decisions within Britain.

4. Ephemeral elements, of no real value but high perceived value in terms of perceived sovereignty, e.g., imperial measures, crown stamps on glasses, blue passports. These are also dishonest.

For comparison, here is a shortlist of EU Freedoms overleaf. This book includes 350 Brexit benefits in Part IV and this is a taster.

"The real Brexit freedom is that rich tax dodgers will benefit rather than those who voted for it. We should keep making that point. What was going to be Singapore on Thames now looks more like Venice on Thames.

A once great trading metropolis parading former glories for the tourists".
Don Adamson

Suffer little children – Image by Cold War Steve www.coldwarsteve.com

WHAT HAS THE EU EVER DONE FOR US?

I am often asked this by leave supporters, so here are a few facts....

- Over 40 years of peace
- Erasmus and overseas study
- A home market of over 500 million consumers
- Cheaper flights and compensation for delays
- Help with tax avoidance
- Maternity and paternity leave
- Stronger voice in the world
- Consumer protection
- Investment in arts and culture
- Cleaner air
- Paid holiday leave
- Maximum working hours
- Cheaper mobile calls and international roaming
- Visa-free travel across Europe
- The right to work in the EU
- Funding for UK regions
- Opportunities for young people – our future leaders
- Funding for start-ups
- 44% of UK exports
- Safer food standards
- 3 million jobs
- Lower prices in shops
- The world's strongest animal welfare rights
- Rights for part-time workers
- Single market with no export charges of red tape
- Product safety standards
- Standards in the workplace
- Europe-wide patent and copyright protection
- Free healthcare across Europe
- Cleaner beaches and waterways
- Co-operation on counter-terrorism intelligence
- Rights in equal rights pay for men and women
- Protection against discrimination based on gender, race, religion, age, disability and sexual orientation
- Strongest wildlife protection in the world
- Investment and collaboration in science
- European arrest warrant
- Improved standards for farm animals

I'm sure this list is not exhaustive. So, Brexiteers, my challenge to you – can you match it?

Russian connections

50.   What is now clear is that it was in fact counter-productive, in that it offered ideal mechanisms by which illicit finance could be recycled through what has been referred to as the London 'laundromat'. The money was also invested in extending patronage and building influence across a wide sphere of the British establishment – PR firms, charities, political interests, academia and cultural institutions were all willing beneficiaries of Russian money, contributing to a 'reputation laundering' process. In brief, Russian influence in the UK is 'the new normal', and there are a lot of Russians with very close links to Putin who are well integrated into the UK business and social scene, and accepted because of their wealth. This level of integration – in 'Londongrad' in particular – means that any measures now being taken by the Government are not preventative but rather constitute damage limitation.

Re-Putin Britain – Paragraph 50 of the redacted Russia report

I set myself the task of explaining to my sister how Brexit was instrumental in destabilising Europe and how Putin's invasion of Ukraine is part of a long-range strategy by Russia to undermine the most successful peace project in the world. She is of the view that we must look after our own and not worry about other nations. She laughed at me, as did a lot of Brexit voters at the time, when David Cameron said that Brexit might precipitate war in Europe. As I write, here we are at that point with a possible escalation to mutually assured destruction. If you are not reading this, then we will clearly have taken that step. If sense prevails and taking it one step at a time for my sister and others who are experiencing the Dunning-Kruger effect

- It is a **fact** that Russian money was used to pervert the Brexit vote. Had it been anything but advisory, Brexit would have been declared **null** and **void** by the Supreme Court. Feel free to fact check this statement if you don't believe it.

- It is **known** that Aaron Banks donated £8 million to bankroll the Vote Leave campaign. This is an unprecedented amount and should have been deemed illegal as it materially affected the fairness of the election.

"We have reasonable grounds to suspect money given to Better for the Country came from impermissible sources and that Mr Banks and Ms Bilney, the responsible person for Leave.EU, knowingly concealed the true circumstances under which this money was provided"

- In case you forgot about the relevant detailed connections, read up on Cambridge Analytica, Carole Cadwalladr's work and The Russia Report. Banks attempted to single out Cadwalladr by taking a vexatious defamation case against her, circumventing her role as an investigative journalist by taking a personal action. Banks lost the case.

- It is a **fact** that there are significant ties between the hard right (and quite probably, the hard left) via The Brexit Party, Aaron Banks, the ERG and the Conservative party with Russian money. Some of this has still to come to light as I write in March 2022.

- Putin got his way when Brexit was voted for. This was an important moment in his ideological battle to leaven unity in Europe. By starting on the western front in Britain, we now see his attention turn once again to the eastern front as part of his legacy to restore the Russian Empire.

- Putin has also been injecting support and dissent into some eastern European states to destabilise the situation there and create dissonance with the European Union as the most successful peace project in the world.

- It also serves Putin's agenda to wage war now, to distract his citizens from the COVID crisis raging in Russia and various other problems. The opening up of social media in Russia means that ordinary Russians were able to see what life outside Russia was like. This is a key difference between the Cold War and the information age.

- With the bond between Britain and the EU weakened, Putin is now able to enact the next stage of his strategy, hoping to exploit disunity in the West to take back control of parts of Eastern Europe.

- The Russia Report, released many years after it should have been, is sufficiently redacted to make it fairly opaque in typical 'Yes Minister' style. However, if studied forensically it makes for interesting reading. Some samples are included.

- It is beginning to emerge as I write that certain actors such as Nigel Farage, Boris Johnson and many more ERG types are up to their neck in Russian backed corruption and kompromat.

The Dunning-Kruger effect in aspic

The Dunning–Kruger effect [6] is a cognitive bias whereby people with low ability overestimate their ability. It extends to the notion of not trusting experts or even believing that naïve wisdom trumps intelligent research. In microcosm, the Dunning-Kruger effect can be seen alive and well in this Facebook thread, following Guy Pratt's thank you statement on social media to members of Pink Floyd for standing up for Ukraine:

Peter : Brexit Begat Bloodshed www.brexitrage.com/brexit-and-wwiii

Steve R : my used bog roll has more clue than you

Peter Cook : You will have to justify yourself as I have in the article.

Steve R : I read it unfortunately. Malevolent angst is not justification it's simply hate

Peter Cook : The article is fully referenced. Please explain what is untrue with your own evidence sources or join me for a leader's debate on Zoom.

Steve R : "Leaders" 😂😂😂😂 Joker

Peter Cook : So, you have no answers then ...

Steve R : My answers to you can be summed up with a single finger

Peter Cook : That is not an answer. You have just been found out to have no argument. But I may use this thread in my next book as it is comedy gold.

Steve R : The remainder bins at Works await with no interest whatsoever

None of this is surprising given that the interaction was conducted online and it seems that our Steve is probably at the end of the Leave – Remain continuum. See our piece on online Brexorcisms in Part IV.

---

[6] Find out more on the Dunning-Kruger effect at https://www.psychologytoday.com/gb/basics/dunning-kruger-effect

40.   Open source studies have pointed to the preponderance of pro-Brexit or anti-EU stories on RT and Sputnik, and the use of 'bots' and 'trolls', as evidence of Russian attempts to influence the process.[42] We have sought to establish whether there is secret intelligence which supported or built on these studies. In response to our request for written evidence at the outset of the Inquiry, MI5 initially provided just six lines of text. It stated that ***, before referring to academic studies.[43] This was noteworthy in terms of the way it was couched (***) and the reference to open source studies ***. The brevity was also, to us, again, indicative of the extreme caution amongst the intelligence and security Agencies at the thought that they might have any role in relation to the UK's democratic processes, and particularly one as contentious as the EU referendum. We repeat that this attitude is illogical; this is about the protection of the process and mechanism from hostile state interference, which should fall to our intelligence and security Agencies.

Paragraph 40 of the redacted Russia report

Boris Johnson has been unable to act on the problem, due to the need to pander to his ERG and Russian handlers. Even Tom Tugendhat commented that we failed to step up to the plate in 2021 by placing military hardware in the Black Sea. Our obsession with getting Brexit done, the need to obey Tory Russian masters and a low appetite to work with Europe after Brexit are contributions of our reticence on the matter.

The EU, US and the rest of the world see the posturing of Boris Johnson and Liz Truss as utterly pathetic. Putin knows this and has actively exploited this division.

The EU has been able to move faster without Britain in its shadow and has signified a fast-track EU entry for Ukraine without question. Our own approach requires people fleeing from war to complete onerous paperwork in a foreign language, pay via fees and travel to Paris or Brussels from Calais. The Home Office and Priti Patel are perfectly able to do better, but they must pray at the altar of Brexit whilst pandering to the racist gallery of xenophobes in Brexit Britain.

Alexander Vladimirovich Yakovenko, British Ambassador for Russia reported of Britain

"It will be a long time before they rise again'>

History shows that a tyrant or despot usually meets a violent end, either at the hands of his own people or at the hands of his enemies. For now, the West, or liberal democracy, must balance two distinct risks – the risk of action versus the risk of inaction. Our Brexit coup is complete and Britain stands as an international joke alongside other world leaders whilst Putin enjoys our castration as a world leader. So much for 'taking back control'.

Big table, but no cat food.

Re-Booting Britain

A Better Britain in a Better Europe for a Better World

www.brexitrage.com

Every day, people of all persuasions tell me "Brexit is done – we can do no more". More than many, I understand just how wearing nearly six years of gaslighting, shapeshifting and obfuscation is on the soul. But, despite it all, we can and we must target politicians, mainstream media, social media and individuals / groups to :

1. Break parliamentary paralysis – lobbying MPs using a variety of means, from letters to direct participation in reformed democracy.
2. 'Take Back Control' of MSM via press and media activity in national and local print / radio and TV media.
3. Develop much better reach into social media, in terms of honesty, depth of penetration and reach outside the Remain bubble.
4. Change minds on Brexit 1 : 1 and / or in communities via online leaders' debates, events, educational seminars and other strategies. This book is a physical manifestation of this goal.
5. Eventually, to cultivate relationships with the EU such that we can ease the pathway to joining the EU anew.

Re-Boot Britain is a pan-political advocacy and lobbying network. We aim to restore humanity, humility, democracy and truth in politics to Britain. Forty years of lying, gaslighting, shapeshifting and obfuscation gave us Brexit. We aim to put the populist genie back in the bottle, by bettering (not copying) the populists at their own wicked games.

Brexit has consumed Britain : three elections / referenda, three Prime Ministers and three failed attempts to Brexit. It has left us weak and vulnerable in our response to the Russian invasion of Ukraine, COVID and contributed to 170 000 unnecessary deaths under Boris Johnson's junta. Brexit consumes all its children.

Furthermore, a political backbone has been absent in Britain for nearly six years and probably longer. The diverse and disparate Remain movements have sometimes gold-plated the strategy that lost them the referendum, albeit with the best of intentions. Various attempts to build cohesion and collaboration into our movement have failed, rather like some of the biggest silo-based monolith organisations.

Yet we cannot allow the greatest disaster next to climate change to threaten the next generation's futures to continue. Our continued resistance is both moral, a fight worth having and certainly not a waste of time, given how much people have sacrificed over the last six years. Would you like to be able to say that you contributed to the re-establishment of an honest government? I would.

Our aims

Re-Boot Britain aims to be a professional movement with one goal : To end Brexit by all reasonable means. Embracing reverse, rejoin, reform, reframe and renew.

- Popular but not populist, reaching across the binary two-party system. We aim to restore honesty to politics. Imagine how much better life could be if you could trust politicians?
- We are non-politically aligned but will campaign in local and national elections to leaven the two-party system to fundamentally encourage better politics, better politicians and an effective opposition.
- We aim to break the deadlock of 'dead cat' politics.
- We collaborate with national European movements but are more edgy to reach our target communities in ways that the long-term organisations are unable to do.
- Our work will be complete when 2/3 of the people no longer back Brexit and the Brexit culture carriers have been removed or totally discredited.

Strategy

RE-BOOT BRITAIN : FIVE GOALS

Targeting **Politicians**, **MSM**, **Social Media** and **individuals / groups** :

1. Breaking Parliamentary Paralysis – lobbying **MPs** using a variety of means, from letters to direct participation in reformed democracy.

2. "Taking Back Control" of **MSM** via press and media activity in national and local print / radio and TV media.

3. Develop much better reach into **social media**, in terms of honesty, depth of penetration and reach outside the Remain bubble.

4. Changing minds on Brexit **1 : 1** and / or in **communities** via online leaders' debates, events, educational seminars and other strategies.

5. Eventually, to cultivate relationships with **The EU** such that we can ease the pathway to joining The EU anew.

www.brexitrage.com

reboot@academy-of-rock.co.uk

On a weekly basis we try to take actions on these areas via a Zoom call that takes people in from all over Europe – see www.brexitrage.com/diary

parliamentary paralysis gave us Brexit and the main political parties are also running scared of the B word. We must help them to face facts through various advocacy approaches. At the time of writing, it is fair to say that Brexit isn't working. Later, it will be possible to say that Brexit has failed although, of course, the problem with that is that much of the damage will have been done.

In Part III of this book, I look at ways to make a larger footprint on mainstream media and social media. We run various amplifier groups on social media to improve our presence.

This book itself deals with item 4 on the list and we offer coaching and mentoring to support individuals and groups in this area.

Re-Boot Britain has a network of contacts to help on the area of relationship management within Europe, which will be a pre-requisite to establishing the conditions for what is left of Britain to join the EU anew.

Organisation structure

We have a team-based network structure across Britain and Europe. What we cannot do ourselves, we do with others. We collaborate regularly.

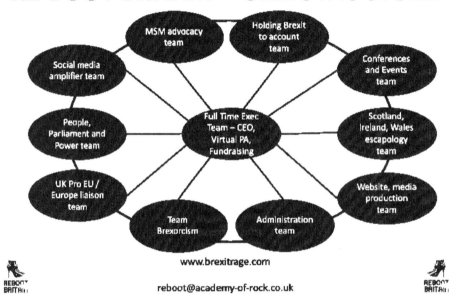

Put your boots on

We meet every Monday at 8 pm via ZOOM – see www.brexitrage.com/diary for details. With members from all over the UK and Europe our meetings offer the most participative online forums to have your voice heard in a diverse group of people. This is how one member of our network describes our events:

"Peter Cook has a talent for drawing people and their ideas together with a practical focus and a bias for action. He also has an eye for the eye-catching on social media. We have worked together in the political sphere, but as a programme management consultant myself I see in Peter a superb ability to recognise the contributions of many and focus them on activities and campaigns that can make a real difference".

Questions and answers

Isn't Brexit already done? A piece of paper was signed

Boris Johnson finally got Brexit done through using COVID and Christmas as a weapon to distract us from the realities of his 'oven-ruined Brexit deal'. This after he promised to die in a ditch if he did not get it done on Halloween. But Brexit is a political process and the law merely a servant to the politicians. We now face a decade of discontent, as the realities start to bite. Anything is possible in such a climate, including the dramatic fragmentation of an 80 strong majority and / or the slow removal of the populist culture carriers from power, just as Trump has been leavened gradually. If you are not sure on the relative powers of politics versus the law, just think of ONE occasion when the government obeyed the rule of law in the last five years, or other precedents. Here's a few where they didn't :

1. Gina Miller's Supreme Court Case which established that parliament was always sovereign, despite the lie that Brexit put forward. This was ignored.
2. The Cooper No Deal amendment – No Deal was deemed illegal, yet it was used in 2020 as a threat to secure Brexit.
3. Prorogation of parliament and lying to the Queen.
4. The 6 million petition was ignored.
5. Breaking international law to get Brexit done.
6. Allowing rapists to continue acting as MPs.
8. Unlawfully killing 179 000 people through a deliberate herd immunity COVID strategy.
9. Offering the DUP a £1 billion bribe to support Brexit.
10. Threatening the peace in Northern Ireland by threats to destroy the Good Friday Agreement with Article 16.

… and so on. Our government is beyond the law. We should not be so keen to give them excuses to continue doing this.

If political will changed, the law would be made to fit the circumstances and lawyers would spend years and earn a lot of money re-arranging the law to fit the will of the politicians.

Is it too late? We finalised things.

We exited the EU via a highly compressed timetable and limited scrutiny of the trade deal. Mark Francois has already declared that the fight for a hard Brexit will continue and negotiations will continue for many years as contradictions and conflicts emerge. We can use various legal devices such as Article 49 and or the formal review process built into the trade agreement. We live in a disruptive political climate with the toxic mixture of Corona + Brexit = Britastrophe and we have no idea whether Boris Johnson's government will survive the oncoming tsunami.

The road will be long and difficult but joining anew is possible if we work systematically towards that aim, seizing opportunities along the way as well as having a long-term focus on an overall strategy. Rejoin movements such as Best For Britain and The European Movement must learn how to marry long term strategy with more agile approaches. All too often, our strategies have been dictated by the other side and / or we find ourselves in the position of ambulance chasing.

PART II

Strategies for Brexorcism

Preparation, preparation, preparation

Like all professional activities, much of the success of a Brexorcism comes down to the preparation. Preparation allows you to be nimble and adaptable in the moment, having gamed the many scenarios that may arise. As in many other walks of life this also means paying attention to small details. Here is some general advice based on extensive experience.

The environment for change

The physical environment crucially influences the context aka the psychological environment for any difficult conversation more than most people realise. Just think about it. Do you have different types of conversation at work meetings or in court as compared with ones down the pub, to a business coach or your hairdresser? I am supposing that not many of you reading this have been to court, but hopefully you get my drift. There is a huge difference in talking with people in a formal setting, when people may have their guard up, or feel they need to defend their prior beliefs in front of family and friends, compared with more relaxed social settings or with a stranger, when people may tell you their real feelings. This may explain why many of you write to me to tell me how difficult it is to Brexorcise family members. In general, the closer you are to someone, the harder it is to Brexorcise them for a host of reasons. Paradoxically, you also need a good bond of rapport to tell people you don't know unfortunate truths. But this does not imply the need for closeness in personal terms. We deal with the issue of how to strike up rapid rapport with strangers later in this book.

However, we cannot always influence the environment beforehand as we are sometimes confined by circumstances. For example, I have frequently 'trapped' my subjects in pubs, or they me, so I can hardly take them to the park for a less confrontational environment. Nonetheless, there are many environmental factors that tend to sway the odds in your favour. For example, if you are in a conversation in a group, find a way to take your subject into a 1 : 1 dialogue.

Environments for Brexorcisms

We don't have to wait for a march or a campaign to do our work.

Seize opportunities as they arise.

Time and timing

Time and timing are everything. One cannot expect a closed mind to open in a single session. Incubation time is often very valuable as a means of 'softening' positions with hardened cases. I estimate from experience, that one may need 3-5 sessions with a hardened suspect, maybe spaced out over weeks or months. This neatly explains why quick conversations on the street or protests do not really achieve much except the reinforcement of previously held positions unless you are extremely skilled. It also explains why protests can simply turn into a 'dialogue of the deaf', with one side shouting their point and the other theirs. I frequently try to detach people from protests to give them more airtime for a conversation.

Targeting ringleaders

All social groups have a hierarchy. The trick is to spot the hierarchy and use it to advantage. In my work in cafés, I noticed that one group of pensioners had a 'big dog', a man who spoke more than the others and whose opinions about Brexit went unchallenged by the group, except his wife. I noticed that she frequently rolled her eyes when he was talking. Over time I began to talk with this group about the weather and other matters. He would always bring up Brexit with me due to my t-shirt which always announced my viewpoint on the topic. For months I mainly listened intently, offering low level facts to gently challenge his opinions and used non-directive interventions in the supporting and cathartic modes of Heron's model, such as "I can see why you might think that", "I'd be curious to find out why you say that" and so on to establish rapport and trust.

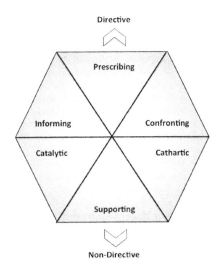

On one occasion I decided I had enough credit in the relationship to launch a head on directive challenge :

ME "You often tell me how great Brexit is, yet you cannot name a single thing that is good about it. Your 'research' comes from The Daily Mail. After months of talking with you I am still none the wiser".

HIM "I are all entitled to our opinion".

ME "Yes, you are entitled to your opinion … long pause … except your opinion is not of equal value to my facts. I have patiently explained facts over many months, but you continue to offer nothing in return".

HIM (slightly indignant) "I'll have you know that I'm considerably older than you. I've been around for a very long time".

Me "But not for much longer …"

This seemingly abrasive reply was met with an almost uncontrollable laugh from his wife. From my observations, she seemed to be someone who suffered in silence at much of the nonsense spouted by her husband. At this point, I considered that my work was done and she would 'finish him off' later at home.

After the couple left the other three males spoke to me. They told me that whilst he wasn't such a bad chap, they did not really listen to anything he said. Two of them also told me that they voted to Remain in the EU and they felt they had to endure his daily digest of nonsense just to keep the group together. In groups, people systematically avoid difficult conversations to maintain social cohesion. As a brexorcist, your job is to skilfully enter the social system whilst maintaining sufficient distance to be an effective agent of change.

Focus, focus, focus

My experience in holding difficult conversations for thousands of hours indicates that when these become difficult, there is a tendency to change the subject. This is an important social strategy to keep the relationship going and avoid difficulties, especially to strangers, who don't really have to listen to you. I call this strategy 'shapeshifting'. But, like James O'Brien on LBC, we must eventually return to the subject to work through the issue at hand. Since we are not on the radio, we are not confined by fitting our work between radio ads and the news. That offers us the luxury of iteration, letting a subject drop but then returning to it much later, sometimes at another encounter altogether. Time produces reflection and this makes it easier to tackle difficult subjects the second or third time around. We must normalise conversations about Brexit rather than allow the government to airbrush the word out of the lexicon.

Unconditional positive regard

Counsellors and therapists use the term Unconditional Positive Regard or UPR, coined by Carl Rogers, to describe the notion that they must believe that their clients are doing the very best they can in the situation they face. However, this does not imply agreeing with them. I know many Remainers who say things like "I don't know how you can talk to them" and so on. Truth be told, we must, unless we are to wait for millions of Brexiteers to spin off this mortal coil. Heavy doses of patience and belief that your client / victim is doing the best they can are needed if you are to successfully Brexorcise someone. This was brought into stark reality when I was talking to someone in a pub. To give him a relief from talking about Brexit and get some context for his Brexit beliefs I started a conversation about his family. He told me he had two kids in their thirties, both with quite serious social problems. He mentioned that one was suffering a great deal of racism (the family was white British). Eager to find out more I asked how this was and he explained that his son was in Parkhurst maximum security prison for some major unspecified offences and he was getting "beaten up by black guys". Hmm, I wondered to myself internally. Just who was this dude I was talking to etc. Externally I replied with the neutral observation of "oh I see" which allowed the conversation to continue. My apparent acceptance of his family circumstances and his 'story' both helped me contextualise his belief systems and know where to press, whilst increasing his confidence to tell me more of the workings of his mind on Brexit. After some time, I got him to volunteer the fact that he had no idea why he voted for Brexit.

Online Brexorcisms

There are massive differences when trying to hold a deep conversation in real life as compared with doing this on Facebook, Twiiter, instant messaging and so on. 90% of your tools to gain rapport are unavailable to you and this makes an online Brexorcism much more difficult than a real life one. We will explore the reasons why this is so and what you can do about it later in the book.

Communicating to influence

Influence and persuasion are at the heart of a successful Brexorcism. This is what we must do to change hearts, minds and souls on Brexit. People have their own preferred ways of being persuasive. I have noticed over nearly six years and thousands of hours of working on the street with grass roots Remain campaigners that there is a preference for what I call 'push marketing' methods as the weapons of choice. These approaches manifest themselves in placards, chants, songs and other forms of 'telling' the other side to reform their minds. There is nothing wrong with these as a means of mass communication but, seen as a means of influence and persuasion on their own, they are what negotiators refer to as the 'dialogue of the deaf'. Even I have had my moments at doing such things, on the street at No 10 Downing Street and via our song projects at 'Rage Against The Brexit Machine' www.brexitrage.com However, there are many other styles. Arguably some of the less demonstrative ones are better in terms of influence and persuasion when the subject of your attention already has strongly formed views, as we shall discuss here. So, we begin with an overview of the anatomy of influential communications.

Communications and influence

We live in an increasingly fragmented and busy world, with many competing activities and stimuli for our attention, time and money. Compared with 50 years ago, we have multiplied the number of ways we can communicate many times. These provide certain freedoms to live spontaneously. For example, we can literally live in a 'Last Minute' economy, booking theatre tickets and social events on demand. Yet, more communication devices and faster communications do not always make for better communications when careful planning is needed, as opportunity is missed.

Success in any form of influential communications can be reduced to four elements :

1. We need a very potent message.
2. We need a messenger who will be heard and listened to.
3. We need to choose the right communication channel(s).
4. We must avoid shouting at the wind. That means making sure that the receivers of our communication are awake, alert and receptive. Preparation is perhaps the most important part of any successful piece of influence.

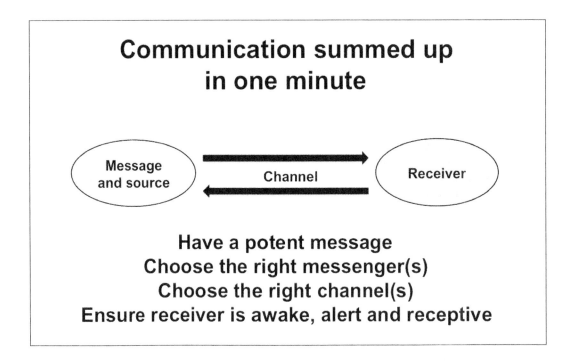

1. The message

Successful communicators use very clear, potent messages to engage and coalesce people around a goal or a project. Fuzzy messages drive fuzzy actions and fuzzy outcomes. In short, fail to plan, plan to fail.

Applying this to the EU referendum, it becomes clear as to why people believed the message that we could spend £350 million per week on our NHS instead of the EU by 'taking back control'. Although the NHS message proved to be false and was retracted the day after the vote had been cast, this did not matter to people who wanted to believe the message. Interestingly, although most people now know that they were lied to about this they still hold on to the belief that it was true at the time to avoid internal 'cognitive dissonance'. Irrespective of your views on the matter, people felt it was an undeniably clear and potent message. The £350 million message was calculated to create what academics call 'order control certainty' in the minds of voters. It could have only been improved by making it seem to be a calculated number by using something like £357 million.

However, the phrase 'taking back control' is a **nominalisation** in linguistic terms. Nominalisation is the process of turning a word from a verb into a noun. It has become painfully clear that people did not realise what they were taking back control of, when, where and so on. For example, since Brexit happened, we are no longer be able to send refugees back to Europe, an obvious consequence of leaving the bloc but not one that the Brexiteers realised at the time. Nor was it apparent to some Leave voters that the controls might work in both directions, with Brits abroad now subject to controls over the time they spend in Europe. At the time of writing, we appear to be 'taking back control' by leaving the borders open, a different interpretation of control than most people have. It is unclear as to how this will lead to less immigration and it has not stemmed the flow of people wishing to risk their lives to travel to Britain, much to the irritation of Leave voters.

Research on the psychology of communications also has wide implications for those of us who aim to undertake Brexorcisms. Consider carefully what we can learn from these findings :

1. Firstly, let's consider the issue of one-sided versus two-sided messages. One-sided messages work best when the receivers already agree with your argument, or when they are unlikely to hear counter arguments. This may explain crudely why people read newspapers that already accord with their views. It clearly worked to influence voters in our example of the £350 million every week for the NHS. This rather demonstrates that we are essentially in echo chambers for much of the time. In other words, we are only ever confronted with views that we are already consonant with. The brexorcist's job is to ensure that they balance hard to hear with ones that create some sense of consonance for our subjects.

    Two-sided messages tend to be more effective when the receivers initially disagree with the argument, where they are well educated, or when they are likely to hear counter arguments from others. The ramifications of this innocent sounding sound bite are massive in terms of thinking about your choice of persuasive communications. Many of us do not like to appear to argue away from our preference by offering counter-arguments, yet it can be very effective when trying to see things from a Leave voter's viewpoint. For example, I know many people who loathe Theresa May so much that they could not bring themselves to agree with anything she says, even if they agree with her point. I'd go so far to say that the ability to argue from multiple viewpoints separates the sheep from the goats in terms of influence. This example from the street demonstrates the wisdom of seeing things from both sides :

We're in the army now

I was talking to three people who turned out to be Vote Leave professionals on parliament Square. They assumed me to be of low intelligence initially as I had my FUCK Brexit T-Shirts, my hi-vis orange jacket and my anti-Brexit hoardings on my bicycle. I therefore looked more like the gasman than a business academic! I, in turn, thought that my 'opponents' were Remainers, as they were at SODEM.

We started with a casual chat, which turned out to be a massive advantage. Within a few minutes, it became apparent that they worked at Millbank at Vote Leave HQ.

They started to rehearse the usual set of Vote Leave issues such as the EU Army, unaccountable bureaucracy and a host of other concerns they had. I answered all the issues raised politely and each one with evidence. On some issues I conceded that they had a point. They were very surprised when I pointed out that the EU needed reform, as did all political systems. The army dialogue was most interesting :

Vote Leave : "Are you not concerned about an EU army?"
Me : "Not really. Despite my appearance as a bit of a yob, I used to tutor MBA students and am in my 'cycling wear' today. I have taught a lot of senior army people on the MBA. One told me an EU army would be pretty good idea" :

- Firstly, as one of the most experienced armies the British Army would likely be at the head of an EU Army.
- British soldiers in the EU army would also be properly resourced, unlike the British Army. No more broken-down tanks in the desert and soldiers without the right equipment and so on.

Setting aside union flags, Queen and country. my army officer pointed out that an EU Army is a pretty good idea from a pragmatic viewpoint. My subjects did not challenge this. After we finished, they complimented me, saying that they had never had such a reasonable conversation with a Remainer at parliament, having mostly been shouted down by the regulars. Although I could not have possibly converted them, we shook hands and there was mutual respect in our exchange.

When is two-sided approach best? When is it right to go for the one-sided approach?

2. When communicating to persuade, it is generally better to draw a conclusion in the message rather than letting others attempt to infer it themselves unless they are highly intelligent and open to persuasion. By not drawing a conclusion we invite the possibility that a different one may be drawn. Or, that no conclusion will be drawn from the passive supply of information. When thinking about persuading voters of your viewpoint, it is always be better if they drew the conclusions themselves. In general, people much prefer their own ideas and thinking than that of others. However, if there is a risk of them drawing a different conclusion, drive your point home with a conclusion and then deal with objections. A typical example would be when saying that the Brexit we now have is not the one that was offered in the 'brochure' in 2016. This is typically met with the objection 'that's because the EU have bullied us' or 'you traitors have brought the country to its knees'. It is relatively easy to push back such challenges.

3. Repetition of a message can increase persuasiveness if used cleverly. However, over-repetition can wear out a message as well. Just note how many people have become irritated by the phrases 'Strong and Stable', 'Deep and special partnership', 'Get Brexit done' and 'Brexit means Brexit' for a graphic illustration of how a robotic approach can offend. Repeating ideas rather than exact messages may be the best solution to avoid message fatigue. For example, the word Remain has suffered from fatigue and was never as exciting as the prospect of . It was quickly converted to Remoan by the media, which further degraded the value of the term. Our populist media are experts at such things!

4. Rather than presenting features, it is better to present benefits, as some people do not translate features into benefits. A good way of forcing yourself to do this is to ask yourself the question 'What does this mean for the person I am talking with?' For example, our membership of the EU has cost us 37 pence a week [7] or half a Mars Bar (feature) means we have had 70 + years of overall peace in Europe (benefit). This requires the use of what we call the 2nd position in Neuro-Linguistic Programming (NLP). I will return to NLP later in this book. Nigel Farage is a master of presenting benefits over features, even if they turned out to be unicorns or outright lies. We would do well to study the artform of Farage, so that we can better his strategy.

---

[7] In 2018, full fact reported that the UK contribution to the EU was £9 billion and not the £39 billion put forward by Brexiteer MPs. Ever had the feeling you've been conned?

Thinking about Brexorcism

Use the information above to refine your messages for your chosen subject :

Communications model element	Applications to me
One-sided versus two sided messages Think about the intelligence level of your recipient. Are you presenting them with new information or are you attempting to 'over-write' an existing belief?	
Drawing conclusions When to draw it yourself? When is it best for others to draw the conclusion?	
When to repeat and when to rephrase? Rephrasing may be better if your subject is resistant or intelligent.	
Present benefits more than features Ask what the feature means for the recipient of the message?	

2. The messenger

Successful communications professionals use a messenger or messengers that will be heard. I have tried many experiments where I have taken the visuals and audio away from the person delivering a hard to hear message and found considerable differences in the receptivity of the messages. This is especially so when the messenger is themselves controversial in some way such as these examples demonstrate.

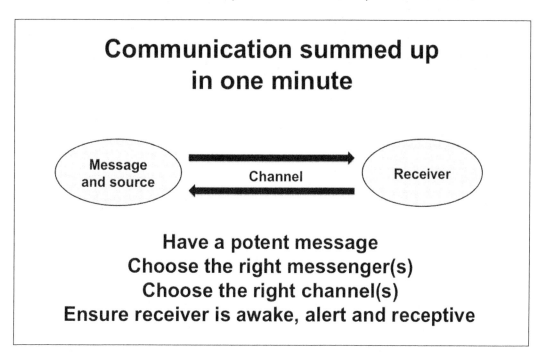

I tested a speech given by ex-Prime Minister Tony Blair, talking about the need to end Brexit. When I simply showed the text of his speech to a group of people on social media who did not know that Blair had said it, their agreement with the messages was overall very good. However, when I tested Blair's words matched with video and audio of him speaking to the same people, the receptivity of his message was severely impaired or fundamentally disagreed with. People made several visceral reactions such as 'Warmonger', 'Liar', various expletives and so on. Sadly, we appear to confuse the message with the messenger. For this reason, whenever I post content by controversial figures such as Tony Blair, I usually soften the post with a caption using the title of George Michael's classic album 'Listen Without Prejudice'. This softens the impact of the messenger unless I am dealing with the most hardened cases. As with all things, preparation is everything.

Gone fishing

I did a kind of live 'clinical trial' or social experiment on communications using Bob Geldof's famous standoff in a fishing boat on the river Thames with our 'UKIP fisherman' Nigel Farage. Firstly, I tested the contents of Bob's message out on a social media post without people knowing who said it. It gained a great number of approvals. Then I repeated with the video and audio of Bob's speech. I was surprised to note that even people who totally agreed with Geldof's message rejected it once they knew who had said it, with reactions such as 'Elitist', 'Rich Irish Wa...ker' and various other insults. The successful influencer chooses the right person or people to deliver their message. This is not always themselves. So, remember that you are not always the best person to influence someone or a group on a particular subject.

We must balance our innate passion for the pro-European / anti-Brexit cause with the need to persuade others of its value. Remember our discussion about two-sided arguments being more persuasive than one-sided ones in many circumstances. This is especially so when people believe that the messenger has something to gain from the outcome. If you find it impossible to be dispassionate and balanced about your obsession, find someone who can represent your interests in an appropriate way to your subjects.

In general, a messenger is perceived to be more influential when the receiver perceives them to be high rather than low in credibility. This explains why leaders need to operate from a strong platform of expertise to be successful and why Boris Johnson's premiership is problematic for many, since it is largely founded on a base of comedic and inept public speaking, rather than deep expertise in any of the needed subject areas. Of course, the impact of expertise is complex and Michael Gove was instrumental in reinforcing this in the 2016 referendum, by suggesting that we should not listen to experts. Once again that goes back to preparation and the need to establish rapport before overwhelming someone with your expertise on a given subject area. One often needs to gain permission to be a smartass in the Brexit debate with someone who disagrees with you and this is part of what I mean by patience. In the world of changing minds, sometimes the tortoise outperforms the hare.

Honesty and trustworthiness are also vitally important to be an ethical influencer. Therefore, the messenger's influence is weakened when the subject or audience perceives that the person has something to gain from the communication. This is another reason to argue on both sides of an issue when people think you are biased. The process of showing that you are balanced can also deal with unspoken objections to accepting your arguments. Sometimes you will not be told verbally that people disagree with your point although it may leak out in their body language. I deal with this later in the book.

People are more easily persuaded by people they perceive to be like themselves. Yet the paradox for those reading this book is that we are trying to change people's minds. We may therefore be opposites of the people we are trying to influence in various ways. They also begin by being diametrically opposed to our viewpoints. Therefore preparation and rapport matters, by finding something in common with your subjects to give you even just a small bond of trust for a dialogue. Some of the most difficult conversations I have had with voters have been preceded with comments in pubs and music venues such as "You are a brilliant musician mate, but I don't agree with you on Brexit". Over many years, it seems that they value my musicianship more than my views on politics. But that's just enough to make a conversation work. Importantly, I find that it is better that they make the approach to talk to them rather than me preying upon them. By doing this we are implicitly indulging in 'pull' communications rather than 'push'. By doing this, most have, at some level, already agreed to be influenced by their approach. With subjects that don't know me, I 'announce' my presence through t-shirts and other devices that let people know where I stand about Brexit.

All this information on communications and influence can be used with congruence and flair as well as an instrument of manipulation. So, none of the above techniques are 'tricks' one can use to be perceived as more honest. Simply stated, if you argue on both sides of an issue for effect, but you don't believe in your counter argument, you will get found out. Successful leaders, change agents and 'brexorcists' know the difference between influence and manipulation and influence with integrity. If you don't believe in your counter argument the best way to deal with this is by using what NLP calls 'mind reading', for example : "You may be thinking that I would say that ...". followed by the counter argument.

3. The channel

Successful communicators choose the best channel(s) or media for the job at hand, not just the most convenient or efficient one(s). Face to face interactions may take longer but it is often the most effective channel, but of course all depends on our goals for the communication.

We communicate to :

- Inform
- Persuade
- Question
- Collaborate
- Confront
- Facilitate etc.

Impersonal channels such as text, instant messaging, WhatsApp can be counter-productive when giving 'hard to hear' messages. This explains why people sometimes fall out on social media channels when trying to deliver complex and emotional messages. The clue of instant messaging is in the title : for messages! If your message is any more difficult than making simple arrangements such as a meeting time or venue and you don't know the receiver well, it may be misunderstood. The relative poverty of social media as a channel for communicating nuanced messages is counterbalanced by people's shortage of time to do anything more effective. So, we are now in the age where deaths are sometimes announced on Facebook rather than in person, sometimes for reasons of efficiency but also with some significant downsides in terms of humanity and understanding.

Some examples of the poverty of communications on social media are shown overleaf. These are both hilarious and rather sad at the same time :

Blaming me, blaming EU aha

Facebook conversation about why Julie wants to leave the EU – grammar unedited.

JULIE i voted leave and we won leave but getting tired of all Remain voters that cant accept a simple vote decision .. if we leave and it goes to pot then so be it . but i think its all scare mongering to be honest . to fear Leavers to change votes.. uk will be better out .. at least then we can concentrate on the uk citizens not saving the world problems .. no one helps our homeless our attrocities over time . my trip to france enlightened me alot of things and norway and a few other countries survive out of the EU

JULIE Peter Cook its called financial issue plus lots of things . they say we have no money but we greatfully give away to eu . plus as in my situation i gave up my home to help people of the uk in over crowded situations . my four bed house within me leaving council moved in a two kid family just arrived in uk . i was furious and that made my mind up priority should be given to those here already needing homes . plus if you walk around the streets you will see all those that arrived to a better life in uk brought over illegally and some legal by eu law on ourstreets homeless. . i also could add even in jobs which i will add priority given to the cheap labour workers over rule our own unemployed . our produce in uk destroyed due to EU rules of size , quality etc. . as a person who got laid off work due to cancer ,to have spent alot if time fighting for treatment , for homes for my kids , jobs not easy to get , cuts to servjces required in communities . losing everything i had ever worked for as i got cancer and had no rights to my home of 8 years . to see the nhs mess , now international health service , people fly over for treatment then go back home .i could go on but ive seen with my own eyes not media not politicians . money given to eu could be used here .. we have criminals here that cant be sent back eu laws . so much so wrong .

i dont need to do any fact checking i have my facts and this us simply another case of remoaners bully to my facts of real life . police what do i need to report to police its full known facts to whole of uk .. i live in the real world and nothing anybody says will make me change my mind on brexit .. a uk vote won and should be followed through not all this false un factual scare mongering . other countries survive without the EU .. im not racialist either and have friends and family abroad but i care for great britain nothing more . my view is my life my families life and my grandchildrens life . honest true life situations enlighten me true facts . i also have family in politics and who work at westminster so i am aware of a little more that what media and Remainers want to try tell me to be honest . nothing will make me change my mind any other way .

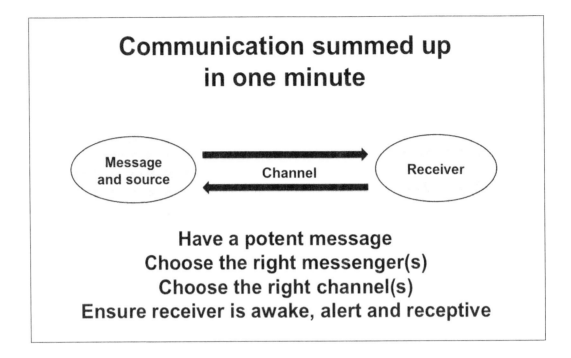

The multiplicity of communication channels has also increased enormously in the last 20 years from text to instant messaging across multiple platforms, video conferencing and so on, yet our fundamental human skills of communicating have not changed that much.

Sometimes the most efficient channels are not the most effective. Personal channels such as 1 : 1 dialogue are efficient in terms of the time they appear to take but they are often very effective. These impersonal channels may seem more efficient but may be quite ineffective. The successful communicator reaches for the best tool for the job rather than the one most readily available. WhatsApp groups of 100 people break all the rules of anthropology for what counts as an effective channel to reach people, apart from when it is one person trying to simply tell 99 other people something very simple. I have watched with some amusement and despair at the efforts of people to run WhatsApp groups of 100 people where 20 different conversation threads are taking place simultaneously, ranging from 'meet and greet' type topics right through to questions of world peace and so on! People rightly leave the conversation or simply switch off.

Two other insights from the field of NLP (Neuro-Linguistic Programming) are worthy of note here in terms of our abilities to communicate effectively.

1. The linguistic aspects of a message are vital in terms of how effective a message is. Professor Albert Mehrabian conducted some research on personal communications in 1970 and concluded that the syntax (words), tone of voice, and body language respectively account for 7% (words), 38%, (voice tone) and 55% (body language) of personal communication. The figures are perhaps less important than the overall point, that the words chosen are but a small part of the overall communication. That said, all we have in many modern communication media (text, e-mail, messenger) is the syntax or words. This explains why there can be so much confusion when trying to explain complex things on these media.

2. We regularly **delete**, **distort** and **generalise** messages through our own filters. This prompts NLP specialists to point out that 'the map is not the territory'. Quite literally, a map of Italy is not quite the same as the experience of visiting the country or eating a fine meal in Rome. For example, the London tube map **deletes** superfluous information, for example elevators, roads etc. It **distorts** by making the centre of London relatively bigger than outlying areas for clarity. It uses only 45 and 90-degree bends to help us to see the big picture. It also **generalises** information to make it easier for you to understand – colour codes for different lines, circles for interchanges etc.

What then is the relevance of deletion, distortion and generalisation in terms of giving clear, potent and accurate messages to people?

Firstly, people are fond of **deleting** context sensitive information when sending brief instant messages or texts. Simple messages do not tend to suffer from this strategy, for example 'I'll meet you at the Kings Cross St Pancras Café Nero at 6.30 pm' is specific and clear (unless there are two Café Neros at Kings Cross!). However, some people try to use the same channel to discuss matters of strategy, complexity, love and so on with some amusing and disastrous consequences. Vote Leave used deletion to great effect by suggesting that Turkey would be joining the EU. They omitted to mention whether Turkey would be successful, that they had tried to do so for many years without success, when this might happen and so on. My sister clearly swallowed the message when she told me about the two million German rapists coming to Tonbridge. Of course, she meant Turkish people.

Deletion of information is also quite common in my experience, when people take for granted information that you don't have access to, without which the message makes no sense at all, for example :

"Farage is a failure"

"A failure at what?"

Many people reading this book may well agree with the premise that Farage is a failure. Yet he is a convincing public speaker. He also is a credible liar since he persuaded Britain to leave the most successful peace project of the last 100 years without even getting elected to the UK parliament.

Distortion of information occurs when there is an inferred cause and effect relationship, for example :

"He never brings me flowers, so he doesn't love me".

There are, of course, lots of reasons in life why flowers may not appear … availability, the weather and not just due to an absence of love …

Generalisation is the tendency of people to assume that what happens to them is true of **all** people. Words like **all**, **everyone**, **never**, **always** contain the hallmarks of a generalisation. Jacob Rees-Mogg and Tim Wetherspoon are fond of generalising specifics to make sweeping statements about Brexit. Spot the language patterns that Jacob and Tim have mastered :

"Because a sweet shop in my town is coping with Brexit transition, it means that Brexit will be plain sailing for all shop owners, towns and the country".

"My pubs are booming, so the whole of British industry will be fine after Brexit".

"Training shoes will be cheaper after Brexit, therefore Brexit will be a success for everyone as everyone wears shoes".

To diffuse a generalisation, sometimes it is important to point out that you have spotted the 'game'. I come on to specific language strategies to do this later, but the beginning comes when you listen intently to what is being said and deconstruct the deception.

Communication errors

Deletion

Missing information, either accidentally or deliberately

"Take Back Control"

Distortion

Twisted information, either accidentally or deliberately

"Turkey is joining the EU"

Generalisation

Making an all-time statement out of a specific or exception

"All immigrants are benefit scroungers"

4. The receiver

Successful communicators ensure that those they are communicating with i.e., the receiver(s) are awake, alert and receptive. Sometimes preparation is the most important work you can do, to ensure people hear and **embrace** what you have to say. Time and timing can be crucial determinants of success. Hard to hear ideas may need some 'warm-up' to get the receiver in the mood to receive and this is where repetition and rephrasing of your message may come in. Sometimes a skilled communicator will use several staged attempts to build up interest and desire to hear what is to be said. Many of the more successful Brexorcisms I have seen and conducted are the result of a multi-stage approach with considerable warm-up and relationship building prior to any challenge. The example I mentioned in the café with the 'big dog' is a classic example of a gradual but deliberate approach to work on the issue over time.

Timing and location are also crucial if you are to reach your intended receiver and have the desired outcome. It is what I call the 'Martini' effect after the retro advertisement – **not** anytime, anywhere. More like the right time, the right place etc. The successful influencer chooses the right time and the right place to change someone's mind. That sometimes means choosing not to act just because you have your target in your sights.

Salvador Dali's 'Mountain Lake' [8] sums up perfectly the problem of no-one receiving. In this prophetic piece painted by Dali in 1938, the disconnected telephone signifies the state of meaningful conversation between Neville Chamberlain and Hitler over Sudetenland. It is vital that our subjects are engaged rather than just present and much of this relates to the importance of preparation.

---

[8] Mountain Lake, Salvador Dali – Tate Gallery, London

Thinking about Brexorcism

Reflect on the communications model and plan your interventions with key subjects :

Communications model element	Applications to me
Have a potent message How can I ensure my message is personalised? How do I ensure I respond to the other person's needs and expectations?	
Choose the right messenger(s) If the messenger(s) is not you, how can you coach the relevant person(s)?	
Choose the right communications channel(s) Remember that influence is mostly a face-to-face activity. If you are doing this on social media take note of the 7/38/55 factor.	
Ensure receiver(s) are awake, alert and receptive? How can I activate people to listen? How can I increase the odds that they will receive the message?	

Insights from psychology

If you are wishing to communicate to influence and know your receivers, it is also worth considering some general personality traits that can help or hinder your cause.

The impact of self-esteem

People with low self-esteem tend to be more persuadable than people with high self-esteem. This explains why people in distress will often take any advice even if it is inconsistent with their needs and why counsellors are never supposed to give advice. It also possibly explains why some people were willing to listen to Nigel Farage in 2016, as he was supportive of the little people who felt ignored by mainstream politicians. He also boosted their self-esteem by telling them to use their limbic system to inform their decision (vote with their hearts) rather than challenging them to conduct analysis or weigh options etc. Vote Leave visited underprivileged housing estates with high proportions of non-voters and people who felt left behind, just as Donald Trump did in the USA. Vote Leave built rapport with disenfranchised communities whilst the Remain campaign presented graphs and spreadsheets to their traditional voting communities. These simple presentation issues lost them votes. Worse still, it is a strategy that various Remain movements have gold-plated to some extent ever since, reinforcing the 'us and them' divide.

The impact of hierarchy

Authoritarian personalities who are concerned about power and status are more influenced by messages from authority figures, whereas non-authoritarian types are more susceptible to messages from anonymous sources. There are important implications here for the so called 'metropolitan elites'. Remain tried to establish authority with people who don't respect hierarchies in 2016. Quite simply it was doomed to failure. A proportion of the Leave vote can be attributed to people simply deciding to 'stick it to the man', as David Cameron tried to talk down to them with disastrous results as they rejected the messenger.

Jacob Rees-Mogg is a master of the art of encouraging deference. Feigning the appearance of an 18th century lord of the manor, Mogg uses language to befuddle people and create the impression that he is intelligent.

The impact of anxiety

Those high in anxiety are hard to persuade. If you face an anxious person in a difficult communication, your first job is to remove their anxiety. In some interactions with Brexiteers, it is fair to say that some feel like they will be made to look stupid by speaking with you. I have made this mistake on some occasions and it is a very easy trap to fall into if you know more than they do on a given subject. Quite why it is sometimes better to use social spaces rather than formal occasions to challenge viewpoints. Social spaces level out power differences. If we wanted to really change minds on Brexit, we would enlist the nations hairdressers, social workers, nail bar technicians, waiters etc. to work on people's unconscious minds. Such people often operate with no hierarchy, just relationship power.

The impact of emotions

People who are high in rich imagery, fantasies, and dreams tend to be more empathetic towards others and are more persuadable. In plain language this explains why salespeople often like being sold to! Simply stated, unicorn salespeople find it easy to sell unicorns to people who believe in unicorns! Given that some Leave voters eschew facts and often use simple analogies to describe their feelings, they are quite persuadable if we find ways to enter their limbic systems. Phrases like "all I know is ..." and "at the end of the day I see it like this ..." typify some of the ways in which this is evident in conversation. Typically, these phrases lead to dead ends in their thinking. We must open these dead ends if we are to make an impact on their thinking. This usually involves lots of empathy and supportive interventions before attempting any inductive change. I will come on to look at John Heron's six factor model [9] to help you think about your interventions later in this book.

The impact of intelligence

People of high general intelligence are more influenced by messages based on impressive logical arguments and are less likely to be influenced by messages with false, illogical, or irrelevant arguments. They may be especially sensitive to short messages that appear to be unsubstantiated in our 280-character world of Twitter soundbites. There are important implications for short versus long messages here. In practice, I spend a lot of my time finding headlines for complex issues, as well as writing longer pieces for those with longer attention spans and those who need verification of

---

[9] John Heron's six category intervention analysis – available on Amazon

headlines with underpinning facts. To better Vote Leave at their own game, we must sell on emotion and justify with facts for those willing to look beneath headlines.

Of course, generalisations can be generally unhelpful! It is always wise to work with the specific realities of each situation you face, perhaps holding the above general principles as a set of heuristics or rules of thumb rather than absolute truths.

Summary

1. To communicate in order to persuade : Have a clear, potent message; use the right messenger; use the correct communications channel and; ensure the receivers are awake, alert and receptive. Flexibility is key.

2. Ensuring your subject is ready to receive is the most important work you can do. If they are not listening, all your work is wasted.

3. Some of the people we deal with present a barrage of issues mixed up in a ball of confusion. Alongside the skills of clear communication, we also need calmness, exceptional patience and forensic skills to help them unpick their 'story' and separate general angst out from things that were related to our membership of the European Union. Sometimes no clarity or listening can come until they have unloaded the whole story on you.

4. Studies of persuasive communications and personality teach us that there are certain things we can do to increase our influence in any situation. It is always good to be able to see things from your subject's viewpoint, even if you don't agree with them.

5. Clear communications suffer from three basic problems : **deletion**, **distortion** and **generalisation**. I will come on to some remedies for these conditions in subsequent chapters.

Thinking about Brexorcism

Reflect on the above choices and make your own notes about your strategies for working more effectively with your target subjects :

Personality traits	Applications to me
Choose different approaches for people with low self-esteem as compared with those of high self-esteem.	
Authoritarian personalities are more influenced by messages from authority figures. Non-authoritarian types are more susceptible to messages from anonymous sources.	
Those high in anxiety are hard to persuade. Remove anxiety to be more persuasive.	
People who are high in rich imagery, fantasies, and dreams tend to be more empathetic towards others and are more persuadable.	
People of high general intelligence are more influenced by messages based on logic.	

Defence against the dark Brexit arts

Here we drop down from the strategic heights to street level. I examine strategies to help you defeat foes, win friends and influence people in the great 'Brexorcism' exercise that needs to take place to alter the 'will of the people'.

I have spent thousands of hours in cafés, bars, on trains, at bus stops, on the street etc. doing what J.K. Rowling would call 'Defence against the dark Brexit arts'. I have combined some 25 years of business consulting, which is all about influence and persuasion with mastery in the psychological discipline known as NLP (Neuro-Linguistic Programming). Alongside this I have the advantage of a masters' degree in the 'University of Life', gained working around the world as a business trouble-shooter and with hardened musicians in rock bands. Musicians are artistic by definition. Some may be autistic which is why they are so good at music. A few are just p...ss artists ☺ In my social world, musicians offer a great opportunity to practising skills of getting things done with difficult and diffident people. Despite what people often think, some artists are strangely disinterested in politics and world affairs. That makes them an excellent set of 'laboratory rats' to practice upon ☺ Doubtless you will find your own 'clinical trial group' to sharpen your skills!

I cannot possibly deliver a full tutorial in the skills needed to convert even semi-hardened Leave voters in one chapter. A 'Brexorcism' needs time, patience, UPR and skill and I have practised them over 20 years. These skills need hours of experiential learning through deliberate practice [10]rather than just knowing what to do. Nonetheless I can provide the key principles and stories that illustrate these principles in practice. With practice, your skills will mature rapidly. This is really an experiential art. Practice really does make perfect in the field of changing minds on Europe and Brexit.

You are welcome to contact me for the purposes of direct coaching, mentoring or group events in the gentle and sometimes abrasive change of changing hearts, minds and souls. I also run 'defence against the dark Brexit arts'' workshops for direct experiential practice on the skills.

Before we begin, I'd like to offer you eleven operating assumptions from the field of that will help you be the best you can be in this area :

---

[10] Deliberate practice, K. Anders Ericsson

Defence against the dark Brexit arts

Operating assumptions

1. We do not operate directly on the world. We create 'internal maps' from our sensory experiences (sight, sounds etc.) and operate from these maps. However, the map is not the territory. Part of the job of a good change agent is to understand the operating maps of your Brexit loving clients / victims / targets, from now on known as subjects ☺ This is why you must understand them deeply as part of the relationship building process before attempting to intervene.

2. Choice is always better than no choice. Always seek to widen the notion of choice. We have been conditioned into binary choices with 'Deal – No Deal', In – Out, British – Foreign etc. Refuse to get trapped by binary thinking as it does not open any space up for your subject to move to.

3. If you do what you've always done, you'll get what you've always got, so if what you're doing isn't working, do something else! Flexibility is key. Flexibility can come from many places, the environment, what you do, what you decide not to do, how you speak with your subject and so on.

4. There is no failure, only feedback, no mistakes only results, no errors, only learning. If you don't succeed in a Brexorcism, learn from it and move on. Picking the ideal subject is key but if you are not in that position, work as much as you can do on the person before you and be satisfied that you have done your best.

5. Experience in itself has no meaning - all meaning is context related. When a Brexiteer tells you to get over it, this may just reflect their own frustrations and anxieties. We live in a fully stressed society. Try to ignore the prod or at least don't take it personally. UPR suggests that they are doing the best they can.

6. You cannot not communicate - 93% of communication is non-verbal. So even breathing and not speaking is an intervention when speaking to Brexiteers is an intervention. Breathing is especially important when your subject is unloading more than five years of pent-up Brexit angst on you! Remember, some of these people will not have had the profound experience of being listened to.

Defence against the dark Brexit arts

Operating assumptions

7. The meaning of communication is the response you get, which may be different than the one you intended. By making small talk to the drugged-up youths that eventually punched me, I had hoped not to draw them into a communication loop. Clearly this did not work! But I have only had a few difficult encounters in five years of this and I do attract difficult cases by my clothing so my experience is not the norm in this respect.

8. There is a positive intention behind all human behaviour. The youths that punched me were trying to fulfil something positive for themselves even though it seemed less positive for me. With more time and skill, I may have helped them to find less violent ways to realise their intention. Sadly, sometimes in the thick of it, there is not time to get a flip chart out and run a focus group on attitudes to anger … ☺

9. What is possible for one person is possible for others since all humans share the same neurology. If I can wander into a café and change minds through tea and empathy, so can you.

10. Each of us has or can create the resources we need to do whatever we choose. We must become opportunity seekers as there are opportunities to change minds at every bus stop, in every bar and bedroom.

11. The individual with the greatest flexibility of thought and behaviour can (and generally will) control the outcome of any interaction. Therefore, we must be agile when talking with Brexiteers. You may have noticed how some will keep changing the subject when cornered on Brexit specifics, what I call shapeshifting. This allows them to control the conversation. Ensure that you control the agenda overall, even if you allow them to drift occasionally for the purposes of rapport.

A key skill in personal excellence is the ability to try on new assumptions. So, imagine that each of these operating assumptions is a coat which you can wear for one day to see what differences emerge. You may be surprised at the results you achieve if you act as if these assumptions are true. Daily practice is the key to personal mastery.

Blowing Brexit bubbles

Some Remainers tell me that they don't like talking to people who voted to Leave. I understand that. It can be like dealing with dementors in the Harry Potter sense of the word. In other words, people who suck your very life force and happiness away! Typically, with catchphrases such as :

"We won two wars and we can win this one".

"We can grow are own doctors, nurses and vegetables"

"I want food rationing. It will teach the young respect for their elders".

"Brexit Means Brexit. End Off".

"War will make men of the young people"

My own sister told me without the slightest shred of evidence that she voted Leave to "prevent Sharia law on Tonbridge high street" and her husband points out that "there are two million German (she meant Turkish) rapists just waiting to get into the UK from Berlin", although they have a German daughter in law. These are bizarre thoughts. My sister co-locates the onset of Sharia law in her mind with the rise of kebab shops on Tonbridge high street. It is one of my greatest frustrations that I have not succeeded at a full Brexorcism of my sister. However, if we don't work outside our comfort bubbles, we achieve little that will contribute towards 'moving the dial' in terms of public opinion for a General Election, referendum or to heal the nation after Brexit ends. We are in effect, 'forever blowing bubbles', so take courage people. A little confidence, a lot of time, extreme patience and lots of skills are needed. Renew yourselves and begin again.

I am aware that many families and friends now avoid conversations about Brexit in social situations. However, attitudes towards Brexit have changed if you have not dared to use the B word in polite conversation for some time, with people more willing to listen to informed dialogue in many cases. The war in Ukraine, sadly, is a game changer in so far that it has made people much more aware of the need for a united approach to world problems. If saying the B word is too much, find a new word for Brexit. Perhaps start talking about being European. One thing is true. Silence is assent. It won't move the dial on Brexit.

Thinking about Brexorcism

Reflect on the 11 assumptions and make your own notes about your views.

NLP assumptions	Applications to me
1. The map is not the territory.	
2. Choice is always better than no choice.	
3. If you do what you've always done, you'll get what you've always got.	
4. There is no failure, only feedback.	
5. All meaning is context related.	

Thinking about Brexorcism

NLP assumptions	Applications to me
6. You cannot not communicate.	
7. The meaning of communication is the response you get.	
8. There is a positive intention behind all human behaviour.	
9. What is possible for one person is possible for others.	
10. Each of us has or can create the resources we need to do whatever we choose.	
11. The individual with the greatest flexibility of thought and behaviour can (and generally will) control the outcome of any interaction.	

The Brexit psyche

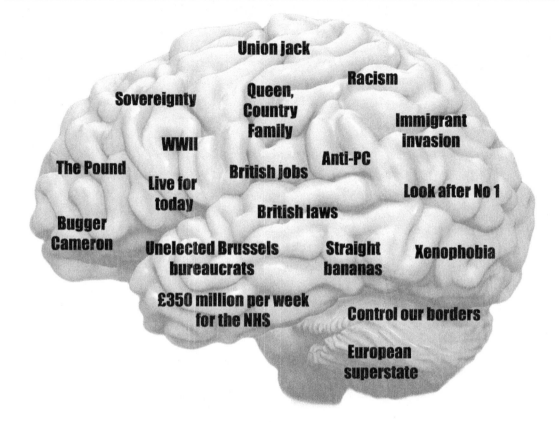

Conversing with hundreds of Leave voters in cafés, bars and on the street over thousands of hours reveals some general traits of what the psychological discipline NLP (Neuro-Linguistic Programming) would call 'meta-programmes'. These are akin to the unconscious operating programmes or algorithms that inform people's thoughts, feelings and behaviours. Leave voters often, but not always, because one can never generalise, think in these kinds of dimensions :

Temporal : Their time perspective is often very short term. Today, this week, this month, possibly as far ahead as a summer holiday. But there's rarely much point talking to Leave voters about Jacob Rees-Mogg's 50-year Brexit scenarios, as it frequently provokes responses such as 'But I'll be dead' or even 'Who is Jacob Rees-Mogg?' Of course, many Leavers do have children and grandchildren, which can change matters, as we discuss later. Speaking about families is also a good way to build rapport as it is usually something that they can and will engage with.

As well as people's time horizon there is also the question of people's orientation in time, in other words, whether they look to the past, present or future as their main reference points for making judgements. It turns out from thousands of conversations that many Leave voters use the past as a reference point for a 'golden age' when things were good, the assumption being that now or the future cannot compare in any way, shape or form. The 1950s to the 1970s seem to be the most quoted times from Leave voters when 'we' in Britain were doing well, even though much of Britain was a bomb site in the 1950s, we had the three-day week in the 1970s and we joined the EEC as the 'sick man of Europe'. Or even longer ago, as this nostalgic Leave voter tweets :

"The East Coast Main Line did work rather well under the real LNER (1923-47), complete with the setting of a speed record in 1938, which stands to this day .".

Of course, history tends to delete some of the more challenging aspects of people's memories as they age. So, typhoid, measles, rationing, the three-day week, electricity blackouts, bearbaiting, electric shock treatments of homosexuals and so on are often deleted from people's longer-term memories. The 'lost paradise' input to our Brexit vote was poignantly summed up by Billy Bragg [11] in his song 'Full English Brexit' in ways that words alone cannot achieve. Check the song out. Broadly speaking Bragg artfully illustrates the point that 'nostalgia ain't what it used to be'.

My neighbours don't drink at the local
Or have kippers for breakfast like me
The food that they eat smells disgusting
They'd rather drink coffee than tea

I cheered when our side won the Cold War
Spread freedom and peace all around
Now there's folks speaking Russian in Tescos
It's a shame the wall had to come down

Spatial : In terms of geography, a Leave voter's compass often centres around their house and family, their street, their town, possibly England but rarely further. I was listening into a café conversation, where a small group of OABs (Old Age Brexiteers) were 'celebrating the advent of blue passports'. I was quietly bemused to find the café

---

[11] Billy Bragg – Full English Brexit www.billybragg.co.uk

Status Quo, gammon, chips and beer

Tim Wetherspoon cleverly capitalises on the 'lost paradise' aspect of older Leave voters though his political campaigns in Wetherspoons pubs, his fine taste for old buildings, no-nonsense cheap food and beer. In fairness the pub environments are not 1970s, the staff are friendly but most other things are. I am just surprised that 'Chicken in the basket' is not on the menu. I can only assume that the damned EU banned the baskets as unhygienic!

A pub chat with the manager and staff in one of their outlets tells me that staff like the social atmosphere of their fellow workers. They mostly hate Tim but keep quiet rather like workers in Putin's Russia. We cannot blame them for that in a gig economy that provides little in long-term employment or career opportunities. Amazingly, they were not only happy for me to place anti Brexit stickers in the pub, but they also actively encouraged it!

So, be nice to Wetherspoons' staff. It is not exactly their fault! Whether you love or hate Tim personally you cannot deny that his strategy is future focused, for him … it seems to me that Tim seeks market dominance by pushing prices down to a level where independent pubs cannot compete in a kind of Soviet style 'alegarchy'. Once Wetherspoons has achieved that, Tim can do what he likes … except that large segment of his clientele are quite literally a dying breed … we'll see what happens with his idea of a full English Brexit food menu … I guess that will be curry then …

owner asking them when they last left the country, whilst winking at me. It turned out that none of them had ever travelled abroad. Three of them (from four) had never even visited London (30 miles / 49 minutes by train) in some 60 + years on planet earth. Globalisation does not mean much to such people. It is bewildering and we achieve little by discussing it, apart from sounding like elitists, unless they bring it up as part of their rationale for leaving the EU, for which there are clear answers.

Self-centredness : In terms of self or other centricity, I note with some sadness that there is rarely any ability to see Brexit from any viewpoint other than their own. Human beings are basically animals and our sense of self-preservation is a primal instinct unless we actively choose to over-ride it consciously. So, appeals based on worldliness, selflessness or greater good type approaches can fall on deaf ears. We hear this played out when people say "we should look after our own" when they criticise charitable activity or world aid programmes. In NLP terminology, I note that some Leavers have trouble getting into 'second' position, certainly 'third', where they can see things from a dispassionate perspectives outside their own. At the same time these people can demonstrate remarkable detachment where they seal themselves off from the awful implications of Brexit as if they have been wrapped in cotton wool. In the extreme, this is demonstrated graphically by faux celebrity Katie Hopkins who reported :

"Show me bodies floating in the water, play violins and show me skinny people looking sad. I don't care".

The F words : in a lot of cases, Leave voters want to Leave the EU based on **feelings** which have been carefully and consistently ingrained as hard beliefs over many years through consumption of lies from the populist media. These were reinforced in the referendum through catchy slogans by the likes of Nigel Farage. **Fighting feelings** with **facts** can be a very difficult game to play as you are confronting quasi-religious beliefs with information and this is not an equal contest for someone who has almost been radicalised. Hence my use of the term 'Brexorcism' in this book. Even broadcaster James O'Brien finds it difficult to gain acceptance from his callers when he provides facts that counter their firmly felt feelings. We must recognise that change may occur **after** an interaction and his LBC Radio show is necessarily limited by the fact that it is mostly a time constrained and single shot theatre for conversation. But, of course, people can hear themselves not listening on playback if they so choose. This must be a painful experience for some, as they experience the pain that comes from 'cognitive dissonance' as they try to hold two opposing thoughts in their minds about a topic simultaneously. It is well worth listening to James' programme as he does his job under incredible time pressure and there are many parallels in his work with what we must do.

We could rant on here about what is wrong with such people but it does no good. Seek first to gain rapport, understand their viewpoint, however dissonant it is with yours. You then stand a better chance of changing hearts and minds if you respond flexibly.

NLP offers a different take on how we think, via what it calls meta language patterns, meta meaning 'above' the actual words that we use, the structure of our communications and the embedded assumptions.

Language Pattern	Behaviour	Brexit applications
Towards or away from	Whether people move towards pleasure or away from pain.	This neatly explains why some Brexiteers discount project fear and why others are persuaded by vague promises of better times.
External or internally referenced	The extent to which people evaluate things using their own internal filters or using external criteria.	This may partly explain why Brexiteers were persuaded to vote with their hearts by Nigel Farage and why external data was ignored.
Self or other centred-ness	The 'what's in it for me' factor versus a more systemic view i.e., what they can do for themselves or others.	We have already discussed that some Brexiteers seem to have a more limited field of vision regarding the meaning of Brexit.
Sort for the familiar or difference	Familiar things are given preference than difference.	Conversations with Brexiteers suggest that some feel alienated by many things these days. Although few of these things are caused by the EU, it is a convenient coat-hanger to hang problems on.

[12] To read more about language patterns, check out 'Influencing with integrity' by Genie Z. Laborde – an accessible read on the subject.

Language [12] Pattern	Behaviour	Brexit applications
Convincer strategy	What does it take to convince someone that something is true?	A fundamental error in the referendum campaign was the belief that if people thought they would be worse off they would vote to stay in the EU. Instead, many voted to 'stick it to Cameron', others swallowed the lies about the NHS, Turkey and so on.
Possibility versus necessity	The extent that people focus on just what they need or what they want.	The Leave campaign offered an opulent vision of freedom and a land of milk and honey without specifying how any of this might be deliverable. This is now coming to light but the journey back will be difficult.
Independent thinking versus group think	The extent to which people are independent thinkers or whether they follow the herd.	The importance of this cannot be overstated when considering broadcast media such as The Sun, Mail, Express, consumed in cafés and so on. I note that many Brexiteers operate in 'herds'.

Characterising the Brexit psyche

I wrote a song to characterise the feeling of 'buyer's remorse' that exists within some people who voted Leave. I set the song up as a nostalgic football anthem called "Alo' Vera – Brexit's Comin' 'Ome". The lyrics convey some of the stereotypes of lost England and so on. Coincidentally Vera Lynn died on the day I released the song! Find 'Alo Vera on Apple Music, Amazon, Spotify, Bandcamp and the video on our EU Tube channel www.youtube.com/academyofrock

'Alo Vera Lynn Don't know where u have bin I've bin fightin' Brexit with Victory Gin

Soon we will be fruit pickin' Cos we are the Brexit fishermin'

It's comin' 'ome, it's comin' 'ome Brexit's comin' 'ome and the nurses are goin' 'ome

Que sera, what will be will be

Some will live, some will die But I've got a passport, a coin and a tie

While Boris tells another pork pie I leave the snowflakes to cry

From Nigel Farridge to Bobby Moore 48 : 52 we knew the score

After Corona we want more It's gonna be just like the war

It's comin' 'ome, it's comin' 'ome Brexit's comin' 'ome I'm home alone and my hair I cannot comb

It's comin' 'ome, it's comin' 'ome Brexit's comin' 'ome I'm home alone and I can't afford a scone

I'm not a remona We drink the Corona We are the doctors, nurses, scientific persona

We are the Brexit land army .. From Verona We fear no ill For we have Bojona

'Alo Vera All Cor Blimey We're gonna take back control of Old Blighty

The M20's blocked all nighty But Bulldog Spirits' gonna make it alrighty If you just take off your nightie ...

It's comin' 'ome, it's comin' 'ome Brexit's comin' 'ome etc.

Restoring blank canvases

How then do we re-format minds that have already been 'programmed' over many years? With great difficulty is a starting answer but it can be done. In the world of art, it is much easier to paint on a blank canvas than one that has already been painted on ... In other words, the populist press had already etched firmly held beliefs on these people's minds over many years. Challenging such ingrained views is rather like trying to apply an aggressive paint stripper to their minds or undo a writeable CD that has already been written on and finalised. The technical term for this is unlearning. It is much harder than learning as it requires the 'undo' step. Yet, this is not like pressing the undo process on your computer. It is an analogue process. People are analogue.

To stand a chance in this dark art, extensive preparation is required. You almost need to get permission and agreement to perform the 'Brexorcism'. Sometimes it helps if your subject does not even know that they are being reprogrammed. Social settings are good for this and sometimes understated methods can seep into people's minds better than the standard tools of selling and persuasion. Great influence is often an artform which is almost invisible to the recipient. Therefore, I sometimes wander into cafés and bars with apparently no agenda, letting my subjects or 'victims' come to me, usually via an initial interaction with one of my T-shirts, badges or artefacts. Over nearly five years of doing this I find that some of my best work is almost invisible to the untrained eye.

The Great Mistake

Tommy and Nigel are moving to Europe
Ever had the feeling you've been conned?

Let's Re-Boot Britain
www.brexitrage.com

Brexitosis

A delusional condition. If left untreated it can lead to FBFR (**F**ull **B**lown **F**ar **R**age), characterised by continuing to make statements such as :

"We need them more than they need us".

"We can have our cake and eat it too".

"The EU are going to tell us what type of toilet roll we can use".

"There are two million rapists waiting to invade Tonbridge from Berlin".

NLP unplugged

Neuro-Linguistic Programming (NLP) comes with a mixed reputation. It is said that NLP master Paul Mc Kenna helped Vote Leave create the snappy slogans that helped them win the referendum, as a friend of Aaron Banks. If that's not a good enough testimony to its power, then I am not sure what is. NLP has, of course, been linked with ideas about mind manipulation, spin and other things which some Remainers see as 'negative'. However, it is not 'positive' to walk on by and let such people have their way. We must better them rather than moan that it's not fair. Life is not fair and we need to lead the conversation rather than lag.

The degree to which NLP is used or abused lies with the people using it. But I am aware that some find it hard to separate the tool from the person. I am however going to do that in what follows, offering you a digest of the main ideas of value to people trying to achieve change in the minds of Brexiteers. I have spent many years studying NLP and related psychologies and a casual read of this book will not make you a master of the art and discipline.   But it will supplement your own experience and common sense in making better interventions. It would be worth your while reading up on related matters to gain a wider perspective.

NLP is not a theory. It is a model of what works. The test of a theory is whether it is right or wrong. The test of a model is its usefulness. Unlike other models that tell you **what** you need to do, NLP shows you **how** to do it. There are numerous definitions of NLP - one of the most practical ones is :

NLP is the study of the effect of language, both verbal and non-verbal in producing excellence in human communications, to achieve desired results.

The awkward name comes from the developments of cognitive science in the 1970s, when research into the brain and the nervous system began to overlap with artificial intelligence studies in the computer field, producing enormous leaps in our understanding of the 'mind'. Although Neuro-Linguistic Programming is a long title, the separate terms precisely identify its meaning :

Neuro   About your brain and its function.

Linguistic   How language affects the way you see the world, both syntax (the words) and body language.

Programming   About our ability to make different choices in life and be flexible.

NLP [13] offers us a simple and flexible formula for influential communications to get things done. In a nutshell :

NLP in a nutshell

To achieve anything in life, you need to do four things :

1. Gain **rapport** with the person(s) you wish to influence. This means finding something common with them rather than something in difference such as your views on Europe and Brexit.

2. Know what you want with precision. This is your **outcome**. Your outcome is the end result of your interaction, for your subject as well as yourself.

3. Notice responses of others, verbal and non-verbal. This is **acuity**, also known as active listening, reaching beyond the words themselves to the way they are said, the body language and embedded assumptions.

4. Keep changing what you do until you get the outcomes you want. This is **flexibility**. The most creative person will generally control the outcome of an interaction.

---

[13] Introducing Neuro-Linguistic Programming by Joseph O'Connor and John Seymour

Other ways of saying this include :

If you always do what you always did, you'll always get what you always got. So, if what you're doing isn't working, do something else!

... or, more cynically if you are that way inclined :

One definition of insanity is doing the same things and expecting a different result!

The formula is easy to write down. In essence it is a healthy dose of common sense, but common sense is not in common use!

NLP provides practical tools and underpinning values for achieving each part of the formula. Taking these in turn :

1. Gaining rapport

It is impossible to influence anyone if you do not have bond of trust, even if this is limited to the terms of the current interaction that you are involved with. Rapport usually arises naturally when two people share something in common. When working with people who voted to Leave, you are working with people which you have difference built in by their very nature. So, we must look in other places to find a common bond. This can of course be a myriad of things – music, football, fitness, relationships, hobbies, family, travel, place of birth and so on

Where there are no natural sources of rapport but you still need to make progress in an interaction, the idea of **matching** the other person's observable behaviour, e.g., the actual language they use, voice tone and quality, body language etc. may give some basic rapport. For example, when people have natural rapport, their posture is often the same. Do some people watching to learn more, especially social groups or people in love. Using the same language as your subject can be a simple way to tune into their wavelength. We can use this knowledge to gain greater rapport with people when we may be offering them more challenging thoughts. If you are going to tell people stuff that they don't agree with you need a bigger 'bank balance' of things in common to ensure that they listen.

Conversely when you wish to disconnect from a conversation or change the subject, try **mismatching**. This can be subtle. We do it all the time in social situations by looking at our watch, using gestures and so on, but it can be done deliberately without causing offence. I find that Leave voters also do it quite naturally by changing the subject when challenged. I sometimes allow them to get away with this to maintain rapport, whilst promising myself to return to the issue once we have re-built rapport, rather like following them in a dance when they put a foot wrong.

Once you have rapport, focus on your outcome for the interaction. This is different than a goal. An outcome describes the end product of the interaction in terms of what you wish to see, hear and feel different, for your subject and yourself of course.

2. Know your outcome

Well-formed **outcomes** are ones that drive success in an interaction. For example, do you really need your Brexiteers to become enthusiastic advocates for the EU or is it merely sufficient to move them away from abject hatred of the EU to a point of indifference. The tactics to achieve the former are much harder than the latter. Too many people seek a full 180-degree evangelical conversion when a move to what psychologists and Ken Clarke call a 'zone of indifference' or a 90-degree refocus (no longer wish to Brexit) or complete indifference to voting again (ambivalence about Brexit) may be sufficient for a pragmatic approach.

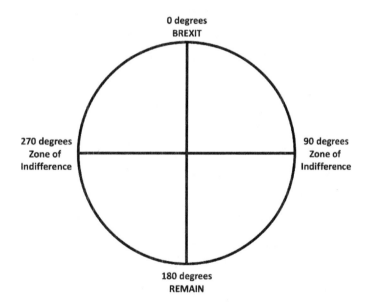

NLP offers specific tools to help you clarify goals and outcomes which are outside the scope of this book. Outcomes are often shared in the world of business as it is essential for others to share in the goal. In the case of influencing a Leave voter there are occasions when the goal will be shared, for example in a panel debate or radio interview when the other person will know that you are taking an opposing view. In other cases, you may be working 'underground'. Machiavelli would advise that you can only have a conspiracy of one person! So, it is sometimes unwise to broadcast what you are doing in the game of Brexorcism. Some of the best work happens between strangers when there is no need to 'win' an argument. Practise the gentle art of naïve conversation for those occasions when you find yourself just 'shooting the breeze' with a stranger.

3. Acuity

'Seek first to understand'.

Acuity [14] is a fancy word for using **all** your senses for the purpose of listening, rather than just using your ears. It has been shown that body language represents 55% of any interpersonal communication message, voice tone 38% and the words only 7%. This helps to explain the myriad of misunderstandings that occur on social media when you only have the 7% of communication plus a few emoticons in your toolkit. In the case of Brexit, we are often trying to explain quite complex concepts using less than 280 characters on Twitter to people that may well be on a completely different wavelength, so there is no basic rapport or shared outcome. I am not saying that dialogue on social media is pointless as a tool of influence, but it is important to be aware of the limitations compared with face-to-face communications. Read more on this via 'online Brexorcism'.

Listening is thus an active process, going beyond the actual words used. Furthermore, different people use different senses to make sense of what is happening, i.e., sight, sound, feelings, taste and smell. These thinking styles 'leak out in our language', e.g. I can **see** what you mean, I **hear** what you say, I **feel** that it will work out, Brexit **smells** bad and we will soon **taste** the sweet freedoms of Brexit. One can of course match the language of your subject to make them feel that you understand them better or work in their predominant 'meta-mode' i.e., sights, sounds, feelings, smell, taste. NLP zealots insist on using these techniques like a robot. In music, this is the equivalent of merely reading the sheet music when performing on stage at a rock concert. With experience, I prefer to use cold technique sparingly and authentically, adding in your own natural expression rather than working from a textbook. However, if you wish to gain greater rapport, listen well to the language that your subject uses and reflect it back to some

---

[14] In NLP, sensory acuity enables us to stop mind reading and start calibrating (not guessing) what body language is telling them.

degree in your responses. You will then better enter their world without them thinking that you are some kind of bizarre mirror for their thoughts.

4. Flexibility of thought and deed

"If you have no choice you are dead
If you have one choice, you have no choice
If you have two choices, you have a dilemma
If you have three or more choices, you have the makings of a real choice"

The more points of view you have, the better off you are with respect to being influential. Flexibility of thought **and** behaviour are required if you want to get a different response in each situation. One definition of madness is doing the same things but expecting a different result. If your chosen subject for a Brexorcism is not responding, NLP teaches us that the onus is on **us** to change the situation rather than to wait for them to wake up. This calls on our creativity and agility as human beings. For a full tutorial on creativity, read our book Leading Innovation, Creativity and Enterprise. I am also happy to provide 1 : 1 coaching and mentoring in this area, based on 127 proven techniques we have taught over many years on MBA programmes and via corporate workshops across the world.

Human beings communicate in a **system**. In other words, if one party varies their response, the other side usually must respond differently, provided they are listening to you. This is flexibility of **behaviour**. So, if your subject is saying we must take back control, break the pattern by asking what part of control matters to him or her. We can also change the environment and other aspects of the interaction to break the cycle of rapport. In practice, I find that many Leave voters don't hear what they say themselves, let alone the responses to others. On occasion, I have asked them to tell me what I just said to interrupt the pattern of non-communication. Sometimes I have even walked away for 10 minutes, saying that I'll return when we agree to take turns. I had to do this once with one of the leaders of the People's Vote campaign since he was exhibiting the same pattern of behaviour. Walking away is quite an aggressive hierarchical intervention but is sometimes necessary if no listening is occurring. Pattern breaking is an important skill to learn to improve the quality of conversation.

Perceptual positions

Flexibility of **thinking** can also arise if you change your perception of a situation. Expert influencers know that, in any situation of interpersonal influence, there are at least three points of view or what NLP calls perceptual positions:

1. Your own   Known as 1st position in NLP

2. The other person's   Known as 2nd position in NLP

3. The viewpoint of a 'detached' observer   Known as 3rd position in NLP

We spend a lot of time living inside our own world or 1st position. Often people who work in service jobs spend a lot of time working inside their client's shoes or 2nd position. Creative thinkers often see situations anew, as if they are unworldly. This is 3rd position in pure form. These crude stereotypes ignore the notion that we are all capable of working in all three positions if we choose to do so

If you are not getting enough of what you want in a situation, try altering the 'position'[15] from which you are operating, notice what is different and then modify your behaviour accordingly. Practical manifestations of this include asking your subject to switch positions, for example ask:

"How would you feel about Brexit if you were a migrant drowning in the sea?"

"How would you feel if it were your business that had gone down the toilet due to Brexit?"

... or perhaps something less gruesome or direct if this suits your style better. Innocent questions that alter people's world view are the breakfast of brexorcists.

---

[15] Perceptual positions are a form of NLP modelling that allows us to step into somebody else's shoes, and see what they see, hear what they hear, and feel what they feel.

Flexibility in practice

*"You have told me you want your country back.
Where did it go? Who took it? When did it leave?"*

*"How do you know it was taken?
What has been lost?"*

"What specifically do you want back?"

"What do your children think about this?"

*"If you were to look back on your decision in 20
years' time, what would you say?"*

"What will you tell your grandchildren about Brexit?"

On flexibility

If you always do what you always did, you will always get what you always got ...

So, if what you are doing isn't working, do something different ...

Use 1st, 2nd, 3rd position

Thinking about Brexorcism

NLP process	Applications to me
Gain **rapport** – match your subject's language, voice tone, pace, posture, body language etc.	
Know your **outcome** – what do you expect for your subject and yourself from this interaction?	
Have **acuity** – open all the senses to listen intently to your subject and the underlying structure of their communication, what is said and what not.	
Practice **flexibility** of thought and deed whilst keeping sight on the outcome.	

On flexibility

Sources tell me that some of the central Remain / Rejoin movements are in danger of copying the design that lost them the referendum ... hiring the same faces with the same strategies that did not perform well in 2016.

Nigel Farage et al. had clear strategies, the advantage of pliable followers etc. But it is never a good idea to copy someone's strategy. That just takes you to a point of equivalence.

If you can't beat them, better them

How can you be more flexible to achieve more?

Defence against dementors

To be an effective influencer, try finding things you can agree on with your Leave voter. They need not be lies if you are to retain your sense of integrity. In Harry Potter this is rather like dealing with dementors. It is what NLP refers to as 'pacing and leading'. Pacing is when you are in the other person's reality, in their shoes so to speak. Leading is when you are operating from your own point of view and literally leading them to see different realities. A story serves to illustrate the principle :

Trumptown and Brexit

I was talking to a pub owner in Minster on The Isle of Sheppey. He had fought for his country in the Falklands, came back to the UK and felt let down by the UK. This is a familiar story. I have seen it when wandering around military fairs and talking to veterans and 'Help for Heroes' supporters. It is not without some justification. Many people joined the army expecting a cradle to grave care package. It is now largely left to the third sector to provide support for injured forces personnel, but none of this was caused by the European Union.

His pub was empty. Another source of angst, although not one that was caused by the EU. He told me he wanted to leave the UK with his Russian wife to live in the US as a committed Brexit and Trump supporter. He was not expecting me to agree that he was right to feel fed up.

Once we had established that he was right to feel fed up with his lot (pacing), he found it a bit easier to hear my point that, whilst he was right to feel left behind, he was wrong to blame the EU for his regrets. I had separated the effect (angst) from the perceived cause of his angst (the EU). I was helped significantly by the fact that he really hated the Corbynista 'Billy Bragg' protester who also frequented the pub and played Bragg's songs really badly. He told me 'At least you can fucking sing and play mate' ... faint praise ... He also hated Corbyn and the other performer who constantly banged on about a return to Communism in Britain ... The lesson learned here is that we must take rapport from wherever it comes! I found it easy to agree that the other chap was not up to standard, even though he himself agreed with the landlord about Brexit as a hard left hater of anything vaguely democratic.

I had given the landlord credit for some of his analysis. This gave me the smallest of 'bank balances' to draw upon, to challenge him about the root causes of his concerns.

In truth it took a little time to get him to listen (I did not achieve it in one single session and incubation time is often helpful). I had 'warmed him up' over a few months through musical performances. This included getting him to participate with a performance of our Chas & Dave Cockney Brexit Knees Up 'Boll..cks to Brexit' (See www.brexitrage.com) beforehand. Finding ways to soften your 'client' is all part of the skill of a change agent. It is what Kurt Lewin discussed when he used the terms unfreezing, changing and refreezing. Unfreezing your victim does not have to involve making them do a 'Chas & Dave Cockney Brexit Knees Up' however! It can be as simple as spending time listening to them, buying them a drink and so on.

Summary

- Great communicators systematically create rapport with people they have little in common with.
- They are clear on their outcome for an intervention or series of interventions. This may merely mean gaining acceptance for an alternative viewpoint or a complete 180-degree Brexorcism.
- They pay good attention to their subject through acuity and respect their viewpoints, regardless of their legitimacy or accuracy.
- Crucially they maintain flexibility. This means shifting shapes in response to the other person's response rather than holding onto positions and ideologies. Hold on to outcomes rather than positions, just as a good negotiator does.
- A key skill is that of **pacing** (being in the subject's position and viewpoint) and **leading** when appropriate. This involves the use of what NLP calls 1st, 2nd and 3rd position.
- The use of 1st, 2nd and 3rd position also gives you the possibility of being more influential than your subject. Do it with empathy and authenticity to avoid seeming unethical or arrogant.
- Context is everything and successful influencers warm their subjects up for a Brexorcism, sometimes over time.

Six styles of Brexorcism

It ain't what you do, it's the way that you do it

Great communicators adopt a range of styles that are consistent with the Brexorcism outcome they seek. They systematically work through the flexible process for changing minds that we described in the last chapter :

- Gaining **rapport** with their subject(s).
- Setting clear **outcomes** for an intervention or series of interventions.
- Paying attention to their subject through **acuity** and respect for their viewpoints regardless of their legitimacy.
- Acting with **flexibility**. This means shifting shapes in response to the other person's response, environment, behaviour etc.

Skilled communicators use the entire spectrum of behavioural styles available to them. Sometimes they use 'push' approaches. At other times they 'pull'.

In this chapter we consider the full range of styles of interpersonal communications' styles available to you. I find John Heron's model of intervention styles especially relevant, since these cover interventions across the spectrum from **directive** to **non-directive**. Heron's model was originally developed for therapeutic interventions. It is therefore very applicable to the act of 'Brexorcism', since we are often working at the level of fundamental beliefs change, even identity in some cases. The model flags up the many roles that a great brexorcist must be willing and able to use.

Heron's model covers six styles, broken into two types :

Directive, where you are overall in control of the interaction, and ;

Non-directive, which offers your subject shared control of the interaction.

Directive approaches are usually quicker. However, non-directive approaches offer a greater possibility of ownership of any changes that are achieved by the person you are trying to influence. In practice master communicators move between these modes with flair un-noticed by their subjects. To observe this in practice, tune into James O'Brien on

LBC. His radio show operates under a necessary constraint of time and of course O'Brien is a broadcaster, so he tends to use more of the directive approaches to fit in between the radio adverts and news. Due to his media platform, his callers sometimes allow him to move to the more directive styles. In other words, some callers accept that hierarchy is baked into James' relationship with them. It is possible to hear deference in some of the people who call in and I sense that he uses this with great skill. On occasion with hardened cases, you will hear James using the most delightful catalytic and cathartic approaches, even supporting styles, when he says things like :

"Look, you are a good man and I don't want to fall out with you over this".

"So, which law are you looking getting rid of most?"

Here are the six styles, broken into the two modes of interaction : **Directive** and ; **Non-directive**. These broadly correspond with 'push' and 'pull', although they are a little subtler than this binary division implies. We will next break down the six styles.

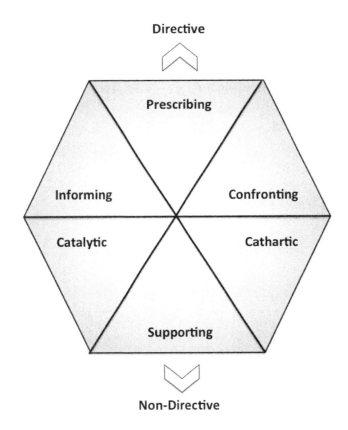

The NLP process

Rapport

Without rapport you ain't got nothin'

Outcome

Stick to your outcome, not your position

Acuity

Open all your orifices to receive

Flexibility

The most flexible person will generally control the outcome

Prescribing (Directive) : Essentially a 'tell' style. For example :

"Take these pills and you'll feel better".

Prescribing is probably the quickest way to get someone to do something. However, the quickest way is not always the most effective way. We know full well that we don't always take the doctor's advice if it does not accord with our own wants, whims and fancies. The Dunning-Kruger effect is relevant here, where people of low ability tend to assess their own cognitive abilities as being superior to experts and vice versa. It is perhaps for this reason that we need the other influencing styles below since we are not that great at taking direct advice if it is dissonant with our prevailing beliefs.

Informing (Directive) : Neutrally passing on information, ideas and knowledge. For example :

"Recent research shows that public support for Rejoining the EU has risen to between 56% and 59%".

This gives your subject the chance to make their own minds up without feeling pressurised or manipulated. Informing does not draw a conclusion. It simply provides information, leaving the recipient to draw their own conclusions and formulate actions. However, one often needs a lot of time for your subject to process the information provided to them. There is of course always a risk that the information will be processed but no action will result or possibly the 'wrong' course of action and you may of course get blanked with one of the usual stock phrases such as "Brexit is done, end off". Yes, I know off is not spelt correctly! Whilst informing may be more effective in the long-term, it requires more time and processing power on the part of your subject than prescribing. It's often helpful to combine informing with other styles on the non-directive end of the spectrum such as supporting or cathartic intervention.

Confronting (Directive) : Involves challenging viewpoints and requires the examination of motives. For example :

"You said that you are not a racist, but you keep saying that you hate people from Eastern Europe and want them drowned. That sounds like racism to me".

Confronting should not be confused with aggression – it can be done with a soft pillow as well as a hard edge, depending on the other 93% of the communication mix. Quite why I always smile or at least look blank, when telling Leave voters things they find hard to hear. Confronting is one of the more difficult interventions that you can undertake as it usually results in some level of cognitive dissonance, where people are held to account or get 'found out'. Done with skill, it can be very effective and relatively quick, but once again the Dunning-Kruger effect applies and people can become actively defensive or, worse still, passively so, which is harder to spot. Time is usually needed after a confrontation and it is also best combined with non-directive approaches to help your subject 'cool off'.

Non-directive interventions usually take longer than directive ones. After all they are literally less 'direct'. However, they may be very effective in more troublesome situations. They also require greater levels of skill and 'sleight of hand' delivery techniques to make them work. The TV detective Columbo is a great place to study these interventions used in a particular direction to nail a suspect. Columbo rarely confronts his suspects, using a series of much more subtle but clever interventions to smoke the culprits out. Far from a simple piece of entertainment, I discovered from the Metropolitan Police Diplomatic Protection Group that they use Columbo at Hendon Police College to train their top detectives for similar reasons that I have described here. They contrasted Columbo's approach with much less-effective approaches from other TV copumentaries such as Morse. One of them explained that 'Columbo always gets his man whereas there are many unnecessary deaths on the way to solving a crime in Inspector Morse. We generally regard unnecessary deaths as bad policing'.

Cathartic (Non-directive) : Interventions that enable people to 'get things off their chest'. For example :

"Can we spend some time exploring why freedom of movement only applies to EU Citizens coming to UK but not to Brits wishing to travel abroad?"

Catharsis can be extremely powerful as a means of allowing people to relive tension about things that are hard to express in more direct terms. One example of this is the use of extended metaphor, where you ask your subject to describe the issue under discussion in metaphorical terms. Sometimes this level of detachment allows people to say hard to say or unsayable things. See also our discussion on 2nd and 3rd position from NLP earlier. Here's a little example of extended metaphor :

"Getting Brexit done is like turning a big ship on the ocean. It will take years and you Remoaners are simply crying salty tears because Leavers are winning".

"OK, following the maritime theme, where are we headed and what should I expect when we arrive on shore? Has Brexit run aground?"

Catalytic (Non-directive) : Providing a sounding board and helping others to come up with their own solutions. For example :

"Would you like to explain more about what Brexit will offer you personally?"

Catalytic interventions build on the idea of catalysis in chemistry. A catalyst is used in small doses to promote a reaction but is itself not involved in the actual reaction and remains unchanged at the end of that reaction. It is once again a detached position to take for the influencer, giving your subjects space to reflect, consider novel ideas and rethink old approaches. Remember your role is to be used in small doses. More is less in this field.

Supporting (Non-directive) : Feedback to your subject in which they are actively listened to and encouraged in what they are doing. For example :

"I can understand why you would feel left behind".

"You are right to feel pissed off that we never took back control of the fishing'.

Supporting is often of great value when using the more challenging directive interventions in Heron's model. It provides the essential positive assets in the 'bank balance' between you and your subject to draw on when dealing with more challenging elements such as confrontation and prescribing. In general, it is always wise to use plenty of pull strategies if you are also pushing for change and a sensible ratio is at least 2 : 1 pull : push. It is also important to consider the 'rhythm' of your interventions. After all, change is like a dance at some level and keeping in step with those you are attempting to engage in the dance of change is important if you are to maintain a high conversion ratio of thoughts into actions.

Great influencers are both well-prepared and also great improvisers to follow lines of enquiry, balancing the need for direction with the need to induce thinking and action within their subjects. Hold on to your outcome but be prepared to vary the journey towards that outcome. That's where flexibility comes in. As mentioned before, sometimes it makes sense to let your subject change the subject to give them space to think.

Heron's model can be taken to new levels when you consider the possibility as to whether you have authority in an interaction. If over time you have developed an authority platform like James O'Brien, you may be given 'permission' to act as if you are in a hierarchy by using more directive interventions. More normally in a conversation with a Brexit voter, we are on a level playing field, even if we think we are smarter than they are. This requires that we move towards the right-hand side of the grid, from co-operation through to giving the person full autonomy. In general, it is a mistake to go any faster than your subject will allow in terms of 'push' and 'pull' strategies. On the few occasions in five years where I had gotten into trouble with Brexorcism, it has usually been down to too much push and not enough pull.

Some examples illustrate these points well :

I often suggest that Brexiteers fact check their own information biases as, of course, they naturally assume I am myself biased! In society, we often operate without any hierarchy and it is not usually feasible to try to pull rank on people you meet casually in cafés, on streets and so on. If the person I meet appears to lack the skills needed to help themselves, I will often help them, for example, by asking them to :

1. Get their phone out.
2. Get on Google.
3. Type in the question or issue that is troubling them. Sometimes I help with the formulation of the question without them noticing.

By using directive behaviour to establish autonomy, we end up operating in co-operative mode and allowing them to use their own phone, it gives greater sense of ownership. Of course, this can take longer, especially if they don't know how to use the phone … again patience is needed!

James O'Brien qualifies for expert status. In theory, he could therefore use hierarchical mode exclusively on his LBC radio show. But, as mentioned earlier, you will often hear him practising what I call 'naïve listening' to promote self-enquiry on the part of his callers. This is especially skilled, given the time pressure he is under to deliver entertaining radio without long pauses as his callers re-arrange their synapses to sort out the cognitive dissonance that arises! Sometimes you can almost hear fuses blowing in their minds as they struggle with the questions and comparisons he uses.

Six styles of Brexorcism

Prescribing

A tell style.

Informing

Neutral supply of information without judgement.

Confronting

Holding the mirror up to your subject.

Cathartic

Helping your subject unload.

Catalytic

Stimulating new thinking with minimal provocation.

Supporting

Giving credit where it is due.

Playing to your strengths

Reflect on the six intervention styles and consider which ones are your strongest skills Plan to develop the others through deliberate practice outside your current comfort levels. Consider where they will be of benefit :

Intervention style	Strength / development areas and potential benefits
Prescribing (Directive)	
Informing (Directive)	
Confronting (Directive)	
Cathartic (Non-directive)	
Catalytic (Non-directive)	
Supporting (Non-directive)	

I have developed the model below to show how you can operate in the various modes, from hierarchical to autonomous in typical conversations about Brexit :

	Style	Hierarchical	Co-operative	Autonomous
D I R E C T I V E	**Prescribing**	It would in your best interests to read up about the 270 Irish border crossings.	Let's look at some websites together, so that we can both understand the Irish border question.	What about calling the Irish embassy to find out some information first-hand?
	Informing	Look at your Council Tax bill. The EU costs around 2.0% of your tax. The total for the NHS and social care is 48%	Let's have a look at our Council Tax bills to see where our money goes.	I have some information which I would like you to consider. Let me know how you would like to move forward?
	Confronting	You told me 7 times that we must take back control of our laws. However, you cannot name a single law which affects you.	I am concerned that we don't appear to be able to resolve the dilemma about which EU laws trouble you. Let's look at these one by one together.	Please call this person. He is a respected EU lawyer and will be able to tell you which laws are made by the EU and which by our own government.

	Style	Hierarchical	Co-operative	Autonomous
NON DIRECTIVE	**Cathartic**	Now is a good time for you to tell me what you really think about immigration.	Can we spend some time exploring what it feels like for someone who came to this country 20 years ago and who now feels like they don't belong here?	Would you like to tell me how you feel about the immigrants in your town and your own experience of interacting with them?
	Catalytic	Explain to me what you think you have learned about the benefits of Brexit since the day we left.	Let's explore the differences between what was promised in the Brexit 'brochure' and what has come to pass.	Would you like to come back to me to explain what Brexit has come to mean to you now?
	Supporting	I think you made the right decision when you voted, given our knowledge on both sides at that time.	I sense that you are having difficulty talking about your disappointments over Brexit. Perhaps we can explore how we both feel now.	I'll support you whatever it is you finally decide about your views about a 2nd Brexit referendum.

Most of us are not James O'Brien [16] and therefore must work harder to earn credit to challenge our subjects. If you are fortunate to develop long term relationships with Brexiteers over time, you will eventually get 'promoted' to hierarchical mode informally or otherwise. But you must earn your right to be an expert in a social situation. The café example below shows how a long-term approach using non-directive conversation with catalytic, cathartic and supportive styles can get you 'promoted' and your expertise validated. Once this happens, people will both listen to you about Brexit and may even solicit your opinion on other topics such as COVID, war and other matters. Once that happens, you stand a much greater chance of achieving a Brexorcism.

[16] Find James O'Brien's books at Penguin

Café catalysis

The slow percolation of change is often more effective than a single 'espresso' shot. I have been going to a local café in my area over an extended period. The café owner always talks to me about my anti-Brexit activities. We always keep it light and amusing. Most importantly, I never talk about politics to her regular customers (all Leave voters, 60 + years old). However, I know they listen in to our conversations. Over time they became curious about what I did. They began by asking the café owner if I was a politician (after I'd left of course … it is not English to ask the person directly!)

After some months the café owner told me that they had searched and found me on Facebook. It turned out that they knew more about my daily movements than I do on occasions! The enigma of my activities on Downing Street was amplified by my taking my bicycle into the café with my 'Break Brexit Before Brexit Breaks Britain' signage, my 'FUCK Brexit' T-Shirt and so on. I always talk to the café owner about current developments on Brexit but made a rule never to proselytise to her customers about Brexit. But they continue to listen in. When I speak with them it is simply to join in with the general conversation of the day. I would of course listen in to their conversations about having to queue for the doctors due to immigrants and all the usual stuff, nodding sufficiently and acknowledging their frustrations to gain rapport without agreeing with them.

A tipping point occurred when I got punched by youths who did not like my T-Shirt. I did not mention it but found out from the café owner that they had already found out from Facebook. On my next visit to the café, resplendent with two black eyes, they started asking me about whether I was going to prosecute and so on. They were surprised that I shrugged my shoulders and just said that we cannot let one incident rule our lives. I did not lecture them about the fact that Brexit had legitimised and even encouraged this behaviour as they were so shocked about it. I thought it better to let them draw their own conclusions in what Heron calls 'autonomous' mode. Shrugging is sometimes a more useful strategy than lecturing! All things in their place.

Café catalysis

Over time and by not intervening, they began to ask me questions about Brexit and are gradually forming the view that Brexit is a mess regardless of what they voted for. One couple even asked if they could help place stickers in their neighbourhood, even though they had voted for Brexit. My extreme non-directive behaviour and UPR (Unconditional Positive Regard) over time has paid dividends, but it has also cost me a lot in Earl Grey Tea, empathy and patience!

- Where are your opportunities for a drip feed approach?
- Where and when can you be more laid back, to promote more autonomous or co-operative approaches to self-induced Brexorcism?
- What subtle (or otherwise) signs and symbols can you use to help start difficult conversations about Brexit?
- Do you think that Earl Grey is essential for success? Would Yorkshire Tea or coffee work just as well?

Reversing family hierarchies

I am the last in a line of 6 children with some 27 years between all the siblings. My mother lost her first husband in World War II and started over. It is generally acknowledged that I am probably the brightest of the family but that cuts no ice over family hierarchy through age. My sister adopts a matriarchal approach, having been left to look after me in her twenties whilst my mother used to go out on the town ... I gather my mum was something of a hellraiser even in her fifties. I suspect that my sister still considers me subordinate in most respects. This has not caused us any problems throughout our lives but it came to a head after Brexit.

At Sunday tea one afternoon, shortly after the Brexit referendum, my sister and her husband revealed that they voted Leave and an argument broke out. Incidentally, it turned out that their own children also had heated words with them. One has a German wife. The other feared for his job as he and his children work in financial services. I suspect they have not dared to challenge her too much on the matter. My sister uses the self-defence strategy that she does not understand much about politics and current affairs, but that does not stop her having an opinion about most things.

The 3R's of Brexorcism

Rewind

Reload

Reprogram

Some subjects just want to tell you their life story. There can be a profound benefit in just rewinding their life without doing anything other than listening and maybe making the odd non-directive intervention. The rapport that you may generate from this may allow you to separate their story from feelings that the EU are responsible for their story. In a sense, you can allow them to reload their story.

In other cases, re-programming may be needed. A complete re-boot, challenging beliefs and identity level change. One useful rule of thumb here is that people must change a behaviour something like 20 times for it to become embedded as a new habit. Changing viewpoints on Brexit may therefore be something like the change needed to deal with addictions.

So, when it was time to vote, her decision was influenced by what she saw as informed sources i.e., The Daily Mail / Express. Her main argument for leaving the EU was because she did not want Sharia Law on Tonbridge High Street. Her husband cited his belief that some two million German rapists would come to Britain from Berlin.

A heated argument broke out which I was not able to win, despite being in possession of more accurate information. One hour later we found ourselves in a surrealistic discussion as to whether the 'good old English rapists' were somehow better than the German ones! Remember, this was early after the referendum and I had not realised just how deeply seated these myths and legends had been installed via our media. Eventually I went to the kitchen to make tea and decided I could face no more. I left my own house, texted my wife to apologise and returned once they had gone home.

The point here is that my expertise in the situation was not accepted as a valid part of our transaction. The operating theory in my family is that age is more important than knowledge. You may well ask what I have done about this since to reverse this family hierarchy? Well, I wrote a letter to my sister and her husband explaining in detail how I had found the whole matter extremely hurtful and that I no longer wished to see them as I felt too depressed to meet. This clearly hurt my sister who did have the courtesy to reply. She did however simply point out that she was 78 and that "I would be sorry if she died before I saw her again". I was unmoved by this act of gross manipulation.

We have not yet reached the point where her husband is willing to acknowledge that his illusion about the two million rapists was a lie. I don't need him to do this really. I do however need them to say that they would vote differently if an opportunity arose. Remember, outcomes are much more important than positions in a Brexorcism.

I have since kept the door open to a reconciliation and in August 2019 I wrote to ask my sister if she and her husband would sign the petition to avert a national crisis. I chose e-mail as my medium of communication and perhaps I should have called. But the course of the conversation was quite shocking, especially as she has diabetes and several health concerns which would likely have been affected by a No Deal Brexit :

Hi Sheila, If you wish to do anything to stop the oncoming disaster the very least you can do is sign and share this petition. Peter

"No thank you Peter, we want out".

Good luck getting your medication and food then. I truly cannot understand what has got into your tiny minds. This is the last communication you will ever get from me. I was attacked again recently, and your Brexit vote is, in part, the cause of this. Peter

"We all have an opinion that's democracy, you being attacked is your problem not mine".

Of course, my greatest mistake was using e-mail to discuss the matter, a very poor substitute for difficult conversation, but her preferred mode of doing this. I'd not recommend that to anyone else and this goes to show that we all make mistakes. I am not done yet though.

In terms of our model of Brexorcism, my sister is not a target for change as she is a lost cause. However, because she is my sister and because I refuse to be beaten, I have tried on an occasional basis to change her mind. Her view has however hardened, despite a large body of evidence that probably frightens her, but she holds on to her view to prevent cognitive dissonance. As I write this I suspect that the pennies are slowly dropping with the onset of the Russian invasion of Ukraine. To her, I am still very much the little boy who is acting up with knowledge and intelligence, but she remains convinced that she knows best. Still, I must try with better approaches. Looking back at my 2019 e-mails, they do smell of desperation and they are not my finest work. Ho hum.

So, beware of the trap of acting as if you are in a hierarchy if there is no agreement about that within a particular social setting. Expertise and authority must be earned as with our previous example of 'Café Catalysis'.

Politicians also make the mistake of assumed hierarchy. In their case, they assume that, because they have been elected, they have authority by dint of their position in society. Western society does not always respect position power these days. Just think. When some people get a diagnosis of illness by a doctor these days, they sometimes challenge the doctor or seek a second opinion. The collapse of deference to authority meant that a lot of people did not listen to David Cameron in the 2016 referendum. The Conservatives ran the usual strategy of telling people that Brexit would harm them economically and a lot of people raised their fingers to the Prime Minister in a show of defiance. In the words of Bob Dylan "when you ain't got nothin', you got nothin' to lose".

Summary

1. Knowing what to do in a Brexorcism is one thing. Knowing how to do it is quite another. Your style of intervention determines how well your message is received as much as the content of your message itself.

2. We often think of influence as a sales process and, indeed, it is in part. However, when we are trying to change beliefs, push marketing approaches can be less effective. Try to pull more than you push to achieve a change in mindset.

3. Some of the strategies which we call non-directive can be very effective in helping people rewind, reload and re-program themselves. They take longer and need more patience, unconditional positive regard and skill.

4. Some of the most effective changes are self-induced. A good brexorcist knows when to let the work continue by its own. We must ignite the spark to learn in our subjects and then help them to find out for themselves.

5. Personalisation is key. People notice authenticity and that often comes from your own personal experience. Check out our top tips for defence against the dark Brexit arts.

Top tips for defence against the dark Brexit arts

Play to your strengths : If you are great at push approaches and not so good at the pull ones, plan to develop the latter whilst finding ways to minimise any weaknesses. Perhaps that means working in tandem with someone who is good at the things you are less good at (Tag Brexorcism) or choosing subjects that are more amenable to push style influence.

Know your outcome : Are you planning a 90 or 180-degree Brexorcism? Is it feasible to do this in the allotted time? Do you need several bites of your chosen target with space in between for reflection? Be realistic in setting goals and time for change.

Maintain flexibility : Stick to your outcome rather than your position. If what you are doing is not working, do something different.

Keep focus : Many Brexiteers, when confronted, change the subject. Politely but firmly maintain focus e.g. "You said you wanted to talk about immigration but we are now talking about garlic. Can we return to the subject when you are ready?"

Preparation is key : Don't rush headlong into a Brexorcism until all the preliminaries have been dealt with. Seemingly trivial things matter such as small talk, getting the environment conducive to good listening, establishing the rules of engagement and so on.

Make it personal : Tell your own story if people want to listen. Stories seep into people's hearts and often bypass their heads. Listen to Nigel Farage if you are not convinced as he is a master of the artform. The technical term for this is 'self-disclosure'. Telling someone that you are worried or frightened can be a powerful lever, especially if it runs counterculture to expected societal norms. For example, a man telling another man he is fearful for his family's future may be counter cultural in some settings.

Mind your language

Neuro-Linguistic Programming (NLP) has a whole section on linguistics and there is far too much to go into here, having spent some five years learning from masters of their art and discipline, but I will provide an essential digest. I recommend you read books by John Seymour and Genie Laborde for more depth … suffice to say that the language you use has a huge impact on how another person will perceive you and ultimately how influential your message will be. The principle of pacing and leading also applies. If possible, work in your client's own vernacular and don't impose yours on them. It just gets in the way of success.

This means that we must master communication. In other words, to work in our client's own language patterns. Also, to be a credible person when relating to people of different persuasions, class, status and so on.

My wife tells me that the 'beauty of me' is that I am what she calls 'intelligent scum' … I believe this is a term of endearment! What she says is this :

"You have three degrees and are at home talking with professors, scientists, politicians, media people and so on. But you have never lost your working-class accent and earthiness. As a musician, you have also been used to speaking plainly with people in pubs. People don't always get it, but you really are able to reach across a broad church of people".

This chapter introduces some of the language structures that can help you get further with your subjects. Remember that language is only 7% of the whole communication message when working face to face. Sure, getting the words right matters but it is not the whole package.

Specifically Vague

NLP talks of two language models. The **Meta Model** and the **Milton Model** :

Meta language patterns are highly specific. Whereas the **Milton** model, named after Milton H. Erickson, is the kind of vague language used by hypnotists, therapists, gaslighters and Brexit politicians such as Dominic Raab, Jacob Rees-Mogg, Boris Johnson et al. We can use the meta model to identify and correct deletions, distortions and

generalisations through language challenges. It is useful in conducting Brexorcisms being mindful of John Heron's style model. It is also useful for dealing with what are called 'gaslighting' incidents where people make statements that are untrue for the purposes of getting others to question their own sanity. Here are some of the main 'violations' of clear language patterns with some typical statements that Leave voters use in conversations and some meta model challenges of those statements :

Deletions

1. Unspecified nouns

Conversations with Brexit voters are littered with unspecified nouns. Here are some of the more familiar ones in *italics* with some starting points for responses :

"Get over it".

"What specifically do I need to get over?"

"Out means Out. Can't you get that through your head".

"Which things must I get through my head?"

"But what is out?"

2. Unspecified verbs

"Remainers upset me".

"How exactly are you making them upset you?"

"It sounds like a magic trick. Are you not in control of your own mood?"

"Stop trying to undermine democracy".

"How specifically am I undermining democracy?"

Dealing with deletion

"Cheese and onion crisps will still be available after No Deal Brexit"

Boris Johnson

On occasion, Brexorcisms are confounded by missing chunks of information. This is what NLP specialists call 'deletion'. Boris did not tell an untruth in the above example, yet he failed to talk about medicines and the 80% of foodstuffs that we import daily.

It is entirely possible that cheese and onion crisps are not essential to life …

This kind of gaslighting only makes it harder for people to find the truth in our politics. The intention is to get people to rise quickly to anger or fight, attack. This is then used to discredit any valid point they may make.

3. Nominalisations

Nominalisations convert a verb to make it a noun. They are often accompanied by the words must, mustn't, have to, should, shouldn't, ought to, can, can't, could, couldn't, would, wouldn't :

"Women have no understanding of politics".

"All women? What don't women understand?"

"We want it all. I want Brex .. it now".

"What Brexity thing do you want?"

"I need sovereignty".

"How do you want to be sovereign?"

"You shouldn't wear the EU flag on your blazer".

"According to whom?"

4. Unspecified referential index

A phrase which deletes the person(s) doing the action or which uses a general subject, for example immigrants, Jews, men.

"Eastern Europeans are lazy".

"Which ones? How are they lazy? How do you know?"

"People don't like you going on about Brexit".

"Which people?"

"Muslims stop us having Christmas. I've seen the Muslims, the Bulgarians, they're everywhere".

A word on breathing

Getting our language right is one thing. Developing the other 93% of the dance of persuasive communications right is quite another. A pure focus on the words is rather like a musician just focusing on the sheet music, rather than the performance and the audience ...

Pauses can be very effective in improving your subject's listening. I have even walked away from subjects that don't take turns ... Pattern breaking matters if you are to encourage listening

7% language
38% voice tone
55% body language

Don't forget to breathe when communicating. It also makes a statement ... and it's healthy !

Match your subject's body language to improve their attention. Mismatch when you wish to disagree without having to disagree ...

**"How do Muslims stop you having Christmas? Where are they?
How many Bulgarians are Muslims?"**

5. Simple deletions

"Britain has had problems for a long time, so Brexit is the answer".

"What problems? The answer to what?"

"Brexit is better".

"Better? Than what?"

6. Comparative deletions

"Britain can be great again".

"Great in what way?"

"We can grow our own vegetables".

"Which vegetables grow in Britain?"

"How will that help with the hungry gap?"

Distortions

7. Complex equivalence

An attribution of a cause to something that may have no correlation :

"My local chip shop is doing fine. So, Brexit will be OK".

**"How is your local chip shop an index of the state of
UK industry and macroeconomics?"**

"I hate people coming over here and taking our jobs and they're not even working".

Reframing distorted views

The meaning of any communication depends on the 'frame' in which we perceive it. Reframing is the process of changing the frame in which a person perceives issues, to change the meaning. Reframing is a key component of many jokes, fairy tales and Brexit delusions. It is particularly of value when working with limiting beliefs of Leave voters, where their frame of reference is limited by perspective, time or just plain wrong.

Vote Leave cleverly reframed the idea of recklessness to ideas about being bold. Whereas David Cameron could only manage to say "I don't believe we are quitters". In NLP terms, he was indicating that Remainers were cowards.

Reframes can be simple, trivial or complex and deep :

"the EU are bullying us".

"They must be very concerned about how we are self-harming the country".

"Remainers are killing Britain".

"They must be very organised and intelligent to be able to do such a thing. What do they know?"

"How are they taking our jobs if they don't work?"

"My dad fought in the war, so Brexit would be OK".

"What has fighting got to do with a realignment of Britain with the USA and the destruction of the United Kingdom?"

"How is Brexit anything like a war?"

"Brexit will fix the NHS".

"How are Brexit and the NHS related?"

"Brexit means that Britain will improve dramatically".

"In what respects specifically?"

8. Lost performative

In this conversational conundrum, a value judgment is made without knowing who or what is making the judgement :

"I cannot read graphs and data about Brexit"

"According to whom?"

"A 2nd referendum is anti-democratic".

"Says who?"

"Brexit is good".

"Brexit. What is it good for?"

9. Mind reading

Claiming to know another's thoughts or feelings without specifying the how you came to that knowledge :

"You are trying to make me look stupid".

"How do you know what I'm trying to do?"

"You know how I feel about Brexit".

"I did not realise you read my mind. Can you explain how you do that?"

"I don't know how you feel – please tell"

10.Cause – effect

In this language game, a direct cause and effect are inferred from disparate items.

"Look what you made me do".

"How exactly did I make you do that?"

"If it weren't for the Remainers, Brexit would be alright now".

"Please explain how Remainers are the cause of the Brexit freedoms we have?"

"What have the activities of Remainers got to do with the success "of Brexit?"

11.Presuppositions

The NLP equivalent of assumptions. It is generally held that assumptions make an ASS out of U and ME (see what I did there?).

"Anti-Brexit protestors cause wars".

"How do peaceful protests cause wars?"

"Women manipulate men to give into Remaining".

**"Are all women manipulative? What is their magic secret?
Are men not manipulative?"**

Dealing with Brexit shape shifters

Ever had this kind of conversation with a Brexiteer?

"Let's talk about your job as a stock controller. You said Brexit was ruining it. I'd love to know the specifics"

"That's one thing, but my boss makes my life hell".

"OK, so let's discuss the boss. Is he European?"

"I don't care about him. He's from Basildon anyway. I can't get an appointment at the hospital due to immigration".

"What is stopping you getting an appointment at the hospital?"

"My boss. He says I'm not ill. I just hate this job".

"So, let's focus on the job. You said Brexit was ruining it".

"I'd rather be a bus driver". ....

There is a balance to be struck between letting your subject unload on you for the purposes of venting and just an unfocussed discussion that achieves little. The Meta Model provides you with a wide range of tools for flexibility. However, sometimes you just need to come back to the point. Rather than using the 'broken record' technique by repeating the question it is usually more effective to rephrase the question :

"You said you wanted to talk about how the EU is ruining your job. Tell me more".

"Let's stick to this subject until we are done".

"Brexit ruins your job. How?"

Generalisations

12. Universal quantifiers

These are generalisations without a reference point. Frequently such statements include all, every, none, never etc.

"Theresa May's a Remainer all the time".

"So, Theresa May never argues for Brexit?"

"No one wants to alter the course of fate".

"No-One? What is fate?"

13. Modal operators of necessity

Words that require actions e.g. should, shouldn't, must, mustn't, have to, need to etc.

"We must carry on with Brexit".

"Must we? Who said we must? What would happen if we didn't?"

"We must not interfere with democracy".

"How are we interfering with democracy? What is democracy?"

14. Modal operators of possibility

Words that imply no choice e.g. can't, haven't, won't etc.

"I can't tell you the truth about immigration".

"What would happen if you did?"

"I won't change my mind on Brexit".

"What prevents you from changing your mind in the light of new knowledge?"

Dealing with generalisations

We generalise all the time. Life would be too difficult to endure without using some generalisations to get through every day. Some generalisations are safe and without consequence, for example the generalisation that all cities are busy helps us plan extra time to cross Central London. Just occasionally we are wrong about how busy London will be, but this usually comes without serious consequence.

Our earlier example of the Irish immigrant who told my wife that our local Council was to house **ALL** the London Borough refugees is a good example of a generalisation. It may in part be true, but he had quickly moved from a specific to a general. Generalisations litter the Brexit voter's landscape :

"Everyone in the town wants Brexit".

"Everyone?"

"Brexit was the will of the people".

"Which people? What is Brexit?"

Thinking about Brexorcism

Reflect on the Meta Model language patterns using this stream of consciousness from a Leave voter below.

- Identify the various language patterns inherent in the conversation.

- Where are the opportunities for intervention?

- Where would you begin?

We are an island, tunnel or no tunnel, and if it comes to war, the tunnel will go. If the EU and Paris play sufficiently silly buggers, to the point it becomes militarily necessary, we can always pull the plug on the tunnel and flood it. In a war scenario, I don't think we'd be too bothered about compensating Paris or shareholders. The Armed Forces are largely pro-Brexit, even in Scotland. England and Wales are not in doubt. All the army people would love to get involved in a war with France, Germany and the other EU nations.

And we could take back control of our railways. The East Coast Main Line worked well under the real LNER (1923-47), complete with the setting of a speed record in 1938 which stands to this day. Go back to the Big Four or pre-grouping model, where TOCs owned their railways. It worked very well. Southern Railway coaches were a lovely shade of green and carriages were made of wood. German railways survive only on subsidy from Britain. SNCF is bankrupt.

Old age Brexiteers speak out ...

Some people are a mixed bag of tricks. They don't fit into just one of our meta model categories. Here is a particularly difficult example with what I call OABs (Old Age Brexiteers). How would you tackle the person involved?

A female friend of mine posted this on social media :

"I've just realised that my pension will be worthless after Brexit".

It is possible that she voted to Leave and has just realised that it will affect her badly.

A mutual acquaintance posted this reply (grammar and spelling left as posted) :

"Your pension will be worth it worth ... Having worked in the major banking sector ... in black Wednesday ...I do not understand your worries . Yes, this a weather report but we the brittish people will win so tell your MP.s that unless they stand with us"

I am quite sure that this person has never worked in any significant position in a bank if that provides some reassurance by the way. There is a deletion in here 'will be worth it worth', plus a host of other meta model violations. Any possible resolution is made much worse. as the post is on social media. Therefore, it cannot be guaranteed that a communications channel exists, that the person will listen to any answers and so on ...

Your reflections :

The **Meta Model** has been extended by the originators Bandler and Grinder. However, I feel this is quite enough for an introduction to the topic. I will leave discussions on the illusion of choice, delusional thinking, pseudo words and so on to the politicians and perhaps an update of this first book on the topic of Brexorcism subject to feedback on the usefulness of this guide.

In contrast, the **Milton Model** derives from Milton H. Erickson, a therapist who used hypnotic language patterns and looser language postulates to help his subjects make dramatic changes. Milton language patterns are very vague. Politicians and some rock stars like ambiguity for different reasons :

Take Back Control

Simply the best

Breaking point

Whole lotta love

Brexit Means Brexit

The winner takes it all

In our Abba example, who is the winner? What is being taken? Is all everything? What is all? Is it all the sausages, the seats on the train, the Brexit benefits or what? Who lost as a result of them winning, and so on …

In the case of the Dominic Cummings 'Take Back Control' catchphrase, I have had many a conversation where it becomes embarrassingly apparent that people have no idea as to what is being taken back. They don't know what control has been lost, when, who caused it and so on. However, the fact that people repeat the phrase in the same way as they might sing a chant at a football match is testament to the hypnotic power of these gaslighting phrases.

Some hypnotic Milton language patterns are shown below, so that you may spot them and neutralise them when appropriate as part of your 'Defence against the dark Brexit arts' strategy.

Hypnotic language patterns

"Brexit will create new understandings".

"David Cameron made me to vote for Brexit".

"People can change their minds on Brexit".

"No Deal is better".

"Your perception of Brexit is changing, isn't it".

"Do you want to have Brexit now or later?"

"Would you rather have Brexit or shall I torch you with a hot flame?"

"It's my deal or No Deal".

"It's now or never".

"I will not suggest to you that Brexit is easy".

"It's important we get on with Brexit before time runs out like sand".

"It's essential to save Britain from immigrants".

"You are feeling sleepy as you listen to me talking about Brexit".

"I'm not sure which eyelid will close first as you hear me reading Article 50".

"Others cannot say whether Brexit will happen now or later".

"Let's get (Brex)it done".

"Brexit means Brexit"

Most of the Leave campaign slogans were essentially hypnotic language patterns. They were completely consonant to the voters, playing to things they already thought or had heard and building upon these illusions. For example :

For people who did not like immigration and immigrants, the idea that the entire population of Turkey would invade the UK was a powerful anchor.

For those who felt that the country had lost its way, the idea of taking back control was extremely attractive.

For those who felt that the NHS had been brought to the point of destruction, the idea of giving large sums of money back to the NHS from the EU was another supremely potent idea. This is part of what is known as 'gaslighting', using things that are near and dear to people's hearts to persuade them.

Boris Johnson also promised £1.9 billion which is approximately five and a half weeks of NHS funding at £350 million per week. The £350 million was to be continuous.

In contrast, much of the Remain campaign was spent on specifics and 'project fear'. These messages were quite dissonant to people that already believed the Vote Leave generalisations and who did not like what they saw as negative messaging.

Like it or loathe it, voters preferred messages that appeared to be consonant with their own beliefs. They also preferred positive hallucinations of the benefits of leaving the EU and gross exaggerations or outright lies about the perceived problems of staying in the EU.

Much of the persuasive strategies of the Vote Leave campaign can be explained using the Milton Model and the ideas of **Deletion**, **Distortion** and **Generalisation**.

A word on integrity

Tools and techniques will take you so far in the dance of influence and persuasion. Without heart and soul, you ain't got nothin' ...

Donald Trump, Nigel Farage and Boris Johnson have great technique as orators, but seemingly no moral compass to temper their words. Thus, their strategies are ultimately morally and practically bankrupt ...

In the words of Annie Lennox :

"Be yourself tonight".

And Lou Reed :

"I do me better than anyone else".

I use NLP language skills on a regular basis in my pub and café Brexit conversations, plus heavy doses of experience. Usually, people come to me to talk, triggered by my selection of provocative anti-Brexit T-Shirts. Getting people to want to talk to you rather than the other way round is by far the best way to engage them. Here's a shortened story of one successful interaction with a hardened Brexit voter in 'Brexit Central' aka North Kent that illustrates some of these principles in action :

We're goin' down the pub

Oh my … one-hour Brexit conversation in a pub in Gillingham started by my T-shirt … 66-year OAB (Old Age Brexiteer) ex BBC radio engineer, two kids in their thirties, one in Parkhurst maximum security prison the other on the dole … key points :

"I love your T-shirt, it's very clear, FUCK BREXIT".

I explain (at great length and very slowly) "yes, FUCK BREXIT, says it straight, unlike our lying politicians on all sides" yada. He nods in agreement … (pacing).

5 minutes later I must tell him that we are on different sides as he has not worked it out … but he agrees and we continue … (leading).

We covered all kinds of things … being invaded by the infidel … the need to get our country back … the future of life with Trump … the fact that Vietnam is not in Europe and I made the mistake of saying that not many people in the high street would know that … he then admitted that he did not actually know where Vietnam was!

Eventually after he had 'unloaded' on me, I said that it seemed that he really regretted the decline of British industry, he wanted his son to come out of prison and we needed to get back being an island (he had never travelled). I went on to agree with his sense of disappointment and then asked what part of his sense of alienation was due to the EU. The subject changed. After a while he started to talk about his grandchildren. I asked him what he thought we would get from leaving the EU and when. He really did not know.

To maintain the relationship, we talked about his kids and grandchildren. His daughter is 33, has never worked. His son is older, in Parkhurst Maximum Security prison (I decided not to ask him why his son is there). He does not like his son being in Parkhurst because he tells me he is getting a lot of racist abuse and "It's full of blacks", although he is quick to point out that he is not a racist.

He moved away from London because of the blacks 19 years ago and now finds them invading his town. He claims that this is the fault of the EU. I point out that immigration is under our own government's control … he agrees … I spend some time trotting out the story of my sister and the two million rapists coming from Berlin. I ask him why rapists from Berlin are 'worse' than 'great British rapists' … he does not know … I leave the subject hanging.

We carry on with kids. I tell him that my son will be 75 by the time we've paid for Brexit.

He nods … there was a lot of nodding … (leading).

Subject changed towards food for some reason … he told me how much he hated all the food in the high street because it had garlic in it. He did not like garlic. I pointed out that it grows here and summed up the lengthy conversation by saying :

"So, if you were to explain to your grandchildren that we were leaving the EU because you don't like garlic and that they would be paying for this for the rest of their lives, would that be enough for them to agree with you?"

His reply "Not really – I'd need another dozen reasons …"

I asked "and what are those?" He did not know …

I considered I had done enough to begin his journey at this point. We changed to talk about music and beer …

Gaslighting unplugged

Gaslighting is a form of manipulation whose purpose is to cause the victim to doubt their own perception, memory and sanity; to destabilise.

In November 2018 Theresa May said that her Brexit deal was in the national interest six times and that her deal delivers on everything she promised seven times.

"If a little bit of Guinness is smuggled over the border, I don't mind".

Jacob Rees-Mogg on the Irish border.

"Lock her up".

Donald Trump on Hilary Clinton.

Final remarks

I could go on at length about the question of style and whether you should use more directive or non-directive approaches, the gentle art and discipline of storytelling, body language, challenging viewpoints without tears and so on. We have already discussed some of these issues and getting the language right is but part of any successful Brexorcism. Authenticity wins ultimately in the game of influence and persuasion, but people are sometimes taken in by some snappy lines. In the words of Nick Clegg :

"If it sounds too good to be true, it probably is".

Summary

1. The Meta and Milton Models can help you spot the language patterns in conversations you have with potential Brexorcism candidates. Having spotted the language patterns that others use, you can then intervene skilfully. They also help you understand your own values, beliefs and behaviours.

2. People do not operate in one mode at any one time. The models help you to adapt your own behaviour in each interaction. Flexibility is key to success.

3. Begin by identifying your own language patterns as a start. By improving your own awareness, you will equip yourself to help others challenge their own habits and thinking traps.

4. Remember that, whilst getting your language right, our body language and voice tone also make up the communication message. Learn to use these well.

5. Act with integrity if you want to be influential. Honesty cuts through.

What should pro-EU people do with NLP?

Quite a lot. Remain lost the referendum due to a brilliant campaign by Vote Leave and a lacklustre strategy by the Remain side. There is plenty to learn, but here is a taste of what must be done should the need arise :

Find better mantras : Remain is a weak concept and sounded dull to Leavers. Our suggestion of 'Better Britain Better Europe, Better World' is positive but perhaps long. It can however be reduced to Better Britain. 'Re-Boot Britain is also a more useful catchphrase than 'Remain', as the re-boot element respects the concerns of Leave voters from 2016 and it also has Britain in the phrase.

Kick ass : Lacklustre and long messages do not reach busy people or ones with lower general intelligence. The Remain campaign's wishes to be in the quality newspapers ignores the fact that Leave voters tend not to read them. Love it or loathe it, the phrase 'Take Back Control' captured the zeitgeist of those who felt left behind.

KISS : Keep it simple stupid. To reach some demographics Remain needs much simpler and more hard-hitting messaging. Remain may loathe Nigel Farage but we need to learn from him. Our language and messages must reach Sun readers, like it or not.

Facts or Fantasies : Facts were considered as project fear last time. Now that we have experience, we can point to facts about what Brexit looks like. We should challenge Brexit fantasies with facts whilst dealing with the question of why Remain and Reform gives us better futures.

Emotions win : Remain's campaign was unemotional last time. We need to get personal to persuade. Personal testimonies seep into people's hearts.

PART III

Tales of Brexorcism

Simple Minds

To give me target practice at Brexorcisms and conduct qualitative research, I like occasionally to go for very hard targets. It is probably the reason why I have suffered a few attacks over the last few years, but the learning I gain from these conversations is well worth the occasional bit of punishment for my 'sins against Brexit'.

I was enjoying a drink at an open mic in 2020 when the wife of the local UKIP mafia approached me. She wanted to find out my views on COVID. As a can opener to the conversation, she wondered why I was wearing a mask as COVID was not really a serious condition. She told me that she had contracted bird flu and SARS years back and cured them by rubbing some herbal remedies on her arms. I appeared non-plussed and replied "Good God, bird flu and SARS in the UK. You really were unlucky".

The conversation rambled as I attempted to pull rank on her by explaining that I was once a scientist and that COVID is a serious disease and it **does** exist. I asked for the basis of her expertise but, as usual, there was none.

So impressed was she with my willingness to talk that she offered me a bundle of the stickers that her UKIP friends had been placing around the poorer parts of town. These were well designed to recruit vulnerable young people to a fascist cause. This is how the contagion of fake news spreads to vulnerable minds at all life stages.

People in 1940s Germany didn't realise they'd been brainwashed by the media and government, either.

The only way to deal with an unfree world is to become so absolutely free that your very existence is an act of rebellion.

STAY FREE ▸ DITCH THE MUZZLE ▸ THE MEDIA IS THE VIRUS

Isas, Isis and Brexit

I spend a lot of time talking to Brexit supporters in pubs. People ask me why? Because the environment allows for a non-confrontational atmosphere in which to have what are often 'difficult conversations'. These have only become potentially aggressive a couple of times out of many attempts, so they are generally low risk. However, one must keep one's temper, sometimes against the odds of some breath-taking revelations. One such revelation came from a pub landlord 'John' who told me he wanted to get rid of all the ISAs. In case you are confused.com, an ISA is an Individual Savings Product. Of course, what he meant was ISIS. He was saying that all Muslims in the UK were members of terrorist cells. An important difference from savings products and I am quite glad I clarified the matter!

Here are some snippets from a recording I made of John. I found him a fascinating but slightly sad character. He had worked much of his life as a carpenter and had managed to afford a pub along the coastal road at Sheerness. The pub had had a glorious past but was now reduced to a shadow of its former glory. I noticed that every time I visited there was just one other customer who quickly left as soon as I took over the conversation. The landlord was full of regrets about his life and had decided that most of his angst was the fault of the EU and the 'system' in Britain which did not reward the 'little man'. You can find the 'Brexit Monologue' interviews on You Tube in their entirety. Go to youtube.com/academyofrock and then look for the 'EU Tube' playlist.

On laws, hoovers and saving the planet

"I tell you what … You can't have a hoover over a thousand Watts …"

"Isn't that a good law, to stop us killing the planet?"

"I don't care about the planet. I just wanna have a powerful hoover".

On human rights and game boys

"I tell you what … What about the human rights law?"

"Yes, it's a good thing?"

"It ain't. Bloody prisoners, done rape and all that. They give 'em game boys. We should bring back hanging".

"Can we hang everyone?"

"Yes, they wouldn't do it again"

"I guess that's true"

The first time I met John, I could not quite believe some of the things he said, so I recorded our conversations. Some people who heard the recordings thought that I had set them up as with actors alternative comedy interviews. Remainers used to ask me why I bothered talking with John. Although he had a certain abrasiveness on the recordings, I sensed a man in his late sixties who was incredibly lonely, feeling left behind by society and who looked for someone else or something else to blame. The European Union was a convenient container for his many problems. He told me that he felt he could have been the President of America like Donald Trump, whereas in the UK he had only amounted to be a carpenter and then a pub landlord. He said that this was due to the class system in Britain and it was out of his control. John failed to recognise that none of his disappointment was anything to do with the European Union when I eventually mentioned it but he wanted to continue the conversation, so I kept working on him slowly and gently.

This seems to be a direct analogue with Trump voters in the Mid-West who want their steel mills back and Brits who feel left behind in England. I return from time to time mainly to listen to John's changing views on life. The more I listen and gently question, the more he reflects on his situation. John has few people to talk to who give him time despite his anger and this makes the conversation worthwhile.   He is impressed that I cycle 15 miles to Sheerness and this provides a good counterpoint for shooting the breeze in between the conversation on Brexit and politics. John always starts our conversations with "You're not gonna change my mind on anything", which I always smile at and reply with "Of course"

Find the Brexit Monologues at our You Tube Page under 'Business and Politics' via our EU Tube channel www.youtube.com/academyofrock

Did you vote to have your UK bank account removed?

Did you vote for US styled private health insurance in Europe?

Did you vote to lose UK job opportunities if you live in Europe?

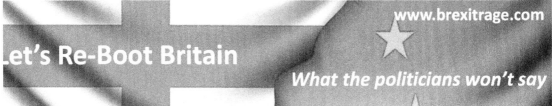

Suffer little children

I attended parliament square on the day of Boris Johnson's 'meaningful vote'. For some two and a half years we had hardly seen a Vote Leave activist on the street, but recent events had caused a few of them to turn up. It transpired that a few of them were 'paid hands' to boost numbers, but however … The typical tactic of the 'Yellow Vests' in UK is to walk through the Remain protest to incite trouble. The standard response is no response, so that we keep good relations with the Metropolitan Police who have tended to look after us at such events up till the point that Priti Patel converted the Met into a 'shoot first, ask questions later' American styled militia. They have a range of quite clever tactics including Nigel Farage's 'grid girls' [17] who chant "Paedo, paedo" to every male who tries to hold a meaningful conversation with them.

A gathering of Vote Leave people had formed inside our protest and Police were surrounding them … yellow vests on yellow vests! I was on the outside of the circle, standing next to a woman who had been marching with a young child, perhaps eight years old, both in Yellow Vests, shouting and swearing. I decided to set aside my personal views about the wisdom of teaching her eight-year-old daughter to F and C at her fellow citizens and wondered why she was not at school.

After a while I mused : "I wish I had 1 : 1 bodyguards like you lot do. It's great!".

She looked surprised : "They are not bodyguards! Why would you want the Police with you?"

I opened my phone and pulled up The Daily Mirror article below. I showed the woman the picture of my two black eyes, saying : "Well, this is what some Leave voters have done to me". Her daughter stepped in to see what was going. I paused for a long time whilst they looked in horror and worked out what might have happened …

---

[17] Nigel Farage's grid girls were Alice and Beatrice Grant, proof that sex sells.

Peter Cook shared photos of his injuries after the incident (◎ Image: Peter Cook)

NEWS	POLITICS	FOOTBALL	CELEBS	TV	MONEY	TRAVEL

Remain campaigner left with two black eyes after attack 'sparked by his Stop Brexit T-shirt'

Peter Cook feared he had broken his nose and visited A&E after the attack – which he claimed was an example of hate crime

By Dan Bloom, **Online Political Editor**
13:26, 25 Oct 2018

    I COMMENTS

A man was left bloodied with two black eyes after an attack he claims was sparked by him wearing an anti-Brexit T-shirt.

Peter Cook feared he had broken his nose and visited A&E after the attack – which he claimed was an example of hate crime.

Police are investigating and have appealed for witnesses to the incident, which happened at around 9pm on Monday 22 October.

The 60-year-old said seven youths taunted him on a train while he wore a garment emblazoned with "Break **Brexit** before Brexit breaks Britain".

He claimed they read out the slogan and called him names similar to "Brexit t***er" and "Brexit w**ker".

The situation escalated and one of the "gang" later punched the 60-year-old in the face after he alighted at Gillingham, Kent.

There was visible shock. The daughter did not even realise the picture was me initially. Eventually she said : "Is that you?" I nodded. Her mum said very firmly : "We don't do that to people".

I thought it best to say : "I know **you** don't, but that's what some of your associates have invited in through the side door …" I was mindful of the fact that a minor was with us, so I kept my contributions brief and reasonably light, but firm. After all, the mother had taken her daughter out of school to an 'adult event' but I considered it unhelpful to force my personal opinions upon a young person. Judging by the look on her face and the fact that she kept looking to her mum for disapproval of the violence, there was no need to do so anyway.

Her husband noticed me, walked over and started speaking with a slightly aggressive manner. The daughter related the story to him (much better than me repeating it). Once he heard the story he pronounced : "Ah, this will be George Soros behind this. He pays people to do this to people like you".

I looked puzzled and said firmly : "So, you were there then? You seem to know more about it than I do?" There was stony silence …. The daughter looked for some atonement from the father. I concluded that I'd made an important intervention that asked enough questions for a brief encounter.

After some small talk we all shook hands. I am left wondering what questions the daughter will have had around the dinner table that evening and at school …. Sometimes one needs to leave a Brexorcism half done, to be continued inside its own social circle. Uneasy endings can be more useful than a tidy life in the world of change, leaving people with difficult questions, backed by powerful stories and imagery.

Reflections for handling difficult conversations

- This was a good example of mostly non-directive interventions using 'co-operative' and 'autonomous' modes mostly in John Heron terms. A reminder of the model is at the end of this story. We must become fluent in the seamless movement between the various styles to be effective brexorcists.

- Silence was a key component of the strategy. I find that one must manage silence in these interactions, using body language and other devices. In this example, looking away or focusing on one person can prevent others from filling needed gaps in conversation. In conversations at parliament, it is extremely important to establish authority and to insist on a two-way exchange using body language and other approaches.

- The exception was a confrontation strategy when I challenged the husband's attempt at mind reading with his George Soros remark. I took the dull thud of silence to mean that he had no answers and decided not to press him for closure given that others were watching. Saving face is important for Brexiteers..

- Leaving endings open may on occasion be a better way to open space for reflection rather than trying to tidy everything up in a conversation

One of the familiar Vote Leave patriots at the Home Office.

Heron's model – Style variations

	Style	Hierarchical	Co-operative	Autonomous
D I R E C T I V E	**Prescribing**	It would in your best interests to read up about the 270 Irish border crossings.	Let's look at some websites so that we can both understand the Irish border question.	What about calling the Irish embassy to find out some information first-hand.
	Informing	Look at your Council Tax bill. The EU costs around 2.0% of your tax. The total for the NHS and social care is 48%	Let's have a look at our Council Tax bills to see where our money goes.	I have some information which I would like you to consider. Let me know how you would like to move forward?
	Confronting	You told me 7 times that we must take back control of our laws. However, you cannot name a single law which affects you.	I am concerned that we don't appear to be able to resolve the dilemma about which EU laws trouble you. Let's look at these one by one together.	Please call this person. He is a respected EU lawyer and will be able to tell you which laws are made by the EU and which by our own government.

Directive approaches with John Heron's [18] model tend to be faster but sometimes the tortoise outperforms the hare in this field of adventure.

---

[18] Find John Heron on Wikipedia at https://en.wikipedia.org/wiki/John_Heron

Heron's model – Style variations

Style	Hierarchical	Co-operative	Autonomous
N O N D I R E C T I V E			
Cathartic	Now is a good time for you to tell me what you really think about immigration.	Can we spend some time exploring what it feels like for someone who came to this country 20 years ago and who now feels like they don't belong here?	Would you like to tell me how you feel about the immigrants in your town and your own experience of interacting with them?
Catalytic	Explain to me what you think you have learned about Brexit since the day we voted.	Let's explore the differences between what was promised in the Brexit 'brochure' and what has come to pass.	Would you like to come back to me to explain what Brexit has come to mean to you now?
Supporting	I think you made the right decision when you voted, given our knowledge on both sides at that time.	I sense that you are having difficulty talking about your disappointments over Brexit. Perhaps we can explore how we both feel now.	I'll support you whatever it is you finally decide about voting in a 2nd referendum Brexit.

The brilliant work of Cold War Steve www.coldwarsteve.com
In this piece he sums up Russian influence, Johnson's spaffing sprees and the improprieties of Brexit. Find his work daily on Twitter.

Love, sex, saunas and Brexit

In July 2016 I made a tongue in cheek suggestion on social media that Remain voting women should deny their Brexit husbands certain … er … sensual pleasures … This was not an idle suggestion. We knew that the Brexit vote was a triumph of visceral reactions over logic. In this same vein, the supply (or denial) of other 'basic instincts' may well have been more effective than asking partners to read lengthy academic articles or to interpret graphs and tables in the intelligent press. As a male in a politically correct age, I cannot possibly go further in offering practical advice on this subject, so I must leave it to your imagination …

These stories from some friends illustrate the point well :

Sexual Brexit healing

A very good friend of mine voted to leave. I had been going on about how thick people must have been to vote in that way and he admitted that he had. When challenged, he said "because I'm a patriot and I love my country". Around this time, he was single but meeting various ladies online, mostly in Scandinavia. We asked him how that would work out if there were no planes after Brexit, he looked shocked. Since then, he has met a lovely German lady who lives in Bavaria. They got married this weekend in Denmark! He has completely changed his mind. He has promised me that he will return to vote Remain if there is a second referendum.

Love changes everything …

The love I lost

In October 2015, I started doing some occasional freelance work in the civil service as an internal communications filmmaker. They liked what I did and asked me back to undertake many other shoots. The following March, one department decided they wanted a full-time position with me in mind. A position went up on the Civil Service Jobs website and I was one of more than 230 who applied. I was told in the week running up to the referendum that I was on a shortlist of 10, but that was a formality as they preferred me out of the others. Basically, the job was as good as mine and the official interview (to be confirmed after the referendum result) was an open door.

But this assumed that the Remain side would win, and no changes had to be made inside. I'm obliged not to say what those changes were. But any interview was put on hold, leaving me in limbo. Barely weeks later, the job listing had been taken off the website, leading me to assume the position had been taken. But my colleagues later confirmed that the position was one of 60 jobs which had been cancelled due to Brexit.

When people tell you that Brexit won't affect people, there are thousands of small examples like this. Uncertainty produces stasis and risk averse decisions.

Anon

Sauna Brexorcisms

After brunch with a friend in 2018, I had a joyful if somewhat shrivelled three-hour session in the sauna. I ended up in a dialogue with a teacher from South America (Remain), a human rights academic from India who wanted to Leave the EU because of the idea of taking back control, but thinks we'll stay now. Also, a friend of the Punjabi optician I met in the sauna the other week (Remain) and someone I know on benefits who voted leave but is now reconsidering things.

We discussed Brexit, Trump, the environment, Kashmir, FGM and much more. We found much agreement and handled our differences in an adult way. We used the full range of the strategies for skilful conversation.

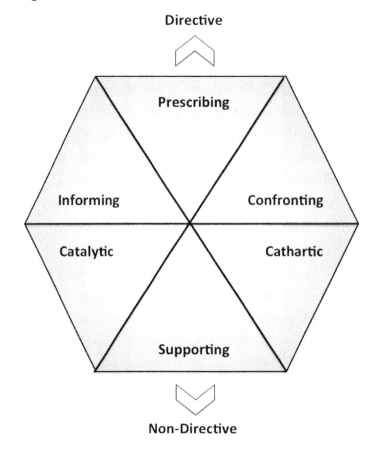

After some detailed dialogue amidst the heat the political academic agreed that Brexit offered no benefits in the mid-term but thought the UK would start to recover after ten years. However, he admitted had not really given much consideration as to how poor people would live and work in the intervening years ... and ten years is indeed a long time to be destitute.

We all agreed that if we did leave the EU via Brexit we move out of the EU frying pan into Trump's fire. I have since noticed over time that there was little appreciation that this was perhaps one of the stronger hidden motives behind Brexit to align Britain more with the USA.

Reflections on sauna seductions

- My three-hour session in the sauna demonstrates that Brexorcisms take skill, patience, unconditional positive regard (UPR) and time. ... in this case some three hours passed very quickly. Sometimes it is better to spread interventions out over time to allow for digestion and reflection. Patience is exemplified by the refusal to be drawn into distractions or to become passionate in an interaction. It also means letting the other side 'win' in areas where disagreeing would affect the overarching goal. I frequently try to find areas where I can agree and give credit to the 'opposition' in 'zones of indifference'.

- The other important reflection is that the sauna provides a non-confrontational environment for dialogue. Cafés are also often better than other settings such as pubs. Alcohol may loosen the tongue (and fists) but the quality of the conversation often declines into football chants and so on.

- It's not essential to sit in a sauna to do this! Find other spaces that offer contemplative psychosocial environments that are better for conversation. Find out what works for you based on your own preferences.

THE TIMES

Dozens of Tory MPs prepare new Brexit revolt

Growing anger at bid to breach international law

Did you know that our Government is breaking international law to Get Brexit Done?

Six former Prime Ministers and many senior Tory MP's have said this is a grave mistake. Mrs Thatcher said this was not the way of Britain

Do you know how this will affect our ability to conduct trade negotiations with the rest of the world?

www.brexitrage.com
Let's Re-Boot Britain
What the politicians won't say

Online Brexorcisms

I note how many people become frustrated at how little progress they feel they make when discussing Brexit online via Facebook, Twitter, LinkedIn, You Tube etc. Online is quite different than real life in several ways :

Online is asynchronous. This means that people have time to calculate their replies. This can result in trying to 'compete' rather than to 'collaborate'. The 'I am right and you are wrong' spiral is a pointless exercise and can only serve to reinforce the binary divides that set us apart. Time delays also mean that people shift away from areas where they would rather not answer the questions in ways that they would not get away with in real life.

Online often misses out on the 'relationship'. You may find yourself talking with someone you don't know and therefore have no investment in as a person - and the same applies to them, as well. This often results in you not knowing their background or motives for the conversation. I often refuse to engage until I know who I am talking to and 'where they are coming from'.

Online misses out 93% of the message. You cannot see someone winking on Facebook, save for the use of emojis. In NLP terms there is much deletion, distortion and generalisation in online exchanges. Some examples of this follow.

Online is often brief and therefore lacks nuance. Given that a Brexorcism often requires an extended period and sometimes needs punctuation by space and time, this limits the effectiveness of such interactions.

Brexorcism is a social process and not necessarily assisted by the exclusive use of social media as the medium of choice. If you only work online, you can mitigate against these limitations by following some basic principles :

1. Take your time. Find out about your 'opponent', their motives, background, hopes, fears and fantasies. Refuse to be drawn into debate before you have some relationship collateral to build upon.
2. Take a break. Allow for pauses in the conversation so that your client may reflect and learn. Invite them to go beyond commenting on social media. I offer an online debate with an invited audience on both sides.

3. Be specific rather than vague. Generalisations may be the realm of some Brexiteers, but it does not do to contribute to the confusion with your own fluffy generalisations. At the same time, do not be too nerdy, detailed or intelligent, as it tends to frustrate and they will probably run away. Saving face is even more important on social media when you cannot see their face!

4. Be disciplined. If your client changes the subject, firmly bring them back to task. However, don't be a Brexit bore by driving them into a dark corner by insisting on answers when they don't have them. Returning to the subject after a break is a better strategy ... "last time we were talking about ...".

5. Timing is all. If someone lacks facts to support their feelings and you don't know them, they are unlikely to accept your expertise. Remember Michael Gove said "we've had enough of experts". Sometimes it is better to supply them with places to go to check facts on their own and then to reward them when they tell you that you were right. Never make the mistake of replying with "I told you so".

Here are some ham-fisted examples of online interaction from "British Life" on Facebook which illustrate the point of how difficult this medium is, especially with the few remaining hardcore Brexiteers. This is where industrial levels of patience are needed.

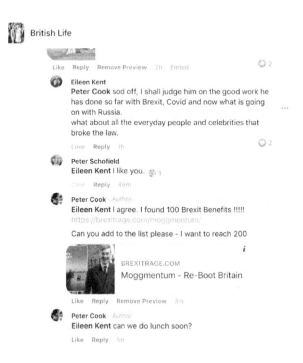

Barry Fitzgerald
I'm all for people having the right to express their opinions in a peaceful way and with complete transparency but Is this really about taking back control of our laws,it doesn't appear to be the sole object of this organisation.This seems to be more about trying to reverse the voters decision to leave the EU and has references to Rage.
The screen shot of their
" Reboot Britain" campaign comes from a site named
Brexitrage.com and the header contains a comment
"Rage against Brexit".
The dictionary explains the definition of the word "rage" as "violent uncontrollable anger".
Make your own mind up if you want to be associated with this organisation that wants to promote RAGE now you know exactly what that means.

Barry is very angry about the word rage on British Life …

Peter Cook Author
Ahem, you clearly don't understand democracy which is a continuous process. If it were a project, women would not have a vote and bear bating would be legal, all things that perhaps Jacob probably wants as his end game for Brexit

… as for your projection about "Rage", it is an allusion to the original title of the music project Rage Against The Brexit Machine RATBM and Rage Against The Machine

I'm afraid that you cannot have "Quiet displeasure Against the Brexit Machine" - it simply does not work as an idea 😊

You can find all the RATBM music here - it's rather good Barry
https://academy-of-rock.bandcamp.com/

ACADEMY-OF-ROCK.BANDCAMP.COM
Ignorance is Bliss

Like   Reply   Remove Preview   5m   Edited

Peter Cook Author
You may join us if you want

Peter Cook Author

I cannot help but laugh that "Barry is mad as hell about RAGE" and his implied meaning of the word. Call me Bazza - I can help

Like   Reply   22m

Peter Cook Author

ooh, just had a look at your profile Bazza - looks a bit RAGEY to be frank

Like   Reply   12m

Pots and kettles ...

Barry Fitzgerald

Peter Cook Your replies are no less than I expected having seen your real objective and the subtle undertones of your "Quiet displeasure against the Brexit machine" comment and what it implies.You can imply your meaning of rage if you want when it suits you but I certainly implied nothing but the true meaning that will always remain (that's not a deliberate pun but it's remarkably accurate).Join you,you have to be joking, I'd never join any group that seems to think that the right way to promote their cause includes rage.I certainly don't promote rage so if that makes me mad about it's use by organisations of any sort your right I never approve of anyone who does.

You ask me to call you and you can help,Well don't hold your breath waiting for the call I don't and will never need your help.

Thanks for the offer but you best seek it yourself you need it far more than I ever will.

Dialogue of the deaf

Nick, a UKIP activist befriended me on election night 2019, when I stood a cat for election in Gillingham and Rainham. He offered me a job to revolutionise UKIP's fortunes as he thought I was by far the best candidate at the election count. I politely declined but we kept in touch. He became a fan of my music and told me in 2021 that he had dropped UKIP after they became fascists. At the same time, he still believes that Brexit did not work because we did not cut ourselves loose from the entire world. I kept in touch with Nick by WhatsApp. This sequence demonstrates the poverty of online forums as an instrument of Brexorcism where **deletions**, **distortions** and **generalisations** rule. Also, why face to face contact is essential to do the job properly.

Nick : It was a pleasure to chat to you last night! Thanks very much for the music 🙂. I think the band and pub should now be renamed, how about 'Omicron at The Super spreaders'🙂

Peter : Hi Nick. Good to talk. If you fancy a coffee away from the madness let me know

Nick : 🙂🙂

Peter : By the way, your UKIP mates threatened to smash my face in, later at the pub

Nick : Sent link BBC News - Maureen Lipman : Cancel culture could wipe out comedy

Nick : Sorry about that...

Peter : My experience on Sunday is a direct result of cancel culture - they want freedom at other peoples' loss

Nick : 🙂🙂.. Too many people/organisations think it is their job to control debate, when it is actually their job to encourage debate...

Peter : Yep with their fists

Nick : I've been threatened quite a lot, sacked from a job, shut down on the media ... Just for making points about the economics of 🙂🙂 and my minimal involvement with UKIP.. Such is life unfortunately...

Nick : When is the next 'music evening'....I will try to come...

Peter : I'm not returning to the Ship

Nick : You're a good musician. Gillingham needs you☐

Peter : I'm not playing for knuckle dragging gammon

Nick : There was quite a diverse crowd their that night....

Nick : So after our 'superspreading event' ☐ we should have symptoms by now [Link]

Peter : Not necessarily. We are not all susceptible clearly

My latest article www.brexitrage.com/brexit-has-failed/

Nick : 'The National Farmer's Union reports that the Australian Trade Deal will break British farming. Listen to Farming Today on Radio 4'. One of the reasons I campaigned for BREXIT is the massive distortions in the ☐☐ Agro Economy caused by the ☐☐ subsidy system and tariff barriers.... ☐☐ ended up growing the wrong stuff and poor ☐☐ consumers paid far too much for food, whilst at the same time subsidising ☐☐ and French Farmers....crazy. Farming Today refuses to put a 'zero subsidy' option out there...

Nick : Well written... Keep trying with the NLP!

Peter : Brexit is a systemic problem. One cannot vote to deal with a single issue. As is becoming apparent now

Nick : I think BREXIT is a 'systematic solution'...

Peter : I don't know what that means

Nick : Got to go and dig my spuds for Xmas day...☐☐☐☐

Peter : Noun is missing ... to what

Nick : ...too the ☐☐ economy....

Re-Boot Britain by changing minds on Europe and Brexit

Peter : This makes no sense - it is why this medium is pointless for a dialogue - if you want a coffee I will meet you in the new year

Nick : ☐☐. Have a good ☐☐ and NY ❣☒ I will be ☐ most of it...

Nick : Because of BREXIT I am on £10/hr more than this time last year... Because of Presidents Xi's bioweapon (I suspect that is what history will tell us) I can wash my hands at work in hot water, for the FIRST time in 30 years! Small mercies..

Peter : But not systemic benefits as I said on Sunday - good for you

Peter : As I said, I find this medium unsatisfactory for a proper conversation - if you want to meet fine, but otherwise it is just a form of interruption to my day

Peter : Latest article "Brexit is Broken" www.brexitrage.com/brexit-is-broken/

Nick : Not my kind of thing... BUT "Democracies get the leaders they deserve, not the leaders they need.". ☐☐ deserved a Comedian... At least he's better (he can speak in public!) Than Treason May☐. I was just listening to JoB on LBC regaling against BJ.... JoB and yourself are missing the point: Britain has no effective OPPOSITION now. Until we have an effective OPPOSITION BJ can continue to blunder along! Another 8 more years☐

Nick : Boris – Most transformative PM since Attlee... More left wing and better for Working Class Northern Britain than TB and GB put together

Peter : Evidence please

Nick Chambers: 1 Social Care paid for NI... Attlee did not do this... 2 Media are at least discussing how to sort out transport across The North...TB and GB never bothered..

Peter : Please see https://brexitrage.com/paying-for-social-care/

Peter Cook: HS2 cancelled

Nick : Labour was against HS2 at last GE. Yes☐

Nick : Got to go to work...☐☐. But glad to here you are still fighting fit☐

Peter : No longer going to gammon pubs

Nick : Next time I'll look after you

Peter : The lorry driver surge lasted a long time then
www.express.co.uk/news/politics/1568297/Brexit-news-uk-lorry-drivers-shortages-hgv-border-rules-eu

Nick : There is a lot of nonsense being talked about this... Some companies say "there is no driver shortage in ☐☐ . Or driver shortage is "just seasonal"... International work (crossing to ☐☐) is still VERY poorly paid. It has been for over 20 years. Minimum wage. BECAUSE it is assumed all the drivers make £ smuggling stuff.... I think the "lack of facilities/antisocial hours etc are big issues...BUT fundamentally delivering around London is hard work. It is a skill. It is not for the feint hearted.....If companies pay enough, they will get the work done....if not then TOUGH!

Peter : https://brexitrage.com/brexit-and-wwiii

Nick : I know a lot of ☐☐ who want to get into ☐☐ today☐☐☐☐☐

Peter : This is all on Farage / Putin

Nick: ☐☐☐☐☐

Peter: A letter to my MP.

Dear Mr Chishti, Well, you must be pleased as Brexit has brought its first benefit ... World War III. And Johnson has put a light show into No 10 to show solidarity. Presumably, he threw a party last night?

It is NOT sufficient to cancel public school places for mini Vlads. It is NOT sufficient to wag fingers about property. It is NOT sufficient to say that NATO is powerless to act when it has made exceptions before. It is your time to act NOW. Even this is yet another example of your boss' "too little, too late" strategy. Britain's soft power has been decimated by Boris' Brexit and we are now an international joke. Listen to Tom Tugendhat instead of Jacob Rees-Mogg.

I imagine you will instead be having a game of tennis? Please make an exception and get serious about Ukraine and world peace for a change. Tomorrow will not wait.

Peter Cook…

Nick : The Russians would have done this irrespective of Brexit…they've been planning it at least 20 years..

Peter: Brexit helped them

Nick : Respectfully that is tripe… But I do not have time to argue….trying to get some

Peter Cook: This is not a satisfying conversation if you are to just reply with your own opinion versus facts Nick. I'd offered a coffee but I'm not continuing this on WA if the Dunning-Kruger effect is to rule your opinions

Reflections

- Nick is not a soft target so one might say there is little point engaging with him. However, he is personable and this makes it worthwhile.

- The medium of WhatsApp is very poor. Asynchronous communications allow for threads to be dropped, for answers to be calculated and so on. Nick is especially good at saying he is too busy to reply to avoid getting into difficulty. He clearly wants to maintain the relationship if only to watch me play some Pink Floyd songs!

- Nick has however detached from his hardcore UKIP friends and denounces the racist stickers mentioned earlier. This is something of an achievement.

- I clearly did not establish any authority in this sequence online. But time changes things. Nick is, of course, towards the end of the hard Brexit spectrum, but, as I said, I like hard targets.

- He demonstrates the psychographic feature of some Brexiteers "because my wages went up due to lorry driver shortages, everything will be fine".

- More time spent face to face would make more impact but Nick seems resistant to coffee! He will give in eventually!

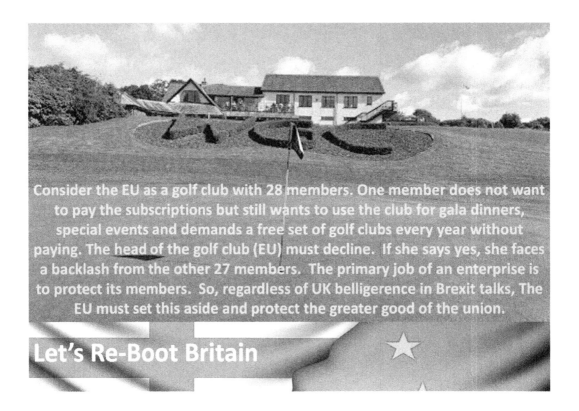

Consider the EU as a golf club with 28 members. One member does not want to pay the subscriptions but still wants to use the club for gala dinners, special events and demands a free set of golf clubs every year without paying. The head of the golf club (EU) must decline. If she says yes, she faces a backlash from the other 27 members. The primary job of an enterprise is to protect its members. So, regardless of UK belligerence in Brexit talks, The EU must set this aside and protect the greater good of the union.

Let's Re-Boot Britain

Police brutality

In October 2020, one of my neighbours took exception to some anti-Brexit stickers on my dustbin and gate post. He first sent a highly offensive anonymous letter to my wife. This was followed by a sustained campaign of placing rubbish in my garden, spray painting my property over a two-week period and using a knife to inflict criminal damage. It turned out that he was an ex-Metropolitan Police officer who had left under mysterious circumstances. As a result, Kent Police seemed totally disinterested in progressing the case, despite a large body of incontrovertible video evidence against him. I was persuaded by Kent Police that it would be better if I handled the matter myself which had the benefit of making sure it was not recorded as a crime. After 18 months of mind-bending hassle, I did in fact negotiate an out of court settlement with 'Ken' of some £3000 which was just enough to make good the frontage of the house.

Below is the transcript of the 'Brexit negotiations' with 'our Ken'. It makes for an insightful read into the art of negotiation under extremely difficult conditions and a case study into the mind of the hardcore Brexiteer.

Ken's contributions are in *italics* whilst I am **bold**, both in typeface terms and in real life, for persisting with the case! Ken still feels that he was "provoked' to attack my property with spray paint and a knife and that he is the 'victim' of the crime he committed. This remains a bizarre reversal of the truth but it is quite common as we have discussed earlier.

Ken's last LinkedIn post from five years ago said "That's why I'm looking to leave no support, constant criticism. Been waiting months to be referred to a counsellor - what a joke. Met officers motto is TJF - The job's F****d - Mets theme tune We're (sic) on the road to Nowhere".

I begin with the court summons which I put in, as this gives you the context for the case. I had sent a hard copy of the summons on 13 January 2022 with a post-it note attached inviting Ken to undertake an out of court negotiation before the case was to be heard on 27 January. I insisted that this be conducted by correspondence rather than by telephone or face to face, given the circumstances of the crime.

In the County Court   Case No xxx

Parties   Peter Cook   Claimant
                           Ken   Defendant

Summary of case

I contend that Mr xxx is guilty of the following crimes:

1. Criminal damage to my property, amounting to £3500 plus court costs in remediation.
2. The premeditated use of a knife to inflict further damage to my property and to intimidate me and my family.
3. Sending a malicious letter, which warned of the above actions.

I have video evidence of the first two items above attached to this report. Kent Police gained an admission from Mr xxx that he was the perpetrator of the criminal damage. Given the timing of the malicious letter at the beginning of this sequence of events, highly likely that Mr xxx was the author of the malicious letter. To avoid further escalation of a criminal case with more serious consequences, I agreed to a civil resolution of the criminal damage with Kent Police, hence this submission.

Mr xxx's malicious letter and the use of the knife have had a severe impact on my wife's anxiety levels, sleep patterns and mental health. As a result of this, I installed video monitoring equipment and procured other personal security items at my own cost. I make no claim for these elements as they are not directly related to Mr xxx's actions.

I offered Mr xxx restorative justice but this was ignored by him. I was subsequently told by a member of Kent Police that he was not entitled to this, due to previous offences.

As a result of the above, I submit a claim of £3500 plus court costs of £185 and £346 in respect of remediation work to be done on the house. This figure does not account for the impact on my family's well-being, but no claim is being made here for the collateral damage.

I believe that the facts stated in this witness statement are true.

Peter Cook   01 December 2021

I, Peter Cook of address, am the claimant in this claim. The facts in this statement come from my personal knowledge and data recorded on video and via photographs.

1. On 17 October 2020 my wife received a malicious letter (exhibit A below) posted through our letterbox. I was away working at the time, my wife was panicked by the language in the letter and phoned me immediately, after which the matter was reported to the Police. The letter complained about some anti-Brexit stickers and posters in my garden and threatened me with further actions if I did not cease and desist. I am a well-known anti-Brexit campaigner in the local area and across the UK and the attacker decided that I must be therefore targeted as such.

> Dear Occupier
>
> Listen you fucking anti-democratic EU loving sad fat ugly turd, stop putting your fucking retarded stickers round Medway and leaving a fucking mess.
>
> Local Residents are fed up of you, your stupid fucking bicycle and putting your sad little stickers on your bins, any labels taken down will all be dumped back in your front garden.
>
> Even somebody with one brain cell like you should understand why your stickers are getting taken down as people are fed up of your pathetic nonsense.
>
> If you don't like Brexit then fuck off out of the country to the EU or stop behaving like a total fucktard.
>
> You are a complete cunt and have been politely warned, carry on putting your stickers up and pay the consequences.

2. Soon afterwards, several 'reminders' of the letter were placed in my garden. These consisted of scrunched up stickers taken from my dustbin and placed to make it obvious that someone had been on the property. As a result, my wife became very fearful going out at night, considering it to be very unsafe. Her anxiety levels dramatically increased. Within 1-2 weeks, this escalated further per the 'warnings' in the letter. Mr xxx then took to appearing every evening at my property armed with a can of spray paint, which he used to

deface the frontage and gate of my property. This was extremely worrying and upsetting to my family and prompted me to install a CCTV camera, hoping it would make him stop. One of these occurrences can be seen at: EU Tube. Another four occurrences were captured on video within just one week and this seemed to be happening every night around 7.00 pm. There were many more occurrences not recorded on film but seen from our upstairs window, as I started to build up a picture of our attacker and his nightly visits.

3. Mr xxx's behaviour escalated to the next level when he turned up with a knife one evening. All the above took place within one month of the 'warning letter'. I contend that these crimes are therefore related to the threats of further action ('pay the consequences'). Please click to view the evidence: EU Tube. With the sound on, it is possible to hear the impact of the sharp instrument. Quite deep marks were made on the wooden gate post which confirm the use of a knife and it can be seen glistening as it is twisted.

4. In order to procure additional evidence, one evening I followed Mr xxx home at a safe distance and ascertained that he lived in an adjacent road. I reported all to the Police and they gained a confession from Mr xxx that he was the perpetrator of the criminal damage. I also discovered in conversation with four independent residents that Mr xxx was a retired policeman.

5. I obtained quotations for the damage to the gate and the exterior walls of the property and attach a quote for the remediation work.

Conclusion

I submit that Mr xxx acted with intent to intimidate me and my family. We have proof that he instigated criminal damage to my property. I allege that he wrote the malicious letter and deposited other warnings to my property. Whilst I fully understand that the country remains divided on Brexit, it is not acceptable to resort to violence to make one's points. Mr xxx's actions have had a significant prolonged effect on my wife's mental health - dramatically increased anxiety levels and fear of leaving the house.

I submit a claim of £3500 plus court costs of £185 and £346 in respect of remediation work to be done on the house. This figure does not account for the impact on my family's well-being, but no claim is being made here for the collateral damage.

I believe that the facts stated in this witness statement are true.

Peter Cook   01 December 2021

Appendix

Examples of posters and stickers used on my property

Police Crimes recorded

Malicious communications
Criminal damage
Use of an offensive weapon

E-mail negotiation thread – Jan 16-27 2022

Sun, Jan 16, 2022 at 4:37 PM Ken wrote:

Ref : Case xxx   *16th January 2022*

Summary of Objection

Mr.Cook,

I'll put things simply for you.

1. *Clear photographic evidence shows spray paint only on the right gate post of your property.*
2. *There is no physical or structural damage to your gate, photos available.*
3. *There is no structural damage to your gate post, photos available.*
4. *There in no damage to any other part of your property, photos available.*
5. *You allege that I wrote the letter, I did not.*
6. *You allege I attacked your property with a knife, I did not use a knife.*
7. *I am not retired I am an ex Prison Officer, my son is a Police Officer, I have never told any neighbours what work I do, even Kent Police will confirm this.*
8. *You made several allegations on Facebook and in your summary that I have a past Criminal Record, apart from a ticket for speeding I have never had a criminal record prior to this incident.*

You have clearly provided a deliberately over inflated quote from a builder based on work you want done to your property which does not need doing and you expect me to pay for it.

I have several reliable honest builder's quotes and a cleaning company quote which I am willing to provide to the court which clearly shows the cost is barely over £200 to repair.

All that needs doing to rectify the damage is simply to paint the gatepost black, or the gatepost cleaned and sanded.

The reason this is scheduled for court is down to myself but also the fact that you refused mediation.

In view of your over inflated quote, I am a reasonable person and am prepared to pay you £500 damages plus costs incurred to a maximum of £1200 which you know is well in excess of the damage caused.

If you are a reasonable person you will accept the offer made and if you supply your Bank Details then I will happily transfer the money immediately.

If you want to discuss the matter on a civil basis one to one prior to attending court then I am off on Monday 17th and happy to meet you in Gillingham park anytime.

These are the honest facts of this incident, please reply with your decision otherwise we will happily see you in court on 27th.

****

Wed, Jan 19, 2022 at 8:20 AM Peter Cook wrote:

Dear Ken,

Thank you for your reply, the first communication I have received from you. I have annotated the various points you have made, so that the court can see the details of our attempts to settle the matter.

All the best

Peter

Ken's comments in italics. **Mine in bold.**

Ref : Case xxx   *16th January 2022*

<u>Summary of Objection</u>

Mr.Cook,

> *I'll put things simply for you.*

1. *Clear photographic evidence shows spray paint only on the right gate post of your property.*

Incorrect. There is damage to both gate posts and the front wall. The court has video evidence of you 'missing the gate' in some kind of frenzied attempt to spray paint the gate and missing, damaging the wall and coping stones.

2. *There is no physical or structural damage to your gate, photos available.*

Rejected. The sound of the attack on the gate from the knife is clearly audible. See point 6. There are also quite a few gouge marks that confirm the use of a knife.

3. *There is no structural damage to your gate post, photos available.*

Rejected. As per points 2 and 6.

4. *There in no damage to any other part of your property, photos available.*

Accepted. You stopped after I reported the matter to the Police. You appear to be making a virtue out of the fact that you did not continue to escalate your actions when you simply got found out. I don't consider this to be to your credit or a validation of your actions.

5. *You allege that I wrote the letter, I did not.*

I indicated that it was highly probable that you wrote the letter, as per the court submission. The actions described in the submission commenced very soon after the threat was received. I repeat that it therefore seems highly plausible that you were the perpetrator.

6. *You allege I attacked your property with a knife, I did not use a knife.*

Rejected. The video makes it quite clear that (a) this is you with your three dogs and (b) there is a frenzied attack with a sharp instrument which glistens as you turn it and which made deep impact marks. The sound on the video also demonstrates the impact of the weapon. There is clear intent. Goodness knows what would have happened if I had been out on that evening. It is simply not agreeable to carry a weapon whilst walking your dogs with intent to cause criminal damage.

7. *I am not retired I am an ex Prison Officer, my son is a Police Officer, I have never told any neighbours what work I do, even Kent Police will confirm this.*

Accepted. I checked independently with four neighbours, some of whom live quite close to you. All volunteered the information that you were a police officer. A couple of them also said that they did not really know you, as you are something of a private person. I imagine that they must have assumed your uniform was that of a police officer rather than a prison officer. And it sounds as if this may have been some while back, so I imagine that they may have seen a uniform and made that judgement. As such this is my mistake and I apologise for getting this wrong in my enquiries. However, it has no material bearing on the case, except that I would also expect better behaviour from someone working in your position as a public servant.

8. *You made several allegations on Facebook and in your summary that I have a past Criminal Record, apart from a ticket for speeding I have never had a criminal record prior to this incident.*

You will need to take this up with Kent Police. I received a call from one of their officers. When I mentioned my offer of restorative justice, the officer said that remedy was not available on this occasion due to previous incidents on your part. I asked what these were but the officer simply repeated the word 'incidents'. I took this to mean that there must have been something they were unable to tell me, due to data protection. In any case, it has no material bearing on the case. If Kent Police have misled me, then I must apologise on their behalf.

You have clearly provided a deliberately over inflated quote from a builder based on work you want done to your property which does not need doing and you expect me to pay for it.

Rejected. May I remind you that:

- It is you who committed the criminal damage with nightly applications of spray paint over several weeks.
- You came to my property with intent to use the knife. This was a planned intervention.
- Given the timeline of these events, it seems probable that you also sent the threatening letter.

I tried to obtain a quote to re-fit the gate posts at the outset, but the builder said it would involve removing concrete and part of the wall. It was in fact more expensive than redecoration, so I opted for this. Contrary to what you say, the damage extends beyond the gate itself per the photos and videos provided. Partial redecoration would

make the rest of the frontage look even more strange. I don't see that I should 'make, do and mend' the damage done by yourself or accept a 'patch up job' from one of your recommended friends.

I have several reliable honest builder's quotes and a cleaning company quote which I am willing to provide to the court which clearly shows the cost is barely over £200 to repair.

All that needs doing to rectify the damage is simply to paint the gatepost black, or the gatepost cleaned and sanded.

Rejected. I feel the need to repeat myself here. I am trying to find the words to support your suggestion that I should 'make, do and mend' the damage done by yourself or accept a 'patch up job' from one of your recommended friends. May I remind you again that it is you who committed the criminal damage, using a knife with intent and who plausibly sent the threatening letter. Given what you have done, please explain why I might want to accept one of your friends to make good the damage that you have caused? The quote provided includes full removal of the previous paint job which is time consuming and is what I had done last time, in keeping with the Conservation area standards. I see no reason why I should accept an inferior job due to your actions.

The reason this is scheduled for court is down to myself but also the fact that you refused mediation.

Incorrect. At no point have I received a request from you for mediation. I offered it at the outset and gained no reply.

At the beginning, I discussed what I wanted done about the matter with Kent Police and I did suggest that I might be willing to accept restorative justice. In the end, the Police recommended that I take a civil case. It was subsequently explained that restorative justice was not available to you, due to previous incidents on your part. I can only apologise again on behalf of Kent Police if they got this wrong. No mediation request was received from you. In fact, when I first lodged the case, you made no response within the required time period and the judge found against you. After the case timed out, you subsequently asked for the case to be set aside and, to my surprise, HMCTS agreed to your request, but there was no explanation as to this or any correspondence about mediation, despite my request to know the grounds for you having the case set aside.

In view of your over inflated quote, I am a reasonable person and am prepared to pay you £500 damages plus costs incurred to a maximum of £1200 which you know is well in excess of the damage caused.

I am afraid the sum you suggest is only 1/7th of the sum requested. As such, it is a perfectly reasonable request to ask you to make good the criminal damage in total. The court costs are already spent and are non-refundable and I have had considerable time wasted by this matter. As such, your proposal does not even begin to meet the costs needed to make a reasonable repair. Additionally, may I remind you of the fact that I had to take other actions to address my wife's anxiety because of your actions, such as surveillance systems and improved security. She did not sleep well for several months during the time that you launched these attacks and up to the point that I installed safety and security measures. The spray-painting events happened nearly every evening over a course of several weeks, in other words this was not an isolated event but a planned and sustained campaign of intimidation. I have much more video evidence of your spray-painting activities than that already provided to the court and, of course, some of your campaign took place before I installed the camera. Furthermore, the whole episode has wasted considerable time, money, effort and caused considerable unnecessary stress and depression for my family who are now contemplating moving away from the area.

If you are a reasonable person you will accept the offer made and if you supply your Bank Details then I will happily transfer the money immediately.
If you want to discuss the matter on a civil basis one to one prior to attending court then I am off on Monday 17th and happy to meet you in Gillingham park anytime.

I am a reasonable person and I appreciate your offer but, as I am sure you will understand, the idea of meeting someone who has previously attacked my property with a knife is not on my bucket list. For such a meeting to take place, I would wish to know what the purpose of such a meeting was in advance. I'd also need the presence of the Police which would be quite unreasonable on their part, given how much of their time this matter has already consumed. I trust you understand that I'd simply prefer that we settled the matter by correspondence or via the court. In terms of reasonableness, I must also refer to the fact that you caused criminal damage, attacked my property with a knife and it is probable that you sent the threatening letter.

These are the honest facts of this incident, please reply with your decision otherwise we will happily see you in court on 27th.

Yes, I hope we'll be able to make progress, but otherwise I too am happy to discuss the case with the judge in a public forum.

****

From: Ken
Date: Wednesday, 19 January 2022 at 08:39
To: Peter Cook
Subject: Response to your objections : Case xxx

You are once again totally wrong I never used a knife you assume it was a metal object not a knife, no damage was caused to your wall photos prove this, you just continuously assume things which appear to differ from your blinkered beliefs.
You clearly overlook that on the paperwork you submitted you refused mediation and didn't have the courage to meet one to one to discuss to resolve this laughable that you would meet only with Police presence shows what a coward you are.
I never had a criminal record once again you believe everything you are told regarding this and me being a police officer.
You are clearly unwilling to compromise so it is patently obvious it is pointless communicating with you.
You know as well as I do this quote is overinflated and honestly does not reflect the true cost but you appear to be a totally pathetic obstinate individual.
For info you are currently under investigation by Kent Police referred by Medway Council for your continued obsession with posting your stickers and degrading the area.

If your not willing to change your stance see you in court and looking forward to it, wouldn't surprise me if you don't report me to Kent Police again as another lie that I chased you down the street.

****

Tues, Jan 25, 2022 at 10.00 AM Peter Cook wrote:

Dear Ken,

Here are my replies to your replies and questions. We are still at 1/7ᵗʰ of the required settlement figure and I hope you will come forward with an improved proposal which

was why I gave a detailed reply. Please read my detailed response and make your proposal.

Kind regards

Peter

****

You are once again totally wrong I never used a knife you assume it it was a metal object not a knife, no damage was caused to your wall photos prove this, you just continuously assume things which appear to differ from your blinkered beliefs.

Rejected : In your previous letter of 16 Jan 2022, you contested my point that you used a knife during your campaign of attacks over several weeks. Now you admit that there was a metal object as was already provided in the video evidence. The gouge marks and audio on the video also indicate that the metal object was sharp and robust. Can you explain what the metal object was please? None of your above points alter the fact that you came out of your house with intent to use a weapon.

You clearly overlook that on the paperwork you submitted you refused mediation and didn't have the courage to meet one to one to discuss to resolve this laughable that you would meet only with Police presence shows what a coward you are.

Rejected : I have the audio transcript of the police interview and I must repeat: Mediation was NOT offered. I have already explained how the Police told me it was not offered due to previous incidents on your part. Your argument on this point is therefore with Kent Police.

I never had a criminal record once again you believe everything you are told regarding this and me being a police officer.

Accepted : See again my reply to your point 8. I have already apologised on behalf of Kent Police for THEIR mistake in inferring that you already had a criminal record.

You are clearly unwilling to compromise so it is patently obvious it is pointless communicating with you.

Not at all. I merely pointed out that we were 1/7th of the way there. The ball is in your court to make a substantially improved offer. Please read carefully what I wrote and come up with a proposal which responds to the points I have made in my reply and which I will give proper consideration to.

You know as well as I do this quote is overinflated and honestly does not reflect the true cost but you appear to be a totally pathetic obstinate individual.

Rejected : I already explained the validity of the quote in my reply below.

For info you are currently under investigation by Kent Police referred by Medway Council for your continued obsession with posting your stickers and degrading the area.

Given what you said earlier about your family connections with the Police, I am a bit surprised as to how you know so much about what is going on inside Kent Police. Can you explain the basis of these data breaches? Who is responsible for this leakage of confidential information? I am not sure how this would look if it came out in any media coverage of the trial.

If your not willing to change your stance see you in court and looking forward to it, wouldn't surprise me if you don't report me to Kent Police again as another lie that I chased you down the street.

Noted and rejected.

Peter Cook

****

Tue, Jan 25, 2022 at 1:00 PM Peter Cook wrote:

Dear Ken,

The court date approaches. I am pleased that you chose to write to me after I offered you the opportunity to reach an out of court settlement. However, there has been no further progress since that time. Instead of negotiating, you have chosen merely to state your grievances, for example, accusing me of cowardice for refusing to meet you in a park, when you were previously armed with what you call 'a metal instrument' and what I call a 'knife'.

Like Brexit, democracy is a continuing process rather than a project, and I'd welcome your further thoughts on the settlement. Of course, like Brexit, the opportunity to reach an out of court settlement runs out on Thursday, so if you wish to make a deal, please let me know asap. Otherwise, we must proceed to court with your offer of 1/7th of the required settlement figure which I do not consider to be in any way adequate.

By the way, per your suggestion, I contacted Kent Police to ask about your suggestion that an investigation has commenced. They can find no record of the investigation. Can you provide the crime number so I may help them with their enquiries? I am still confused as to what the crime is and who reported an incident. Perhaps you can elaborate?

Peter

****

From: Ken
Date: Tuesday, 25 January 2022 at 17:41
To: Peter Cook
Subject: Re: Final opportunity to settle : Case xxx

Your estimate for damages is unacceptable that is obvious to anybody and would be to the court when I provide photographs and quotes for restoration from builders and cleaning companies.
I am in no way paying the full amount of your claim it's that simple, so what would you consider reasonable???
You seem very obsessed with Brexit it appears that's all you have to occupy yourself as for the situation with Kent Police you will have to wait for them to make contact with you as you are aware they aren't the quickest.
I'll make it simple either reduce your costs to something I find acceptable or see you Thursday I will not agree to your overinflated builders quote as we both know that is to be polite excessive.
I await your response.

****

In the meantime, this happened ….

From: Kent Listing
Date: Tuesday, 25 January 2022 at 12:46
To: Peter Cook
Subject: ##VERY URGENT## CASE STOOD OUT xxx , COOK V SPEDDING

Good afternoon,

Please be aware that unfortunately, the hearing on 27 January 2022 at Medway County Court will not go ahead. The matter is being stood out of the Court list due to a lack of judicial time.

Please can you contact the Defendant as we have no contact details for them.

If you have any dates to avoid for the next 12 months, please email them to Medway County Court – within the next 7 days and we will then relist this matter. We apologise for any inconvenience caused.

Kind Regards

Kelly Craig
Kent Centralised Listing
Maidstone Law Courts, Barker Road, Maidstone, Kent, ME16 8EQ

Editor's note : I decided to continue with the out of court negotiation and decided not to tell Ken about this postponement, as the case would have simply returned and he had chased me down the road on the last occasion that I took papers to his house.

****

Wed, Jan 26, 2022 at 7:23 AM Peter Cook wrote:

Dear Ken,

Thanks for your reply below. The ball is very much in your court per my previous replies. To clarify the negotiation process:

    1. **You will recall that I made a claim via the court.**

2. You made an offer of circa £500 plus costs, just 1/7th of the requested amount. I cannot imagine any circumstances in which anyone would make an offer of 1/7thof the claim, expecting to gain an out of court settlement.
3. It is therefore your turn to make a revised offer. Please go back through the detailed points I made in our previous correspondence below and make a substantially improved offer.

I have fully explained the rationale for this in previous correspondence. You have stated that you are a reasonable person. I hope that you will act reasonably, before this becomes a matter of public interest.

You made a few additional points below and I have answered them.

You said "You seem very obsessed with Brexit it appears that's all you have to occupy yourself as for the situation with Kent Police you will have to wait for them to make contact with you as you are aware they aren't the quickest".

I agree that, apart from climate change, Brexit is a major constitutional, political, economic and social change that will reverberate for centuries and affect the lives and livelihoods of all our children and theirs. I therefore cannot apologise for being, as you say, 'obsessed' with Brexit. Rather than obsession, I would call it a simple concern to build a better Britain for future generations. By the same token, I must observe that someone who organised a sustained campaign of attacks over several weeks, procuring spray paint and then taking a knife (or metal object) may also be considered to be 'obsessed' with Brexit.

I repeat that, if you or others have submitted a crime to Kent Police, please give me the crime number. I am quite happy to help them with their enquiries.

I consulted with a linguistics expert on the various letters you have written. They point out that the style of the letters you wrote is similar to the one that you claim you did not write or post through my letterbox (copy below). These similarities include the accusative style, the specific use of language and specific grammatical devices and ornaments. Additionally, the letter originally sent mentions that stickers from my garden and dustbin would be put back in my garden. Of course, this was the beginning of your actions, which you admitted to Kent Police, along with your sustained campaign of spray painting over several weeks. We have now also established that you did use the knife / metal object as part of your intimidation strategy. It therefore seems highly probable that you wrote the threatening letter, since it describes actions which you have already admitted that you conducted.

So, I repeat, the ball is firmly in your court to make a substantially improved offer. I await your offer, at which point I am prepared to discuss a final settlement. This would mean that there would be no need to go to court, or to face public disclosure of your campaign of intimidation. Any agreement must be fully settled and monies transferred before the public hearing if it this to be avoided. To this end, I am happy to provide my bank details if a negotiated settlement can be reached out of court.

All the best

Peter

> Dear Occupier
>
> Listen you fucking anti-democratic EU loving sad fat ugly turd, stop putting your fucking retarded stickers round Medway and leaving a fucking mess.
>
> Local Residents are fed up of you, your stupid fucking bicycle and putting your sad little stickers on your bins, any labels taken down will all be dumped back in your front garden.
>
> Even somebody with one brain cell like you should understand why your stickers are getting taken down as people are fed up of your pathetic nonsense.
>
> If you don't like Brexit then fuck off out of the country to the EU or stop behaving like a total fucktard.
>
> You are a complete cunt and have been politely warned, carry on putting your stickers up and pay the consequences.

Ken's writing became increasingly like the anonymous letter as negotiations proceeded.

****

From: Ken
Date: Wednesday, 26 January 2022 at 07:36
To: Peter Cook
Subject: Re: Without Prejudice : Case xxx

You think you are intellectually superior, unfortunately you're not, I never spray painted your property over several weeks another lie.
I never wrote the letter contrary to your laughable linguistic experts.
I have already told you, you make an offer of what you consider to be honest and reasonable as I'm not paying your bill it's that simple even for somebody with your limited intelligence, the balls in your court if you'd considered mediation it would never have reached this stage that is down to your immature obstinate (I'm always right) attitude.
Message me with an offer as I'm not paying your estimate that's the second time I've requested this try and keep up.
It will be a matter of public interest anyway as no doubt you will gloat all over Facebook and probably gossip to all the neighbours.
Once again message me with a reasonable figure.

****

Wed, Jan 26, 2022 at 8:08 AM Peter Cook wrote:

Dear Ken,

Thanks for your rapid reply. You have until 11 am tomorrow to complete the necessary arrangements once we have agreed a settlement.

To repeat : Mediation was not offered by yourself or by the Police (audio transcript). Please carefully read the detail that I gave.

Regarding your campaign of intimidation, I have a whole series of videos with you spray painting the property. This took place over two weeks. I procured a camera in the second week after I realised that you were coming round every evening to do this. To be frank, it looks a bit deranged. I attach one of the examples of your work in case you doubt the evidence.

The original letter says that you would conduct the actions that you subsequently admitted to the Police. I'd say that makes it highly probable that you wrote the malicious letter.

The clock is ticking. Your move. Once I have seen your revised offer I will consider whether I can make a concession for a settlement of the matter.

All the best

Peter

****

From: Ken
Date: Wednesday, 26 January 2022 at 08:19
To: Peter Cook
Subject: Re: Without Prejudice : Case xxx

I have the paperwork completed by yourself which clearly highlights that you have ticked 'No' to mediation another lie by yourself or oversight.

Incorrect : It helps to get the timeline right. When the Police came round to begin with I did indicate that I was willing to consider mediation. Later, they said that they would simply issue a warning and turn the matter over to a civil court. I filled in no paperwork. When they arrived, they simply asked me to sign to say that I was happy that the matter had been turned over to a civil court. At no point was mediation mentioned and there is an audio recording of the conversation that took place. Subsequently, they told me that you were not eligible for mediation anyway due to previous incidents as I already explained.

For the 3rd time as you're becoming a tedious bore you make me an offer I am offering you your opportunity to submit an honest figure as I've highlighted your figure is overinflated and unacceptable, it is obvious I am trying to resolve this before Thursday but as usual you're behaving like a child no wonder you use crayons for your graffiti.

I am sorry that you feel I am boring you. I would not have even had the opportunity to 'bore' you if you had not conducted a sustained campaign of intimidation which has caused my wife untold stress and anxiety and caused me additional costs to install safety and security equipment. You appear to be making the argument that you were

provoked by some stickers on my dustbin to attack my property over several weeks with spray paint and a knife aka a metal object. This is rather like saying the 'the girl deserved it as she was wearing a short skirt'.

Make an offer it's not difficult.

It is your responsibility to make an offer now. I will then supply bank details if it is sufficient.
The deadline for settlement out of court is 12.00 tomorrow. Any agreement would need to be fully honoured by then.

Kind regards

Peter Cook

****

Thursday 27 January – Judgement Day

From: Ken
Date: Thursday, 27 January 2022 at 07:27
To: Peter Cook
Subject: Re: Without Prejudice : Case xxx

Your conduct referring to girls in short skirts is worrying do you have an issue with children ?
It seems you lack basic intelligence as I have the paperwork you dropped off at my house completed by you were you highlighted no to mediation.
It would appear pointless submitting an offer as you will only reject it but as you are just clearly being an obstinate prat so I'll be the bigger man so I'll offer you £2500 inclusive of costs this is a final offer and is well in excess of the costs of your cowboy builder.
I will pay this immediately if you agree and supply bank details but I won't hold my breath as you appear to get off on being awkward.
Reply with your decision, either way I'll be at court at 12.

****

Thu, Jan 27, 2022 at 8:47 AM Peter Cook wrote:

Dear Ken,

This is a welcome development. In turn I said I would respond in kind.

If you can meet the court costs of £531, I will accept your offer. Sadly, these have already been spent and cannot be refunded.

So, that would be £3031 rounded down. Let's call it £3000 as a full and final settlement figure.

Bank details below

All the best

Peter

****

From: Ken
Date: Thursday, 27 January 2022 at 08:56
To: Peter Cook
Subject: Re: Without Prejudice : Case xxx

I'm not willing to pay another £500 court costs,I'll pay you a final figure of £2750 take it or leave it.

****

From: Ken
Date: Thursday, 27 January 2022 at 09:52
To: Peter Cook
Subject: Re: Without Prejudice : Case xxx

I have transferred £2750 to your account

****

From: Peter Cook
Date: Thursday, 27 January 2022 at 09:57

To: Ken
Subject: Without Prejudice : Case xxx

Dear Ken,

Will you settle at £2950 plus a full apology in writing? An apology at the outset could have changed the course of this case and I would consider this a generous move on your part which would go some way to addressing my wife's feelings on the matter.

I will, in turn, get the work done as soon as the weather allows and provide you with a copy of the final accounts in good faith.

The court will commence settlement at £2750 and it is entirely feasible that you will end up paying £4031. The matter will no longer be a private affair.

All the best

Peter

****

From: Ken
Date: Thursday, 27 January 2022 at 10:14
To: Peter Cook
Subject: Re: Without Prejudice : Case xxx

I will settle at £2950 I have already apologised it's not happening again so you can gloat and publish all over your Facebook account.

Editor's note : Ken never ever apologised at all. The Police told me he had said sorry to them and they wrote it in their notebook. I asked to see a copy of their notebook, but they never sent the apology. I never gloated over Facebook after the event. Instead, I thought the story was an object lesson in negotiation with Brexiteers so decided to give Ken five minutes of fame here without a full name check.

****

From: Peter Cook
Date: Thursday, 27 January 2022 at 10.14

To: Ken
Subject: Without Prejudice : Case xxx

Dear Ken,

Our e-mails crossed in mid-air. Please see my final offer in the previous e-mail.

Meanwhile I have not seen the faster payment in my bank account. Can you send a screen shot of the transfer? This will of course be to your credit at the court hearing.

All the best

Peter

****

From: Ken
Date: Thursday, 27 January 2022 at 10:15
To: Peter Cook
Subject: Re: Without Prejudice : Case xxx

Am not interested in seeing an invoice from your builder don't come anywhere near my property again.

****

From: Ken
Date: Thursday, 27 January 2022 at 10:19
To: Peter Cook
Subject: Re: Settlement agreement

I have just sent another transfer for £200 so final settlement is £2950 as agreed.

****

Thu, Jan 27, 2022 at 10:20 AM Peter Cook wrote:

Dear Ken,

That's agreed then. Please transfer the money and show me a screen shot of the transfer by 10.45 and I will have the case stood down.

All the best

Peter

****

From: Ken
Date: Thursday, 27 January 2022 at 10:27
To: Peter Cook
Subject: Re: Settlement agreement

Look in your account money has been transferred

From: Ken
Date: Thursday, 27 January 2022 at 10:40
To: Peter Cook
Subject: Re: Settlement agreement

Look in your account money has been transferred

****

Thu, Jan 27, 2022 at 10:40 AM Peter Cook wrote:

Thank you for acting with decency and integrity in this matter. I will stand the case down and you will not hear from me again.

The clock is no longer ticking.

All the best

Peter

****

From: Ken
Date: Thursday, 27 January 2022 at 10:51

To: Peter Cook
Subject: Re: Settlement agreement

Never was ticking for me □□□□, maybe for somebody else it's ticking, adios don't come near my property again.

Shows what a liar you and your builder are as you now claim that you will get the work done for less than your builders quote, from your previous email I suggest if you need to see something deranged you look at yourself in the mirror.

Don't spread anymore malicious lies around without foundation as two can play those kind of games.

I'm sure we will bump into each other again.

****

Reflections

Ken remained of the view that he had 'won' and that I was the 'cause' of him taking up arms and spray paint. The abiding theme is once again of someone that is angry about his lot and found a place to place that blame in Brexit and anyone who dared put forward different views about the topic.

I never cancelled the court date and a month later Ken got another summons. He sent an angry letter. I waited a day to reply and for the first time I got a reply which said 'please and thank you'. Someone observed that, eventually, I will get 'Dear Peter' and 'Kind Regards' if I persist. I won't!

Kent Police systematically avoided dealing with this matter, despite all the evidence provided. I can only reflect that people with more serious crimes are just as likely to be given the brush off by our Police service. Brexit has amplified and emboldened a minority of biased Police officers in Britain.

I am grateful to Michel Barnier for teaching me the gentle art of negotiation when face to face conversation is not feasible.

Political correctness and Brexorcism

Nigel Farage capitalised on the current obsession with political correctness and what some call woke behaviour to win the referendum. Granted, it is wrong to be offensive deliberately to disempower an individual or groups, but I sense that the movement for political correctness has now moved way past the point of a practical approach to improve our humanity. In some cases, it has been reduced to a set of personal preferences. Taken to extremes, it can restrict communication on important ideas and becomes the enemy of those issues rather than an asset.

I noticed just how difficult this made life when trying to write satirical songs for the Remain movement and finding that we had a suite of 'keyboard censors' on Facebook, trying to rewrite the songs via virtual committee. Having written a Chas & Dave inspired 'Cockney Brexit Knees Up', I had numerous complaints about the use of the word twat. I had sampled 'Eastenders' star Danny Dyer saying the word about David Cameron. Apparently, it was OK for Dyer to say this on daytime TV, but not OK when sampled into the song by a mere mortal as an 'Eastender'. I was left feeling that some Remainers have had a humour bypass operation.

Undeterred, I thought I'll change it to the very popular 'Bollocks to Brexit' refrain. We initiated this on the street at No 10 Vigil. B2B had been adopted as a campaign slogan by the Lib Dems. I contacted Charlie Mullins OBE, CEO of Pimlico Plumbers, a 'sarf London geezer' and managed to get him to do a voiceover. However, I got just as many complaints, some due to the word and others due to the working class and cheeky non-PC nature of a Chas & Dave pastiche. I don't mind that people don't like a song. Indeed, once I have listened to a song thousands of times whilst I am recording it, I often never want to hear it again for a while! However, I must be honest, that sometimes I wonder if Remainers ever wanted to win the fight against Brexit. Oh well, I went back to the drawing board again ... in Chumbawumba terms 'I get knocked down but I get up again'.

I also wrote a satirical 'Country and Western Brexit Hoedown' called 'Theresa May's a Remainer'. There were no expletives in the song, so all was well, or so I thought. Alas, amidst the lyric was a reference to John Major taking about the Eurosceptics in 1992 who he dubbed 'bastards'. I made a reference in the song with the phrase 'Shoot the bastards, they're all insane'. This was accompanied by a comedy gun shot and a horse 'clip clopping' through the song. It could not be much more obvious that this was a piece of satirical comedy in the same way that comedian Jo Brand mentioned battery acid and milkshakes when talking about Nigel Farage. Yet even this received complaints from angry Daily Mail readers with a humour bypass operation and no sense of political history. No wonder Billy Bragg says that nobody makes protest songs any more …

Find all the Rage Against The Brexit Machine songs at www.academy-of-rock.bandcamp.com or via iTunes, Amazon etc. The lyrics to both songs follow, so you may judge for yourselves the degree to which they offend, along with some of the quotes on 'Theresa May's a Remainer' from the rabid Daily Maul readers.

Theresa May's a Remainer :
A Country and Western Brexit hoedown

Theresa May's a Remainer

May-be we should restrain-er

Stop Brexit luv, Don't abstain-er

No Deal is kind of insane-er

May's Deal is mostly Remain-er

Remain is a no-brainer

Grow a spine, Just don't complain

Stay in Europe, Let's just Remain

Shoot the bastards, They're all insane

Daily Mail complaints

Truth hurts wrote :

The words used in the song is unbelievable. He needs reporting. Clearly, someone that isn't mentally stable.

Cheerful in swale wrote :

Theres a better of the Gov getting the bill through parliament in its current state before Christmas than this getting to number 1..or 2... or 3 in fact into the charts at all. What a terrible song and really do we need to use foul language in songs?

Kmuser1512 wrote :

Perhaps they were offended by the fact his song lyrics advocates violence & shooting political opponents?

Bollocks to Brexit:
A Chas & Dave Cockney Brexit knees-up

Brexshit, Brexit, Brexshit, Brexit, 'ave a banana

Well I've been goin' darn the Brexit food bank for a while
While Jacob Rees-Mogg 'ee's dining out in style
The Banks are leaving Blighty and Dad's Army's on the streets
Whilst us poor buggers stay to fight on Brexit plates of meat

Eggs and gammon, no smoked salmon, traffic jammin', bloody spammin'

I'm really sick of Brexit, why don't you fade away, I wanna find the exit, Please 'elp me
Boris J ... Brexshit, Brexit, Brexshit, Brexit, 'ave a corona

Well I've bin' tryin' to score some drugs for my dia-betes
But I still can't buy no bog roll for me Brexit faeces
And I can't afford a crib in Maracheeses (fake Spanish town)
I might as well end it all in Bognor Regis (Reges)

Diabetes, mega faeces, runny cheeses, big diseases
Russian geezers, in 'Bognor Reges', lemon squeezers, Trump appeasers

I'm really sick of Brexit, why don't you fade away, I wanna find the exit, Please 'elp me
Boris J

My wife's avin' a midlife Brexistential crisis
While me bruvver says I've joined Remainiac Isis
In football speak, Brexit was a quarter finalist
Theresa may need to see a Brexit psychiatrist

Customs union, big delusion, Is Arlene Foster even 'uman?
Barclays bank, J. Arthur Rank, Aaron Banks, sherman tank
Soviet Union, Trump communion, Is this love or Brexit confusion?

I'm really sick of Brexit, why don't you fade away, I wanna find the exit, Please 'elp me
Boris J

We are now speaking of invoking Article 16 which will put peace on the island of Ireland in jeopardy once again, undoing 30 years of peace.

Workers' rights

An elderly man stopped me on a petrol forecourt. He asked for directions to Boots the chemist, as he worked there as a security guard. We got talking. He told me just how ridiculous his shift pattern was, since he had to work in Gillingham Kent until 5 pm and then Sevenoaks at 5.30 pm. I agreed that there was no way he would reach his Sevenoaks shift in time. This moved on to a discussion about how bad his security company was and workers' rights in general.

I unzipped my fleece to reveal my Break Brexit Before Brexit Breaks Britain t-shirt, Superman like, saying "well you have Brexit to thank for this". It turned out that he voted for Brexit. This was mainly because his father had been ridiculed for voting to join Europe in the 1970s. I explained the P&O situation to him and how Brexit would deliver a bonfire on standards and employee rights, pointing out that his situation, whilst not caused by Brexit, would be exacerbated by Brexit. He accepted my reasoning, having had no idea that the Conservatives filibustered the bill that would have prevented P&O from firing and rehiring. He was an easy person to talk to and listened well. This helped immensely.

He admitted that he had no idea what Brexit would bring him and agreed that we had been taken for a ride in 2016. He agreed strongly with the idea that Russia had poured money into Brexit to destabilise Europe and that the invasion of Ukraine was Putin's next step on the master plan. Russia seems to have changed everything.

Sometimes these conversations go very easily. Take every opportunity to influence others, whether at the bus stop, the leisure centre, in a restaurant or on a petrol forecourt. Casual settings can be much more conducive to positive change than the formal ones.

Free roaming has gradually been dropped, because of our departure from the EU.

Music, musicians and Brexit

The EU offered a range of travel exemptions to musicians.
UK refused them, based on faux sovereignty.

It is already apparent that musicians are one of the main sectors whose lives and livelihoods are being radically disrupted by Brexit, to the point that it is causing 21% of musicians to consider changing their career. Lord David Frost just announced that the Brexit deal he negotiated was 'too purist' and has failed musicians on a multiplicity of levels. I cannot forgive him for his candour. He was told numerous times.

Sir Simon Rattle recently stated that it was a miracle that The London Symphony Orchestra got to France, and only after intense diplomatic activity on both sides of the Channel involving French and British culture ministries. These effects were predicted many years ago, ignored by the UK government, who continue to attempt to mask the issues under the COVID umbrella. So bad has been our sleepwalk into Brexit inspired flag waving and racism that the band British Sea Power have announced they are changing their name to simply Sea Power, in a bid to separate themselves from the recent 'wave of crass nationalism'. To misquote The Who "We do get fooled again". Let us remind ourselves Lord Frost left the entire creative sector out of Brexit negotiations on the trade and cooperation agreement. This is our second biggest export industry after financial services. Composer and broadcaster Howard Goodall sums up the issues for musicians:

"The barriers are multiple – visas, haulage and cabotage restrictions, carnets for equipment and instruments, VAT declarations in and out, special certificates for rare or animal-based materials, proof of contracts, health, repatriation and vehicle insurance, and so on".

The EU offered a range of travel exemptions. UK refused them.

The economics of music

Since we ended up with a 'slow boiling frog', in other words, a Brexit deal, rather than 'No Deal', touring remains possible in Europe. The Musician's Union report that 43% of musicians said that they plan to continue working in Europe and 42% are considering relocating, to continue making a living from their music. That said, the economics have been transformed by our government's decision to turn Britain into a 3rd country against their will. Nearly 80% of musicians expect their earnings in Europe to decrease due to new red tape and extra costs.

As a graphic example of what has happened outside the glare of mainstream media, cult psychedelic jazz rock combo Tankus the Henge report the economics of music after Brexit They had to pay for a carnet, additional insurance and an extra night of accommodation due to the travel time. This removed £1500 from the band's income in one stroke. They pointed out that they had travelled to an 'easy country' in so far as France does not need a visa as well. In other countries, they would be looking at several hundred pounds additional costs. That's not where the story ends. .With razor thin margins from Spotify and Amazon streaming sales, many bands make more money on merchandising than the direct sales of their music. Tankus the Henge estimate they lost a further £2500 on merchandise, since they must now be VAT registered and pay duty on all exports.   A £4000 hit on a tour makes it virtually impossible for upcoming bands to even consider touring in Europe. But, to misquote another song "It's not all about the money".

Boris Johnson's government recently announced a deal with 19 out of 27 EU countries, allowing musicians to conduct short tours visa-free after months of campaigning from the entertainment industry. However, as always with matters of Brexit, the devil is in the detail and the visa is simply the tip of a much bigger iceberg for touring musicians.

Former Runrig band member and SNP MP Pete Wishart reminded us that the UK was offered arrangements to make musicians lives and livelihoods better by the European Union during Brexit negotiations, but Boris Johnson rejected them in favour of sovereignty. Try making a living from a fistful of sovereignty as a musician …

Ticket to ride

Money is not really the only issue if you plan to tour in Europe after Brexit Since musicians typically take equipment with them, Brexit affects their freedom of movement in ways that are similar to international lorry drivers, who are restricted as to the number of stops they are able to make before reaching their final destination. Clearly the idea of a tour becomes impossible as Tankus explain:

"Moving equipment through more than two or three countries or doing more than two or three stops becomes illegal. For a musician, band or orchestra who typically tour multiple locations to make the tour viable, it just makes tours impossible".

Due to the specialist knowledge required and the time it takes, I foresee the need for musicians to hire professional agents to prevent obstacles to freedom of movement and delays going forward.

Rachel Ashley is a professional singer, voiceover artist and songwriter who co-wrote the song "In Limbo' for all Citizens of nowhere trapped by Brexit uncertainty. She has worked with industry leaders at close range and has real life insights of the highs and lows of working in the music business in the gig economy. She points out that most amateur musicians are content to play in pubs and, for them, nothing much will change after Brexit. However, anyone that is serious about music will realise that their margins are razor thin and they need to tour to survive. That means travelling.

"It's really no fun sitting in a van for 7 hours at Dover waiting to board a ferry and this could make the difference between doing your gig on the continent and getting paid … and not. Brexit will reduce margins and add hassle to any serious band's touring schedule. For professionals, time = money".

To those who say that it's just a bit of extra hassle, hassle costs money and eventually businesses make decisions about whether they want to deal with the additional hassle. One European opera house has just made a value decision on the topic, by insisting that performers have a European Passport to perform. Opera singer and stage director Leon Berger has direct experience of the issue. Some contracts require people to be abroad for longer than the 90 days allowed. In other cases, artists are hired to stand in at very short notice, but visas, permissions and carnets prevent the agility that is needed to fulfil jobs with a lead in time sometimes measured in hours:

> Thank you to those submitted so far, we sadly have a few roles to fill due to visa/passports deadlines.
>
> Due to Brexit regulations we can only consider performers with an EU passport/Schengen Visa. Unfortunately we are not able to consider anyone with a UK passport at this time.

However, to every logistical problem there is a 'solution' in a capitalist world. There are signs of a relocation of equipment providers and hauliers into Europe so that bands would not need to take their instruments and equipment abroad.

Robert Hewitt of Stage Truck handles equipment for some of the world's most famous music acts. He has just spent £4.5 million on a site in the Netherlands and other costs to offset the freedom of movement issue for acts wishing to tour Europe. This impacts HM Treasury, as all the taxes associated with touring will go into the EU and not HMRC. Additionally, he will have to use European drivers to drive the trucks unless his own drivers can get Irish citizenship at further cost.

For the average touring musician, this freedom of movement comes at a cost as they would be effectively hiring their equipment at each location. The only freedoms musicians have under Brexit are the freedoms not to have to carry their instruments onto planes, trains and trucks and, of course, to become bankrupt in the pursuit of their chosen careers. The music industry contributes some £5.8 billion towards the UK economy at present. Much of this revenue looks set to be lost from Breadline Brexit Britain.

The EU offered a range of travel exemptions. UK refused them based on faux sovereignty. I'll just repeat that.

I guess that's why they call it the Brexit blues

Elton John stands in stark contrast to Iron Maiden's Bruce Dickinson on Brexit. Elton John points out that whilst he can afford to tour and absorb the additional costs and hassle from our decision to become a third country, this is not a choice available to the aspiring musician or ensemble. In contrast, Bruce Dickinson focuses almost exclusively on what academics call parochial self-interest, by pointing out that he is unable to pursue his pet hobby of flying jets to Europe. Even Dickinson was finally moved to anger when he called the government's approach 'guff.' Elton John shows himself as an emotionally intelligent leader with a long-term focus on the needs of future generations of musicians, whilst a host of other artists from Dickenson to Daltrey, Morrissey and Ringo Starr stare myopically at more selfish ambitions, xenophobia and faux nostalgia about mega tours in the 1970s. Mick Jagger saw a different reality in his metaphorical homage to Brexit "England Lost".

Flying the flag

The Conservative Minister Oliver Dowden suggested that artists should use their 'star power' to influence the EU.

"Musicians don't need a visa to give performances. If they get paid, they can stay for up to one month, and if they are only claiming expenses or prize money, they can stay for up to six months".

Dowden's suggestion has proved to be disingenuous at best. It is governments that negotiate treaties. They do not leave it to industry groups to do it for them. So disgusted with this outbreak of nationalism, British Sea Power commented that they did not wish to be associated with isolationist, antagonistic nationalism:

"We have always been internationalist in our mindset, something made clear in songs like Waving Flags, an anthem to pan-European idealism".

The EU offered a range of travel exemptions. UK refused them based on faux sovereignty. I'll just mention that again.

Licensed to thrill

It is currently unclear as to whether music licensing will remain the same, although, judging by the mess that parliament has made of the pharmaceutical regulatory affairs, the settled status of EU Citizens in the UK and passporting arrangements in banking I have zero confidence that arrangements for musicians will go well. This may result in difficulties in selling music to Europe.

In case you think the EU has interfered with our laws, you would be right. It was the EU that extended copyright law from 50 to 70 years to protect artists, music and income.

The only way Brexit is not going to affect you is if you remain in your bedroom, practising and waiting for that day when The X-Factor recognises your talent. Never mind the X-Factor, the BreX-Factor will destroy lives and livelihoods of musicians.

The Bard of Barking, Mr Billy Bragg perfectly articulates the underlying feelings of being left behind and which informed the Brexit referendum.

I cheered when our side won the Cold War
Spread freedom and peace all around
Now there's folks speaking Russian in Tesco's
It's a shame the wall had to come down
I know some are fleeing from war zones
To keep their young children from harm
But my parents stayed put through the Blitz years
And me? I was sent to a farm

Taking back control

In the five years that have elapsed since 2016 it has become apparent that:

1. There remains no long-term plan for UK plc to benefit from Brexit economically, socially, environmentally, ethically and politically. The problems facing musicians are one of a kind in terms of other sectors and industries. As much as I'd like to solve the problems of Brexit for musicians, this is only a partial solution.
2. Jacob Rees-Mogg's best estimate of 50 years 'Net Present Value' for Brexit will see my son's friend's band into their seventies by the time they are likely to 'break-even' from their losses. They will be paying for Brexit for all their adult lives.

3. Musicians face increased costs, paperwork, hassle and losses in freedoms if they want to work in Europe. In some cases, they will lose their livelihoods as a result. Contrary to the assumptions of Leave voters, most of these losses were avoidable, as the European Union offered concessions to travelling artists. These were rejected by our government who are wholly responsible for this.
4. We will eventually Rejoin the EU. Sadly, this will be after a great deal of damage has been done to lives and livelihoods. It will require the removal of the Brexit culture carriers from the corridors of power as a pre-requisite. There are multiple scenarios for Rejoining, some which rely on an incremental approach and others which may result from disruptive changes in society at large. Much of this relies on musicians coming together with other sectors to say that 'Enough is Enough'.

Summary

Before Brexit	After Brexit
Freedom of movement in 27 countries.	Carnets needed. Insurance needed. Visas needed in some countries. Equipment checks. There could also be additional restrictions for filming and other elements. Increased costs.
Ability to sell your products and merchandise freely.	Need to register all products for VAT and this puts a burden on their ability to sell merchandise at concerts and events.
Ability to organise tours quickly and easily.	Agents, specialist advisers and paperwork make it unprofitable to organise short tours and / or short notice trips. For longer trips, the 90-day rule may make them possible. Some music enterprises are starting to only allow people with EU passports and Schengen visas to apply for work.
Ability to perform using your own equipment.	We foresee a slow drift towards an industry springing up in Europe to provide equipment and trucking to work around restrictions inherent in Brexit.

Re-Booting jackboot Britain

I was unfortunate and unlucky in so far that I got punched by seven angry Brexiteers at a train station shortly after the October 2018 People's March. The story was reported as widely as Norwegian TV alongside The Sun, Mail, BBC Radio and TV. It turns out that tensions were heightened in the days following that march and quite a few people suffered violence at the hands of a few extremists. Check out Norwegian TV via the EU Tube channel at www.youtube.com/academyofrock

It would be all too easy to become a victim at this point. I have had so many people either saying that 'I deserved it for being a traitor' or presuming that I would stop putting myself at risk. People rightly fear personal attacks. To be honest, it was not the best day of my life! I had previously assumed that people of advanced years were somehow immune to violence from youths in gangs. Clearly not.
But there are several mistakes that must not be made here :

1. To assume that such things are widespread and therefore to stop campaigning to end Brexit populism. My experience was the exception, not the norm. I have a bicycle with a large hoarding that says 'Break Brexit Before Brexit Breaks Britain' on it and T-Shirts that say the same. My phone has a Boll..cks to Brexit sticker on the back, which is always visible in cafés etc. I do this as I know that these act as incredibly effective icebreakers to restarting the conversation about Brexit with tired Remainers and Leavers in regret / denial. I don't wish to agree with the Daily Mail readers that say 'I deserve my fate'. However, I make myself highly visible and this makes me more of a target than the average person. It does not mean that others will suffer the same fate. I live in a Brexity area as well and refuse to be silenced by a very small nasty element which has always existed in English society, empowered by our Brexit referendum and Boris Johnson's racist dog whistling.

2. To assume that this behaviour will go away if we ignore it. Ignoring bad behaviour is a classic way to extinguish it but the genie is out of the bottle on this and we have a far right which is quietly stoking such behaviour by a few people. I have become aware of breakaway groups from UKIP that are stoking civil unrest amongst the young in my area through conversations with them in pubs. They are armed with very good marketing materials and part of me wishes I had access to their designers.

3. To assume that this behaviour will get worse if Brexit ends. Fear is a powerful motivator, but the statistics don't match people's feelings in this area. Just this weekend when I wrote this, some 100 'Yellow Jackets' demonstrated in London and some other cities, targeting Greggs the bakers for vegan Sausage rolls … I am still having trouble understanding the relevance to Brexit but that may just go to show that I am something of a 'pastry elitist'. But let's also put the numbers in perspective. 100 protestors and 4 arrests. Compare with some 840 000 people attending The People's March in October 2018 with no trouble and no arrests.

Shortly after my attack in 2018, I wrote to Gina Miller with my thoughts on our new binary choice :

- **CARRY ON** with Brexit and normalise misogynism, xenophobia, racism and hate back into Britain as part of the Little England culture.

- **STOP Brexit** and possibly have a few riots from a few extremists. We can then begin the journey back to a civil society and a Better Britain in a Better Europe for a Better World. In doing so, we could begin to address the root causes of the referendum result rather than the symptoms. This is the constant call from those I meet who feel left behind in Britain. Brexit has simply come to represent a totemic symbol for the bundle of issues which people feel are holding back Britain.

Some of the feedback I received from Daily Mail, Sun, Mirror and local newspaper readers makes for comically sad reading. There is no greater fear than fear itself. Do not be seduced into thinking that an end to Brexit will breed a new generation of thugs. We still have the same number of thugs that we always had. Many of them are too busy watching the X-Factor rather than worrying about the BreX-Factor! Since 2018 I sense that a lot of people would be quietly relieved if Brexit ended in some way, but we must still work on those who see this as impossible. The comments are not edited for grammar or spelling at all.

Medway Messenger

Angry of Chatham wrote :

Has this guy got a job? (Sounds not as he has not mentioned having to take time off work for his injuries) If not he should lose his benefits as he is not making himself available for work. Sounds like a drain on society. Loser.

Editors' note : There was no mention of any of this. Total fabrication.

tideyd01 wrote :

Brilliant illustration of what is wrong with Brexit. Who would want to be associated with people who think it's alright to beat someone up for wearing a t-shirt. Compare that with the good nature amongst the 700,000 who marched in London for a second vote. Nasty, snarling hatred is definitely a trait of the right wing as so often demonstrated by the ugly, racist nationalism demonstrated by a lot of contributors to this site. Did you see the pro Brexit supporters deliberately delaying an ambulance with its lights and sirens going on Westminster Bridge did you ? Like to stick up for that would you ?

pip wrote :

We had a vote. Leave won 52 to 48 so that's it. Get over it. If it had been the other way I'm sure it would have been all forgotten by now. You can't have another vote because it will destroy people's faith in democracy. If we have a vote and remain win, will we have the best of 3?
It's really getting to much now. Man up and take the result. We may not like it but that's what the majority wanted. Surely we are not that gullible to believe all the scaremongering. When anything goes wrong in future e.g. shares drop,interest rates go up,bad weather , it's will be Brexit's fault. Before Brexit we never had black Monday. We never had big high street shops disappear. We lost our car industry to Europe. Must of been Brexit. Who owns edf Dartford crossing, royal mail the railways? It's definately isn't British. Is that the fault of the leavers vote?

scott wrote :

Simple..Dont wear the shirt! You know what your doing, so how your surprised by repercussions is beyond me...

The Daily Mail

Lone263, Edmon, Canada

The left finally getting theirs!

Editor's note : interesting assumption. I'm not a lefty

nostalgic, Leicestershire, United Kingdom

Don't condone the violence, but people generally do not like other people views bring thrust in their face. If someone went around with JC's mug on their T shirt, I'd want to throw things at it.

Panda2018, Chengdu, China

Not right to be treated like this in a supposedly democratic country, however the hairstyle could be exacerbating the situation.

Teresa, BRIDGEND

His t shirt doesn't bother me, however, that hair???

Punkawallah, Chandigarh, United Kingdom

He should probably know better at his age?

RobbRaw, Hammersmith London, United Kingdom

Doubt it was just his t shirt that sparked abuse, find some remoaners cannot accept the democratic outcome, and demand a block, or reversal without a debate. That or the mindset, have more referendums until the silly people vote stay.

Bazzy, London, United Kingdom

I fear there will be much more of this violence if the Bexit voters are denied the democracy they were promised in the original vote in June 16.

Alexander, Brackley, United Kingdom

This is wrong poor man ...... However this may happen on a huge scale if the government try to force another referendum the country could end up in anarchy. We must follow the will of the people and democracy

Garry Latjion, London, United Kingdom

not statistically representative enough. Make an experiment in at least 20 towns

billyelton, Peterborough, United Kingdom

Re-Boot Britain by changing minds on Europe and Brexit

So the young don't want Brexit , that shows you how strong the anti EU feeling is right around the country , interfere with it at your peril !

Katieconker, Hornchurch , United Kingdom

Despite what we are force fed by the Remainers, there's a lot of strong feeling for Brexit out there. Best to keep viewpoints private!

Curtis, London, United Kingdom

Don't ware the silly T shirt then.

Tim Fixit, Barrybados

Knowing how much the Brexit issue angers people on both sides of the argument the last thing I would do is go around draped in slogans like that for either side. Keep it to yourself man.

TooMuchTyme, Surrey, United Kingdom

There is no justification for violence. However, this man is wearing a t-shirt that supports stripping people of their democratic vote. That is understandably going to irk people.

Ms Wise one, Beaconsfield, United Kingdom

Brexit is the best thing for Britain especially a managed no deal.

BBI3, London, United Kingdom

Its not an anti-brexit t shirt. Its an anti democracy t shirt.

I190, London, United Kingdom

Violence is not acceptable, ever, but I doubt he was innocent his agitation of these situations. He is stood at a microphone shouting his jargon at innocent people going about their day. I would be annoyed if he was doing that in my town center, and have no issues asking him to pipe down. We voted, it's a democracy, end of Remainers to suck it up and deal with it like adults please. YOU LOST go cry your tears quietly.

Your Last Gasp?

Corona Crisis + Brexit Disaster = Britastrophe

Let's Re-Boot Britain

www.brexitrage.com

Art offends

I had heard that digital artist Cold War Steve had made an installation of several pieces of satirical Brexit art in the Medway Park, a relatively undisturbed natural habitat in the Medway towns, by the river. I had to go and see this. I still want to meet the person at the council who commissioned the installation to shake their hand, as (a) my area was 70% Brexity and (b) s/he must have persuaded Alan Jarrett and his team of sloths at the council that the art installation would improve Medway Council's chances of winning a city of culture award! In my view Cold War Steve should be running the council ☺

On arrival, I could not find one of his exhibits, although I did initially wonder if 'Steve' had entered a new phase of postmodern art as I studied the plywood frame and the arrangement of glue on it (see the Medway Messenger picture). I then realised that Steve's artwork had been dumped in the Medway estuary mud. I decided to rescue the piece and shimmied down the bank and waded out to sea. I also decided to report the matter to Kent police (pointless) and the press (useful). The Medway Messenger had a field day reporting the story. Naturally, regular Brexity readers thought that I'd instigated the vandalism to cover their tracks! I somehow wished I was that clever to have done this. Here are some of the comments, which are comedy gold.

Whilst you want it to start a debate, the people who visit this place don't want a debate. They just want to experience a bit of nature and have some peace. How much arrogance can you possibly have to think it's ok to impose your views on others?

Isn't it amazing coincidence how Peter Cook manages to be right in the centre of the action in Medway and available for a picture? What a peculiar fellow.

Yep, the attention seeking weirdo probably did it himself to get his picture on KOL again and they fell for it...

The truth is somewhat more mundane. Art clearly offends when it points out uncomfortable truths to people. People complained about having their days spoiled whilst walking in the country park by these 'monstrous placards'. You just know you are doing something right when people tear down your work and throw it in the river. I take my hat off to Cold War Steve. Art reaches the parts that spreadsheets, graphs and lengthy academic articles do not.

Cold War Steve artwork at Riverside Country Park, Rainham, is thrown into River Medway

KENT TRAVEL NEWS   SIGN ME UP FOR NEWS ALERTS ❂

By **Will Payne**   Read all comments | 28
Published: 15:54, 23 September 2020 | Updated: 14:10, 06 October 2020

More news, no ads →   **LEARN MORE**

Art which was a part of a satirical exhibition has been torn from its stand and thrown into the Medway.

The piece by Cold War Steve is currently on display at the Riverside Country Park in **Rainham** .

Peter Cook recovered the artwork from the River Medway. Picture: Peter Cook

Medway Council hopes the artist, **who has had worked displayed at Glastonbury** , will help boost its UK City of Culture 2025 bid.

The work in question involves Tim Martin, the owner of the pub chain Wetherspoon.

Gillingham resident Peter Cook retrieved the piece after he spotted it floating in the river and has since handed it over to police.

A fisherman's tail

I met the Faversham fisherman, Mark, at the Bollocks to Brexit bus protest in Faversham. It turns out that Mark is a real character. Quite charming and with many a 'fisherman's tale' to tell. He was a participant in Nigel Farage's Fish protest against Bob Geldof. Mark had even written a song about Bob, who lives in the same town.

Mark was drawn by my guitar as he loved music. Others who knew him well from the town had managed to avoid him, but I enjoy talking, so I listened for one hour in mostly non-directive and autonomous and co-operative mode from John Heron's model. The main points of that conversation are recorded here.

I began by me admitting my relative lack of knowledge about fishing. I made one point, that I felt someone must make rules about catching fish, otherwise we would catch all the fish from the oceans. That duty currently fell to the EU. I then invited him to fill in my knowledge gaps. Mark agreed that rules were needed but felt that the fishermen could self-regulate. I am doubtful due to the human condition of moral hazard, but I say nothing. We move on.

Mark's essential point is that he cannot make a good living from the quotas of fish that he is allowed to catch. In common with around 80% of British fisherman he operates from a small boat. He can catch his entire quota in one day. Quotas disproportionately disadvantage smaller boats and I understand his angst. European boats tend to be bigger and I was left wondering whether our own government had somehow left our fishing industry behind.

The basic economics are that he can catch all the fish he needs on one day per week. The diesel to run his boat is quite expensive and it is barely worth the effort to continue. He spends the rest of his week in local pubs, telling fishermen's tales and so on.

I asked him about leaving the. If we left, would he be much better off, a little better off, the same, a bit worse off or a lot worse off. It appears he had not given this much thought. After a long pause, he said he would be a little better off but not massively. This was a surprise to me (and him, I sense).

Having listened for some 45 minutes, I offered a small insight. I said that I was mainly worried about my kids. We had not discussed families, but it prompted him to tell me that he had a daughter. I asked :

"Does your daughter plan to follow you into the business?"

"No", he answered, "she likes horses".

I left the conversation there. I then asked Mark to perform his Bob Geldof song in the square which he did. It was very funny, even though it was clear that he could not stand Bob. A few Remainers winced as I encouraged him to have his voice heard.

A few hours later, Mark turned up to greet the Bollocks to Brexit bus. He had been home to retrieve a CD of protest songs for me, written by relatives of Pete Seeger. He had also been to the pub and donned an equally offensive Brexit fisherman's T-shirt. He was ready to perform his song again, so I recommended he speak with Madeleina Kay who was leading the charge on the protest. Apparently, he was refused as is sometimes typical from people who refuse to work outside the Remain bubble.

I was told afterwards that Mark was an EDL supporter, which is why nobody would talk to him. He came across as charming. But then again, so does Nigel Farage …

Mark clearly constitutes one of the people 'left behind' by our government. We may not all want to share our homes with such people, but we ignore them at our peril …

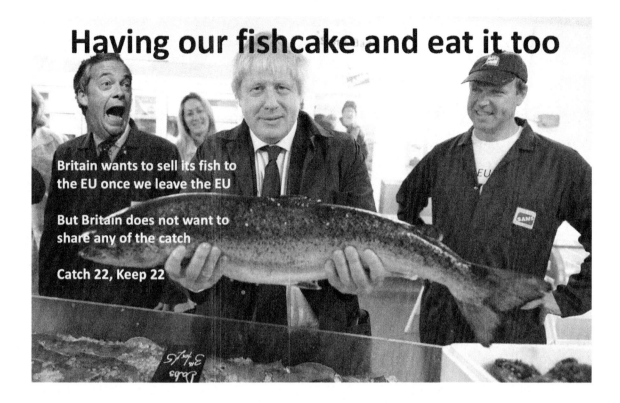

Having our fishcake and eat it too

Britain wants to sell its fish to
the EU once we leave the EU

But Britain does not want to
share any of the catch

Catch 22, Keep 22

The liars that got away ...

Reflections on a fisherman's tale

Although Mark was an incredibly difficult target as a member of the EDL, a real conversation did emerge after putting in all the preparatory work. I doubt he is a convert but at least we did explode some of his own mythologies about fish and fishing. This story contrasts nicely with the UKIP Nick and the other online approaches.

Despite his EDL credentials, I found Mark personable and not so far away from me on many issues. I thought it a charming gesture that he offered me his rare CD and I took good care to return it to him.

This kind of work outside the Brexit bubble has given me the nickname of "The Brexit whisperer[19]"!

---

[19] Brexit whisperer – someone who has a strong affinity with a Brexit voter

The Smiths

I had a great conversation about Brexit with a woman who does not vote nor read newspapers in W.H. Smith today. She will vote against Brexit in any future election or vote. The lack of awareness was staggering, but at least she was pleased to have an intelligent dialogue. We were there for ages though. The conversation started after she saw my 'Break Brexit Before Brexit Breaks Britain' T-Shirt. This validates the importance of triggers to conversation, however subtle or unsubtle they might be.

And complimented for my skills and patience by the young shop assistant who was earwigging in on the conversation with the customer. And I only went in to hide copies of The Daily Mail, Express and The Sun!

Three in one. The T-Shirt is the conversation starter although other things work ... My main asset in the conversation was not judging her astonishingly low levels of knowledge about Brexit and respecting her candour in saying she did not vote. Silence can be an asset.

So, Brexorcism can be simple and swift. Sometimes it's worth looking for simplicity before digging deeper.

Sadly, Morrissey, singer with The Smiths turns out to be a lost cause. Heaven knows I'm miserable now.

Elf and safety

A friend was talking to a woman on the street at an event. She was a hairdresser. She voted for Brexit but admitted that she did not know much about her vote. But she did know about hairdressing. To my friend's surprise, she told him that the thing that swayed her vote was the fact that she could no longer get hold of a hair colourant because the EU had banned it due to it being carcinogenic. She demanded the freedoms to give her clients cancer. I so wish we'd found out which hairdresser she worked for …

In my own case I had struck up a bit of a relationship with The Printers in Chatham. It turned out that the owner was the brother of the 'Artist Taxi Driver20' who has a large Twitter following and who is very anti-Brexit. The owner described his brother as a bit mad and decided I must be the same …

Later in our relationship, I dared to ask him why he voted for Brexit. Like the hairdresser, his answer was pragmatic and came down to what Kotter and Schlesinger called 'parochial self-interest[21]'. He pointed out that the continuing onslaught of 'health and safety' meant that he had needed to buy new machinery and stop using certain types of processes, due to emissions and so on. I explained that I'd once worked in pharmaceuticals. We had, on occasion, to reformulate products without certain dyestuffs, due to finding out that they were carcinogenic. I went on to explain that, however irritating it was to make these discoveries, we called it 'progress' to make the decision not to poison your clients! Since I was paying for some posters and leaflets, I think he found it hard to argue with me about the matter. Staff would ultimately thank him for not poisoning them with solvents. I'm not really sure he agreed …

The printer did make us some excellent stickers, some of which have endured to this day. The slogan 'STOP BREXIT 4 UR KIDS' FUTURES was more persuasive than 'Stop Brexit', as it had a higher-level motive than the simple instruction. This assumes hierarchy in John Heron terms. I will not be attending the woman's hairdressing salon any time soon.

---

[20] Find the Artist Taxi Driver at www.twitter.com/chunkymark
[21] Strategies for Change – Kotter and Schlesinger, Harvard Business School.

Brexit butchers buggered by Brussels

I heard just recently that JC Rook the butcher has gone into administration across Kent. Rooks is a family business with 11 shops and 155 staff who were told not to come into work on Tuesday 15 March 2022.

Whilst I feel very sorry for the staff, the boss of the Gillingham shop told me to fuck off in 2019 whilst I was campaigning about Brexit during the general election. In previous discussions he had told me that Brexit would be great for him as he could charge people extra for his meat and that I was a sad loser. On the day I heard of this I reflected that I was extremely glad that he has had so much 'winning' from Brexit.

In their official statement to the Kent Messenger [22], JC Rook blamed COVID as the easiest 'red meat' for their staff to swallow. Respectfully this is horseshit, for the following reasons:

- JC Rook went online with a range of food some while ago, so they were not solely reliant on high street footfall.

- They had little competition for people's money on the High Street during lockdown, as one of the few essential shops that would have remained open at that time.

- Food purchases [23] went up overall under COVID, as people stayed at home to pamper themselves, so JC Rook should have been able to at least survive and possibly to prosper.

> Main findings
>
> Volume sales of food and drink purchased for consumption at home in the year to date up to the week ending 21 June 2020 is 11.1% higher than the same period in 2019.
>
> The week ending 22 March 2020, which was just before formal lockdown was announced on 23 March 2020, saw the highest ever volume sales recorded (volume sales were 43.6% higher than the equivalent week in 2019).

---

[22] Brainless Brexit bigots butchered by Brussels bigshot bandits – fake KM headline.
[23] HM government report – impact of COVID on shopping behaviours.

- For some people, meat is an essential purchase, so it is COVID-proof to some degree.

I had already decided never to shop at JC Rook again in 2019 and made sure others knew. I doubt that my 'gammon protest' will have been the tipping point for Rooks, but, in the words of Tesco , "every little helps".   The Brexit butcher also inadvertently persuaded me to further reduce our meat consumption, so I have a lot to thank Mr J. C(Rook) for. As Morrissey would have observed 'meat is murdered'.

In the warped words of Alan Partridge :

"Rooks the butchers. Yesterday's meat at tomorrow's prices".

Brexit Britain bar BQ beef butchering beneficiaries!

Citizens of nowhere

Where Windrush leads, Brexit follows …

'In Limbo' is a poignant piece of music I wrote, inspired by the book of the same name by Elena Remigi, to highlight the desperate plight of EU citizens left in uncertainty and fear for their futures, due Brexit. Check out the In Limbo book for the full stories of tragedy, hope, hopelessness and hate which have characterised our Dis-United Kingdom since June 24 2016. The song In Limbo achieved number one status on Amazon, beating chart entries from Ed Sheeran, Abba and Kylie Minogue. This is remarkable for a song produced in a basement studio with no established artist as a brand. Even more remarkable is the back story of the song's production.

Due to advances in music technology I was able to gather voices from all over Europe and as far afield as Thailand to tell the tales of people's hopes, fears and experiences of being treated as 'Citizens of nowhere'. Here are some song facts :

IN LIMBO

FACT FILE

30 + EU Citizens on the song

Contributions from France, Germany, Ireland, Czech Republic, Hungary, Poland, Greece, Spain, Italy, The Netherlands

132 + tracks to mix !!!

3 months in the making

In Limbo started as a piano ornament and developed into a downbeat EDM groove in my basement studio with a major lift via a chorus delivered by professional singer Rachel Ashley and a supremely great animated film from Mark Duffy. Comparisons have been made with Moby, Leftfield, Pink Floyd and Prince. It is one of my proudest musical moments and a testimony to the power of teamwork across continents and boundaries.

Whilst we aimed to achieve UK top 40 chart success with the song, this was not the main ambition. There was a need to mainstream the issues of EU citizens in UK and UK 'Britizens' in Europe via our populist media, having been one of the first people to give the In Limbo book international publicity via www.because.net   Ultimately the song did not reach the chart due to the fragmentation of the Remain movement. As a result, we did not cut through to the Brexiteer's thought space. I was relatively alone at the time in thinking that we needed to break outside of Remain bubbles, nonetheless it was still a great achievement by all that contributed. I remain disappointed that at the time of writing the various groups fighting for EU citizens' rights continue to talk about 3 million people rather than 68 million citizens of nowhere. Although silos are a very normal human feature of organisational life, they are a mistake in terms of giving us scale and impact to fight the monumental resources of HM government.

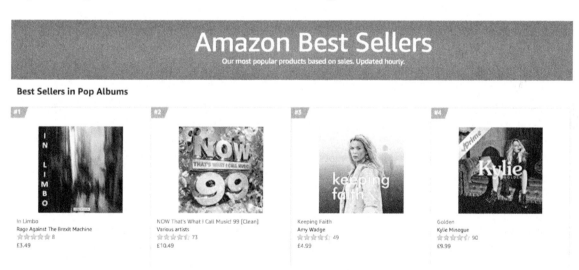

Boris Johnson and David Frost used EU citizens as bargaining chips in their desperate attempts to negotiate a 'Cake and Eat it Brexit deal'. EU citizens in Britain still face uncertainty in terms of renewal of their status as citizens as do Britizens in Europe.

The In Limbo song contains stories of people who were threatened with being burned alive by our so-called tolerant British people. When I make comparisons with the emergence of Nazi Germany, I am often told that this is offensive. Well, it is offensive to be threatened to be burned alive and if the truth hurts in our sanitised society, then so be it. I am too old to worry about political correctness … if you are bored by Brexit, frankly, so am I and I make no apology at continuing to make the argument against it. It is even written in the snow …

We noted that music is the language of the emotions earlier. The 2016 referendum was won by a naked appeal to the emotions of the people when Nigel Farage asked people to vote with their hearts (bypassing their heads). Whether you like or loathe Nigel, his strategy surprised nearly everyone, including himself, but not Cambridge Analytica …

However, it does not do to copy a strategy. Rather we must better it …

There is a long legacy of protest through music, from Nina Simone, Pete Seeger, through Joan Baez, Tracey Chapman, John Lennon, Prince, Marvin Gaye, Kate Bush and Billy Bragg et al. Music reaches people more deeply than a spreadsheet or graph. When combined with video, the effects can be chilling. Find the In Limbo videos on our EU Tube playlist via www.youtube.com/academyofrock

Citizens of nowhere

Where Windrush leads Brexit follows ...

Find 'In Limbo' on iTunes, Amazon and EU Tube etc.

Google 'In Limbo', Voices for Europe'.

Check the In Limbo [24] book out.

---

[24] Find Elena Remigi's In Limbo project and books at www.inlimboproject.org/

It's no longer that way for fishermen held in limbo by Brexit.

Writing letters

One of the more practical ways of influencing people is to write a letter. We are told that letters should be polite, courteous and ask questions to prick the conscience of the people we write to. How then can you increase your chances of writing an influential letter? Here some advice from a lobbyist:

1. Stick to what you know

You will find it easier to write, you will be more convincing, and you are more likely to be listened to if you write from experience. It doesn't matter what that experience is. It will create a punchier piece than if you string together hearsay.

2. Likewise, cite your credentials: in what capacity are you writing?

If you run a business affected by Brexit, that will grab the MPs attention.
But even something as simple as this would do: 'one of my daughter's children benefitted from the Erasmus scheme. The younger one cannot. This has placed a barrier between them.'

3. Rely on the power of your points

Simple factual points in unadorned language hit harder. They build momentum through the letter. Opinion can be flatly rejected. Slanted characterisation too. A pile of facts is harder to resist, it gets the reader's attention and can move them at least towards accepting your premise. This takes us to the next point.

4. Stress practical effects over ideology

MPs have two sides: the ideologue and the pragmatist. Your job is to sidestep the former and appeal to the latter. If you meet a politician with a broad argument of principle, you invite a prepared speech in return. Citing Marx at a Conservative will get as far as arguing privatisation to a Corbynite.

If you show that you, their constituent, encounter a problem because of a policy they support, you give them something practical to engage with, and something about which you know more than them.

5. Understate

For crying out loud, just don't rant, OK?!? The culture in parliament, government and civil service is quite understated outside of gameshows like PMQs. Clearly, being directly abusive is the best way not to achieve anything. You'll just give a junior staffer a laugh as they chuck your scrawl in the bin. But even non-abusive hyperbole is ineffective. A strong statement that can be evidenced is one thing ('Brexit is the single most damaging policy I have witnessed'), but 'the annihilation of model railway hobbyists is clearly another example of this appalling government's plans to absolutely destroy the UK' is a waste of a perfectly good point. Try, 'this obstacle to a much-loved hobby for so many people is a small but telling reminder of the everyday impact of these policies'.

6. What's your main point?

Work out the gist of what you're arguing before writing. Jot down your points, free-form, and chew them over for a bit. What really is the heart of your argument? Democracy has been damaged? The economy has been hit? And does 'economy' relate to SMEs or GDP or inflation or empty shelves in Tesco?

Once you know what you're really getting at, you can marshal your material to support the argument. You can also build a rhythm. Each block of facts can be tied up with a phrase relating it back to your 'gist'. And ideally, enriching it, deepening it, moving it forward.

If you keep your focus, you control the potential scope of the answer.

7. Make it credible

Facts and figures are valuable additions. Make sure to check them. Get the name of the Act right, the years for the GDP comparison, the exact wording of the quotation. The best sorts of figures include well-known economic indicators and time-series comparisons (e.g., hate crimes have increased x% since 2016). International comparisons can sometimes help, although they are always open to the counter-argument that the context in the other country is different.

At the moment, we are seeing dramatic figures for decline in trade: comparative percentages will often work better than disembodied numbers. A 12% decline (on last year? last month?) is probably better than £1.2m losses. (There are always exceptions, as when we learned that around $1.6tn in assets had moved to the continent!)

If you can, cite government policy back at them. 'The Prime Minister stated in 2020 that 'blah'. How does the Albania deal square with that undertaking?' Or cite the government in support of your argument. 'The Trade Secretary said at last year's party conference, 'blah-blah'. Sanctions against Russia would serve this aim.'

8. Formalities

When writing to your MP, cite the fact that you are a constituent and give your address. There's almost no point at all writing to some other MP: they're not supposed to interfere in each other's constituencies and are far too busy to do so. The sole exceptions are government ministers, leaders of parties to which you belong, or in a few cases those MPs who become closely associated with a national campaign.

When writing to your own MP, you can usually find them at firstname.lastname.mp@parliament.uk although a few have variations – check your MPs website or the write to them website.

If you write to a Minister, it is better to use their departmental address, not their MP email. You can find the departmental details with a Google search.

Some example letters follow to help you create your own.

Example letter to The Queen

Her Majesty the Queen
Buckingham Palace
London SW1A 1AA

Wednesday 28th August

Your Majesty,

I write to you as one of your loyal servants to ask you to reconsider the decision you were forced into by our government regarding the prorogation of parliament. I do understand that you were placed in an invidious position by Boris Johnson and colleagues to frustrate British democracy, but I ask you to consider the serious implications for the United Kingdom.

Should the prorogation result in a No Deal Brexit, I foresee the breakup of the United Kingdom, with Northern Ireland reuniting with Ireland or facing a return to what was euphemistically called 'the troubles'. Scotland would have a legitimate case for independence and to Remain in the EU. Doubtless Wales will follow, then Cornwall. Ultimately, the atomisation of the Kingdom threatens the very idea of your role as the head of state, with England once again reduced to splendid isolation. I am a little surprised, as you appear to have signed a 'death warrant' for your family and its standing in the world.

At a simple level, Ma'am, Brexit threatens the lives of people with complex medical conditions, a potential for extreme food shortages and many more unpredictable changes to the lives of your subjects. People will die because of this and I implore you to factor this into your future conversations with Mr Johnson and other key figures.

At the highest level, this political prorogation threatens the very idea of parliamentary democracy. You have been unfortunately drawn into politics at this critical time. I urge you to consider the impact on your legacy as the head of state and that of those who will follow you and act accordingly in the coming days to secure the country.

I have the honour to be, Ma'am, Your Majesty's humble servant.

Peter Cook

Orphaned by Brexit

Alice Boulliez decided that she would not be orphaned by Boris Johnson after Brexit made her and millions of others 'Citizens of nowhere'. A 62-year-old British housewife and farmer, living in France with two children has turned into a Brexit Avenger alongside Claire Godfrey Le Monnier, Grazia Valentino Boschi and a group who call themselves EuBritizens. Unable to vote in the Brexit referendum and are now united in outrage by the careless approach of the Brexit government in looking after their rights. If they succeed in their legal actions, they may help millions of others to gain their voting rights back, freedom of movement and other civil liberties that people enjoyed before Brexit.

"To be disenfranchised is a horrible feeling, like a motherless child. Your orphan voice does not matter. The suffragettes were not fighting for something they had lost, nor something that they had had previously; they were fighting for new rights. I am fighting to regain my right to be counted as a sentient human being".

Alice wrote to Lord Heseltine, The Queen and lobbied people in Brussels. Eventually, she found Julien Fouchet, who was looking to take a case to the French courts. The case was heard in the Court of Justice before Judge Romanello. He, in turn, sent it through to the ECJ in November 2020, having collected over 500 replies from people in similar situations. The case has since reached the UK Select Committee on the effects of Brexit.

We hope to confirm our status as European citizens with full rights, freedom of movement and municipal and European electoral rights as a corresponding status to Settled Status in the UK.

"European citizenship was given to me when the UK joined the European Union. From that moment on, I have been a fully-fledged and exemplary European citizen. I own that citizenship. It is my inalienable right. Since Brexit, my only privilege now is to pay my taxes, with what in return?"

Many other lives and livelihoods rest on the success of this case. What are we to say to Mrs Page who had planned to live out her retirement in a lovely house in the French countryside surrounded by her animals, whose income was severely affected by Brexit and who is now in a sad retirement home near London? To Mr Duke whose Carte Vitale is still not available to him and must pay out of his pocket for health care? To Mike Johnson whose girls who have always lived in France and who now has difficulty getting them a Carte de Sejour? Or to the twins who went for French nationality, one got it, one didn't? We refuse to be orphaned by Boris Johnson's Brexit.

Influencing mainstream media

Whilst most of us cannot afford to buy News International, we can influence what gets reported in the mainstream media in smaller or greater ways. Here is some advice from Mike Cashman et moi to help you get letters into the press.

Where? Choose your publication; whether because they may be favourable to your view or because you want to challenge their readers. Follow their rules – e.g. text in the email, no attachments, provide contact info – not to be published.   Different publications have different conventions and it matters to follow them to succeed.

Brevity : Short is good and may increase your chances of publication. 300 words is a typical maximum. The clue is always to study the form of your target publication.

Bold message : Be clear and strong about your message, but in ways you can support. I spend most of my time on the title, the intro and outro. The rest is then easy.

Insight : Make every word your own. Try to provide personal added value. Show how your unique knowledge contributes to the debate.

Structure : Have a simple structure, for example a beginning, middle and end. If making factual points use the rule of three. Do not use shopping lists in letters.

Goal : Political letters may begin with a problem, or maybe the whole letter is about the problem. The letter may read more positively if it has a constructive next step at the end. If not, then at least a pithy conclusion.

Timing : The ideal time to write your letter to a morning daily paper is in the morning, responding to that day's newspaper for example, and sending before 3 pm, so that it can be considered for the next day's letters page. This is not essential, and you can send your letter in the evening, but sending before 3 pm maximises your chances.

Exclusivity: Media like exclusivity so send your letter to one publication only. Don't share it in advance on social media or elsewhere.

Edit, edit, edit: After writing the draft: rest, reflect, review, revise, reduce. Feedback from others can be helpful. Edit until no words are wasted.

Cuttable: If you write a longer letter, consider writing it so may be easily shortened.

Here is an example from The Financial Times. Do get in touch if you are targeting National or Local Radio or TV.

Letter (+ Add to myFT)

Letter: One minister's chance to lead by example

From Peter Cook, Gillingham, Kent, UK

© PRU/AFP via Getty Images

JUNE 5 2020

I have a suggestion to restore basic faith in our political system, having heard that UK business secretary Alok Sharma felt ill after attending a parliamentary conga session and testing positive for coronavirus (Report, June 4).

Mr Sharma now has a golden opportunity to lead by example, by providing information about all the contacts he made among other MPs and staff. This would provide much needed confidence in our government in the fight against coronavirus.

Peter Cook
Gillingham, Kent, UK

Expect a Brexit fire sale

I am a British business author and consultant currently working in SA. One often has to leave one's country to see it more clearly, and your article on Boris Johnson was spot on in terms of its incisive analysis of the decline of our nation ("Boris Johnson takes a leaf out of Donald Trump's media-bashing book", February 11).

All business, life and politics rely crucially on trust, and Johnson, Trump et al have devalued that currency to a point of negative equity.

Yes, it may rally the mob when the press walk out of Downing Street, when judges are to be interviewed for suitability by politicians, and so on. But long term, it leads to a climate where we cannot get the important things done in a troubled world. It will pay us back when we start trying to trade with the rest of the world.

I trust that Africa is ready to reap the rewards of the "Brexit fire sale".

Peter Cook
Human Dynamics

South African Business Daily

Take every opportunity – I was only in South Africa for a week but managed to get a piece in the main business newspaper there. I studied their style of the letters' column and read the article about Boris Johnson carefully. I played the novelty angle of being a businessperson in Africa well and made sure there was a takeaway point for South African readers (quite literally!)

A major push for a "people's vote" on the final Brexit deal between Britain and the EU has been launched by MPs, celebrities and business leaders. A cross-party lineup of MPs took to the stage at the Electric Ballroom in Camden, north London, on Sunday. They have been at pains to avoid the term "second referendum".

The MPs included Conservative Anna Soubry, Labour's Chuka Umunna, the Greens' Caroline Lucas and Liberal Democrat Layla Moran.

"We have got to get a majority in the House of Commons for the proposition of this people's vote," Umunna told a crowd of more than 1,000 people, many of whom were waving flags and sporting remainer garb ranging from blue berets to stickers proclaiming "Bollocks to Brexit". "That means at the very least my party, the Labour party, needs to be true to its values and support this," he added, eliciting foot-stomping and cheering from the crowd.

'I've been punched in Brexitland, and I can tell you that it hurts, but we have to go there'
Remain-supporting businessman Peter Cook

In the audience, meanwhile, participants such as business consultant Peter Cook shrugged about the optics of holding such a key anti-Brexit event in the arch-remainer territory of north London. "We have taken the easy way in terms of doing this in north London, yes, but the reality of what we're saying is still unavoidable," said Cook.

"What we do have to do, though, is get out there in the Brexit heartlands - places like Clacton and Ramsgate and Sunderland. I've been punched in Brexitland, and I can tell you that it hurts, but we have to go there."

This piece upset James McGrory, head of the People's Vote campaign, mainly because he had no story to offer The Guardian, having failed to plan his media coverage.

If you wish to aim for an article, a press release is needed. An example of a press release follows. This succeeded internationally, gaining publicity across MSM from the Daily Mail, The Guardian, BBC, New York Times and BBC Have I Got News For You.

PRESS RELEASE
Kent residents say NO to toilet conversion
CLASSIFIED CONFIDENTIAL

"I won't shit in our own garden" – Dorothy, Edenbridge

"I voted for Brexit, but I didn't vote for this lorry park" – Linda, Ashford

EU Flag Mafia are to makeover **ALL** the Kent border signs to say 'Welcome to Kent – Toilet of England', as Brexit dumps its toxic waste onto the people of Kent under UK's Winter of Discontent. We will flush out the senseless combined effect of Corona crisis + Brexit disaster = a 'Britastrophe'.

Spokesperson Peter said of 'Operation Pisspot':

"The Mafia have managed to organise people from Erith marshes in South-East London all the way to Jury's Gap in Kent near Rye. This is a military operation to relabel all the signs along the Kent border. We will point out the mindless chaos to come to our county: 70-mile pile ups; rotting food and medicines in lorries; Dogging parks, Portaloos in villages; 30% price rises on some foods in the middle of a global pandemic. We must endure COVID as a natural phenomenon. We don't need to endure Brexit as a man-made project for the benefit of a few disaster capitalists. We may also be delivering some toilets to Nigel Farage's house".

We invite you exclusive coverage of this story, undercover and in complete confidence. Last time we took to the streets, we were arrested by Essex Police with our Bollocks to Brexit Mini Cooper. Sadly, we called 999 and Essex Police had to issue a retraction of their ignorance of the law. To embargo the story, please call our brexorcist in Chief.

"Brexshit has finally hit the fan. The dirty protest has yet to come" – June, Sussex

BBC Have I Got News For You adopted the phrase 'Operation Pisspot'. This underlines the need to have some good soundbites in your press release.

The policeman's behaviour has been described as "bang out of order."

THE NEW EUROPEAN

Subscribe to The New European today!

🏠 HOME   TOP STORIES   OUR WRITERS   STORE LOCATOR   SUBSCRIBE   CONTACT US   DOWNLOADS   SHOP

Try 13 weeks of *The New European* for just £13   SUBSCRIBE NOW ▸

My letter from Nigel Farage

⏱ PUBLISHED: 09:01 31 August 2018 | UPDATED: 09:01 31 August 2018   Peter Cook

Search...   🔍

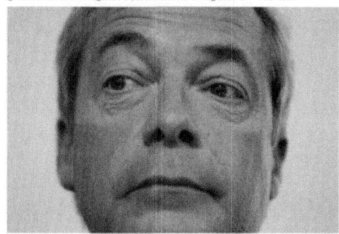

Nigel Farage. Photograph: Daniel Leal-Olivas/PA Images.

PODCAST

▶   Podcast   The

Twinkle toes Theresa and a momentous mo... 48:40

Best for Britain, Raabbling on and Donald ... 1:04:33

More scandal for Jeremy and fantasy politics 38:05

Boris Johnson plays the race card and the ... 43:17

Brexit conspiracies, Hunt on tour and social... 49:30

f 🐦 G+ SUBSCRIBE   B

I wrote to my MEP Nigel Farage requesting a financial assessment of the benefits of Brexit.

I was expecting a mathematical answer but was astonished to receive a reply blaming those bloody Greek philosophers Plato and Aristotle:

"May I suggest some general reading for you: Hobbes, Locke, Von Mises, Hayek, Fukuyama. The EU is based on the philosophy of Plato rather than Aristotle – that's why continental Europe keeps descending into tyranny whilst the UK escapes – we have done so again in Brexit and the EU's tyranny is for example exposed in Greece.

"Democracy is the real Brexit prize and from it flows a stable political system, the rule of law and sustained economic prosperity. Change of course always involves some disruption, and there is a short-term cost to that, but the long-term gains from the above are priceless. The mistake was joining the EU project in the first place – that is where responsibility for the costs involved in leaving should fall."

Who knew that philosophers were to blame for our current business uncertainties? I imagine Mick Jagger would have said "you Kant always get what you want".

Peter Cook, Kent

• Have your say in The New European by emailing letters@theneweuropean.co.uk

ANTI-BREXIT EVENTS

Events: How you can help the grassroots anti-Brexit campaigns

 Is this the real reason why Farage and Rees-Mogg want a speedy Brexit?

 Now Copenhagen airport trolls Brexit Britain

 Spoon-fed manifesto could backfire for Brexit champion

 MANDRAKE: BBC uninvites Gina Miller from commenting on no-deal Brexit papers

 Fox: 'Don't blame me if there isn't a deal'

RELATED ARTICLES

• Shock, horror: No-one wants this portrait of Farage hanging on their wall

Article for Premiere French magazine L'Obs – this came about due to a chance encounter in Whitehall on a Sunday afternoon. The journalist had been visiting the Churchill war museum and spotted my anti Brexit t-shirt. It pays to be 'open all hours' if you wish to influence events with the media.

Once the subway rush passes, the band heads to 10 Downing Street and plants itself in front of Theresa May's office to play her favorite song, "Dancing Queen," from Abba. Peter Cook knows he annoys the head of the government but does not give up. He wants to convey two messages: consider the possibility of a new vote and we are closely monitoring the negotiations with Brussels and the false promises of Brexit.

> *"Theresa May was greeting the Commonwealth leaders in April, we stood on the path of the procession to get our message across, she always had a tough message against immigration, but when she wants to negotiate a free trade agreement, exchange with India or Pakistan, will not they ask for the free movement of people as well as goods? What will Brexit have brought to us? I want her to recognize it and to tell people."*

For Theresa May to understand that opponents of Brexit, who have probably missed the referendum campaign, will no longer be silent, the consultant sang the song Police: "Every step you take, I'll be watching you" (' I'll watch every step of yours, "he hums, laughing. He tells :

> *She glared at me, I would have dreamed that she did like Emmanuel Macron, that she came to discuss, to debate with me, she would have shown that she knows how to negotiate, that she can surprise the other party, disarm it. "*

But no !

LARRY SPEAKS

I fucking hate my life under lockdown. BOJO is a weasel. He never even feeds me the Brexit fish.

Foreign INVASION

IMMIGRANTS set to INVADE Britain under trade deal by Liz Truss

"I want a vote on this attack on are sovrinty"

MOGG : My Victorian Sex Guide : Page 3

"No, Nanny, No. Not the birch again on my bare Etonian bottom"

ILLUSION OF CONTROL

WORLD BEATING DEATHS – **BOJO loses count of COVID deaths, but Britannia rules the waves of death.**

"A good COVID death is one that does not count inside our 28 day window. Some people are refusing to die under the Government's guidelines".

SOVRINTY THREAT
Liz Truss heralds new trade deal with South East Asia with few benefits. *"Geography was my best subject at school. Much has changed since those days, but the UK still is not in the Pacific".* **Jane, Truro**

BOJONA WARS – **after nearly five YEARS of wanting our Sovereignty back, Jim in Clacton complains when EU suggests for two HOURS that Sovereignty cuts both ways. MASS GASLIGHTING exercise begins and Sun readers fall for it ! ☺**

John in Dudley asks if Astrid Sennica is a racing driver.

If all else fails, make your own populist media !

Find our spoof pages at brexitrage.com/gutterpress

Engage your MP

Writing letters is one thing. Stalking out your MP at public or private meetings quite another.   My MP is Rehman Chishti, a nice enough chap who succeeds mostly by avoiding his electorate in the safe seat of Gillingham and Rainham in Kent. Formerly a Labour candidate, Rehman had a religious conversion to the Tories some time ago, presumably as there was a better career to be had as a Conservative in the post Dockyard era. He has consistently voted with the PM of the day and as a result became Party Vice Chair for Communities a while back. I went to the same school as him for a couple of years where he also followed the rules and became a prefect. Sadly, I did not and that accounts for my entire life in working with the establishment, but we all have our crosses to bear.

Life has not been so kind to Mr Chishti of late. He was implicated in taking consultancy fees of £200 per hour from a Saudi think tank, reported on Channel 4 News. Needless to say, there are quite a few people who feel that justice should also be metered out for his tendency to ignore his constituents. One of them contacted me after my assault by Brexiteers, a fellow Remainer and, who it seemed had a long track record of trying to get Mr Chishti to serve his constituents.

This is one of those 'you had to be here' moments but I will try to explain longhand in this story … it is in two parts and I've saved the best till last so read on …

PART I – Don't stand so close to me

I had the immense pleasure of going down to my local Council surgery to speak with the local councillor recently at the request of a mystery Remain voter who dislikes feckless politicians. His intention was to use me as a 'Trojan Horse' to put another nail in Rehman Chishti's coffin. This followed Rehman's resignation from his position in the Conservative party.

On arrival, we were met by the Councillor for Rainham North, Martin Potter. Martin became fixated on my 'FUCK BREXIT' T-Shirt as he opened the door to his office. Caught like a rabbit in headlights, he seemed unable to let us into his surgery, burbling and stuttering, as he attempted to articulate his problem with the T-Shirt at the door … he hesitated endlessly …

Martin : "Erm, I cannot speak with you with that T-Shirt on".

Me : "What is troubling you? We came to speak with you about a local policing issue".

Martin : "It's the T-Shirt – I cannot speak with you with that word".

Me : "What, Brexit?"

Him : "Erm, no …" dithering and fumbling nervously.

Me (very loudly so that front desk person could hear) : "Oh, you mean FUCK. I think you will find much worse out there in Chatham High Street".

Him : "It's just I cannot speak with you with that word on the shirt …"

Me : "Well, to be honest I find your green Lacoste T-Shirt unbearably boring, but I'm not going to mention it. Now, we don't have the BBC filming here. We are not recording this. We are on our own in your office. What is your problem really" … (no answer) … later … "Would you like me to take my top off?"

Him : "That would help".

Fortunately for everyone I did have two tops on … !!! So, I removed the T-Shirt.

Footnote … Martin kept mentioning the T-Shirt throughout the meeting, even though I no longer had it on. Two days later, it was still the main subject of his e-mail response to me. I imagine he has had to receive therapy for this by now …

Dear Peter,

Thank you for visiting my surgery on Saturday, and for removing the t-shirt with the offensive f**k word on it so we could engage in dialogue on reasonable terms.

I was very sorry to hear of the incident on the train in Gillingham, and I do hope my advice regarding the Office of Police Conduct yields a full and proper investigation into what went wrong with the police response. As requested, I have also copied Mr Chishti's office into this email and included the contact details below:

Email: Rehman.Chishti.mp@parliament.uk

Tel: 01634 570118

Best regards
Martin

Eventually, after further nervous hesitation, we entered his office and got down to business. Martin was still completely phased by our initial conversation and kept referring to it, despite my ignoring it. He agrees to getting a meeting with Rehman

Chishti to discuss the failure of the Police after I explain that I understand Mr Chishti really cares about local issues, although he allegedly spends an awful lot of time assisting Saudi Arabia with advice … He looks terrified as he continues to think about the T-Shirt …

PART II – Close encounters with Rehman Chishti

Eventually we left, happy with the outcome (although he has not contacted me since, true to form). I enjoyed the brief encounter with my mystery friend so I asked if he would like a cup of tea. We turn the corner to the café in the precinct. As we walk in, who should be there but the MP Rehman Chishti himself !!! … My friend announces our arrival and begins to introduce me to Rehman …

"May I introduce you to … "

Rehman (interrupting) : "Peter Cook" … somehow Rehman knows me!!

Me : "Oh, we've never met. I'm not the dead comedian".

Rehman : "I know who you are. You were very rude to me on Twitter".

Me : "I wasn't. I wrote you some letters, but you don't ever answer them".

Rehman : "My parliamentary record shows I always answer every letter" (… still living the dream as a prefect at school).

Me : "OK, yes. You do answer the letters, but you don't ever answer the questions. They are vague generalisations or nominalisations in NLP speak. Or, if you prefer, cut and paste".

Rehman : "I personalise all my letters".

Me : "OK, you put Dear Peter at the top. We did not come in here to talk about that, so enjoy your coffee"

Rehman : "You called me a turd on Twitter".

Me : "Actually I don't think I called you a turd, I think it was a twat but they both start with a T" (emphasising the words turd and twat – the café was full and people started listening. They will have known who Rehman Chishti was).

Me : "I'm from Gillingham. Although I have three degrees, I'm told I have a 'Labour accent'. My wife says I'm intelligent scum ."..

Rehman : "So am I from Gillingham. I'd not go so far as your wife".

Me : "But she knows me so much better than you. It's true I am intelligent scum. With 3 and a half degrees but you can't take the chav out of Chatham. We both went to the same school".

Rehman : "The point is that this sort of language is not for Twitter".

Me : "I disagree. If you go down to Chatham, you will find words such as turd and twat are exactly the currency of people in Medway. The vernacular of Chatham is the same as Twitter. I always try to settle issues by personal and private communications. When I don't get any answers, I take the debate public and use direct language as it gets to the heart of the matter. I think you should get outside more. Anyway, I came to speak about another matter (explains what we had done).

We ended up agreeing to meet to discuss police matter. Of course, he never replied I promised not to mention turds twats, Brexit and Saudi arms trade in our subsequent meeting.

We shook hands. He still had a coffee with some mystery guy. Having sat down for 30 seconds or so, they both left the café, leaving their coffees behind. I'm not sure who the other guy was, but I had a distinct feeling that they did not want us listening in … ☺

Lessons learned

A direct approach can be more effective than all the e-mails and tweets.

An unusual artefact can help 'announce' you. However, beware of gimmicks per se as they wear out. But symbolism can cut through words in quite remarkable ways. Martin is probably still under the doctor due to my t-shirt. The faux outrage is of course a device of social control.

A plan for such encounters matters. A good plan allows for the ability to be spontaneous.

Rehman Chishti tried to invoke position power at the beginning of our meeting. I did not accept his attempt to introduce deference and hierarchy. Beware such traps. Nigel Farage, Mark Francois and Jacob Rees-Mogg are also masters of this artform.

"While most other advanced economies have seen a strong recovery in trade, UK exports remain below pre-pandemic levels," said Jonathan Portes, professor of economics at King's College London.

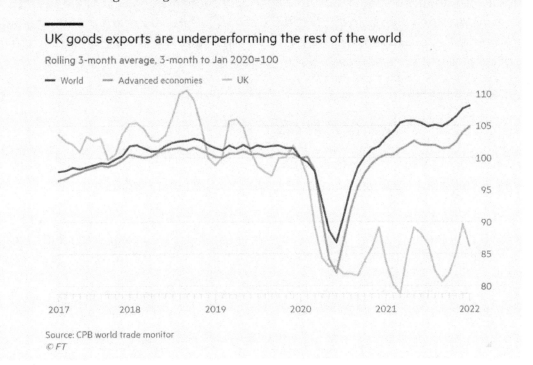

UK goods exports are underperforming the rest of the world

Rolling 3-month average, 3-month to Jan 2020=100

— World   — Advanced economies   — UK

Source: CPB world trade monitor
© FT

Now that the COVID mask has come off, we begin to see the economic effects of Brexit. MPs eventually listen to such things, once these effects have been translated into people's lived experience. The real question is whether the people will make the necessary correlations between the macroeconomic effects of Brexit and the microeconomics of their everyday experience? UK is the line on the graph that has not recovered from COVID. Source : Financial Times.

Microblogging

Everyone can do microblogging. Simply post your thoughts on Facebook or as a Twitter thread. Make sure you have your settings open to ensure you reach outside the bubble and do reply to people as they engage. Pedr Ap Roabt is a master of the artform and one of his pieces is shown below.

STEVE BAKER WATCH

Steve retweets a man called David Scullion:

'The public told us to get Brexit done, they gave us a large majority to do it ... and yet still we seem to be too nervous to do what the country instructed us to do.'

Both Steve and Scullion well know that only 43% of "the public" voted for pro-Brexit parties in the supposedly binary 2019 "Brexit election". Our undemocratic First Past the Post voting system made it look like there was a "large majority" for it. But there wasn't.

So no one told anyone to "get Brexit done", and most certainly very few imagined it would be the hardest possible Brexit that Steve and his fellow ideologues could get away with.

What Brexit would really mean was never clarified, least of all by its proponents. It was made up as a hapless government staggered from self-induced crisis to self-induced crisis while being wagged opportunistically by Steve's rather nasty political misfits in the ERG.

Finally, at no time was an "instruction" issued or received by anyone. In 2016 there was an advisory referendum; in 2017 a Brexiter government managed to lose its majority; and in 2019 please refer to my first point.

Shame on you, Steve Baker.

Retract! Delete, amend or clarify the errors in this tweet! It would be the honest - and Christian - thing to do.

Again, please answer my email of weeks ago. That would be the grown-up thing to do.

Or you could do all of us here in Wycombe a favour - and Get Orf Our Land!

Brief encounters of the 3rd kind

Brexorcisms don't have to take hours. Sometimes a brief encounter is worthwhile as opportunities present themselves, as these examples demonstrate :

I met a 40-year-old woman at a coffee shop opposite Marylebone station. After a brief conversation, she told me she did not vote. After I pointed out that my life was over, but her life mattered re Brexit, she agreed that oblivion was not an overall helpful place. This was surprisingly simple and quick. I suspect she just needed pushing over the line towards caring more.

A North London Leaver with seven friends at the same café, who initially joked that he was pleased he did not have to punch me as I'd already been done! ☺   A good icebreaker. He was subsequently shocked when I showed him the actual pictures of me being punched. It had not seemed real in casual conversation. I'm not sure he even believed me as I joked about it during the 'rapport' building stage. This made him think about the hostile environment we have invited in via Brexit.

A genial conversation ensued. He was pleasantly surprised to meet a Remainer that did not lecture him. No Brexorcism was achieved with him of course but his friends were all giving my bicycle the thumbs up by the time I left. He gave the familiar argument that his dad fought in the war and that came out well, so Brexit would be OK ... I chose to let it be, having mentioned that there were some differences between a war with a common enemy and a desperate situation versus our current situation of a divided nation and a self-induced crisis. We had a cordial exchange on this, and both listened well.

Having boarded the train, I met an old age pensioner with his kids and grandchildren on Chiltern Trains going to Wembley. He initiated a long chat with me about how we can turn the minds of politicians, after he spotted the hoarding on my bicycle. This was the catalyst to the conversation which otherwise would not have happened.

Later, an old woman glared endlessly at the sign whilst waiting to get off further up the line at Ruislip - I could not make eye contact so I said 'sorry' to break her fixed gaze at the sign, thinking her to be a Brexiteer. She then told me she voted to join the EU in 1975, voted Remain in 2016 and was delighted to see people still fighting to stay in Europe. She was almost in tears as she left the train. A heart-warming moment.

On my return journey, I received numerous nervous smiles at Victoria and Marylebone stations ... and a bit of glaring at Victoria ... It's strange how the River Thames seems to be a tipping point for glaring ☺

I returned with the football supporters from Wembley ... I don't know what teams they supported but I thought that this might have led to trouble and was slightly cautious as I did not wish to be punched again. However, all were OK ... mostly amused smiles and a bit of glaring at the sign ... I guess their team must have won ....

Finally, the station attendant at Orpington stood staring at the bicycle sign. I wondered why and eventually made eye contact. He broke out in a broad smile. He then went to get his colleagues to look at the bicycle and could not believe I'd been punched for wearing a T-shirt ...

On another occasion, a young woman approached me having seen my bicycle. She enquired as to whether I thought Brexit was a good thing. I explained myself. She then told me that she voted Leave and said she was fed up with it all. I explained that I too was bored but that was not a good reason to accept a poor decision after three years of wasted time. She agreed and said she had changed her mind. I showed her the picture of my attack and this reinforced her view. She said "nobody should have to go through that" and kept repeating it. I had a sense that she had some personal experience ...

The importance of satire

Remainers still tell me that we must use facts, be earnest, deliberate and measured on our attempts to change minds about Europe and Brexit. Respectfully, I say to them that they are partly right. We need all the tools in the book to reach outside the bubble. Satire and humour reach the parts that other approaches to influence and persuasion do not. Find our 'Private Eye' platform at www.brexitrage.com/gutterpress

NEW VARIANT BREXIT

SILENCE OF THE LAMBS

Mad Cow Liz Truss wants an Australian Brexit so badly that she is SACRIFICING farmers on the BREXIT ALTAR of sovereignty. CHEESE FAN Truss

FROSTY THE NO MAN

FURY as **Civil Service** LOSER **David Frost has** attacked the EU for making Great Britain have BREXIT.

"The EU forced BRITONS

LIFTING THE SKIRT ON BREXIT

"He rolled onto me like a binbag full of custard".

KINGS OF THE NEW STONE AGE

SOVRINTY, SOVRINTY, SOVRINTY

Foul play

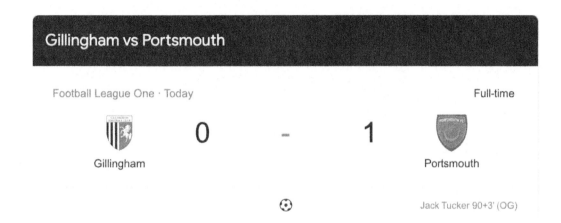

Gillingham vs Portsmouth

Football League One · Today   Full-time

Gillingham   0   -   1   Portsmouth

⚽   Jack Tucker 90+3' (OG)

I was in a local cafe when the football fans emerged from the match. Gillingham lost to Portsmouth by one goal in the 93rd minute. By the way, Gillingham have a habit of losing when they are supposed to win so this was not a total surprise!

A dejected fan came in. When I asked how it had gone, he pointed out that it was totally unfair, as there was foul play and it should have been declared a nil-nil draw.

However, he seemed to think that the Brexit referendum, polluted by foul play, industrial scale fraud and a whopping lie in the '93rd minute' should stand, although this 'match' too was won on the thinnest of margins.

I left him in a state of cognitive dissonance to ponder the parallels …

Incubation

I sat in my usual café in Brexit Central, run by my Remain friend from Ghana. About two years had passed since I'd first had conversations with Brexiteers, based on my T-Shirt. Most of the café goers were Leave voters many are over 60 and 'Brits at leisure'. There is one key opinion former in the café, in practice he is the loudest voice. He is about 65 years old, physically large, lives on benefits, has considerable health needs and has been permanently signed off from work as a result. He appears to have few real health issues and spends his days in the café, telling others what they should think about Brexit, the NHS, the world, life and the universe. Nobody challenges him, but I suspect some merely pay lip service to him, as he often talks about how he will 'smash people in the face' if they disagree with him, telling stories of how he has slapped women in the past to 'teach them some sense', to reinforce his sense of self.

He started talking to me about how the Remainers are a disgrace with what had happened recently (the sit-in on Downing Street) and so on. I tried to reply but he kept cutting across saying that he didn't want to talk to me. So, I agreed and stopped. He continued to talk but I just nodded minimally to begin with and then totally ignored him. Eventually he stopped.

When I went to leave, I walked over to him and said "It's very rude to speak with someone and then you don't allow them to reply. I've listened to you for ages over the years M, but you don't return the favour. I like you mate, but I must be honest when I tell you that you don't listen. None of your opinions are supported by any facts. I understand why you feel left behind and all of that, but you really need to get an education".

I apologised the café owner later, but it seemed that she was delighted that I'd done it as she has to listen to him all day. She also told me that most of the café goers have now changed their minds on Brexit, having listened into my encounters with M. Some even refuse to visit the café if they think he will be there.

This rather illustrates the point that Brexorcisms take skill, patience, unconditional positive regard (UPR and time..

PART IV

Defence against the dark Brexit arts

Defence against the dark Brexit arts

Here's a compendium of commonly asked questions or statements that Brexiteers ask or make about Brexit. There are no magic bullet answers to such challenges since :

- Your subject may not be awake, alert or receptive. See our thoughts on waking up your subjects in Part II.

- Only 7% of the overall communication is down to the syntax. So, snappy responses are one thing, but getting people to understand and accept those answers usually requires much harder work on the preparatory phase. See our thoughts on warming up your subjects. Remember all is different online when compared with real life, when you are mostly working only with the 7% plus the odd meme and video. This is not a conversation. It is one-way transmission. It may also be asynchronous and or fragmented by distance and time.

- Context / warm up is everything. You may well need a bank balance of emotional credit to slay a 'sacred Brexit cow' or roast a piece of gammon.

- The environment may make a massive difference to success. The physical environment and the psychological environment both interact to help you succeed. See my comments on saunas and cafés.

- And a host of other issues may prevent successful two-way communications.

Nonetheless I have attempted to list some general lines of attack in the hope that it will help 'arm' you with ways to 'challenge people without tears'.

Remember that you can challenge people in both directive and non-directive ways. Use the full spectrum of John Heron's model for maximum impact on your subject. You will mostly be working in collaborative and autonomous mode unless you are an acknowledged expert. Even then that expertise may not be accepted by your subject.

Brexit apathy

Typically, people say things like :

"Brexit is done".

"We left".

"Leave means Leave".

"Just forget Brexit, be done with it as that what we voted for".

"I'm really sick of Brexit".

Suitable challenges begin with the following arguments :

"I'm also sick of Brexit. What do you feel we have gained from Brexit after nearly six years of negotiations?"

"What did you vote for? Much later … To what extent have you gotten this?"

Imperialism

Typical objections I have heard Leave voters use include mantras such as :

"They (EU) need us more than we need them".

"The EU need our money. We should threaten not to pay".

"If they ask for the £39 million back, we should just bomb France".

"Why should we pay any money anyway?"

"All Boris Johnson needs to do is to play these EU gangsters at their own game".
"Simply tell them OK. No problem if you don't want to help. I'll just go back to the UK and organise another referendum with just the two options on the ballot for the people to choose from. My deal. Leave with NO £40 Billion and onto WTO rules Just the thought of the British people having the power to tell the EU where to go with its £40

BILLION ransom demand would terrify them all in Brussels because they know full well that given the options above which they are going to choose by a mile I also think that turning the table on the EU gangsters and playing hard ball would make her far more popular than she is right now because the vast majority of the British public have had a belly full of the EU and the way it has treated the UK since the vote to leave".

"Britain is full".

And here is a personal threat I received on social media just for fun.

Trying to make money from the UKs at with Brussels?

I'll give you publicity.

But not the sort you'll like.

Like · Reply · 23h

The EU don't need us more than we need them. This is becoming apparent now. I run a portfolio business. Supposing I juggle 10 clients and one of them decides they no longer want to work with me anymore. I lose notionally 10% of my business. Supposing that client is a good client and they are worth say 25%. I am upset but it does not kill me. I must work hard to make up the shortfall by seeking another client. It is the same with the EU27. They have lost 1/28 in terms of countries and perhaps 1/20 in terms of economic value. It won't kill them.

Clearly some countries and industries are disproportionately affected. France, Belgium, Holland, Ireland and so on. The automotive industry etc. This is in part why we see the EU making trade deals with Japan and so on to help offset losses in particular sectors.

As regards not paying the exit bill there are two points here :

Why do we need to pay an exit bill at all? Well, most macro scale projects require up front commitments on a long-term basis, without which they would not happen. We have committed those payments and we must therefore pay them. Jeremy Hunt recently said that we must pay our debt to Iran and this is no different.

Why can't we just not pay? There are only two circumstances in your life when you can avoid paying a bill. When you never intend ever to trade with anyone ever again and when you are fixing to die. Trade relies on trust. If the UK does not settle its exit bill, our country's 'Trust Pilot' score will be 'minus 3000'. It will set a toxic context for any trade deals we wish to strike in the future, a bit like dealing with a dodgy builder.

The Truss Pilot – a new index of broken promises and Brexit fantasies

£39 bn sounds like a lot but it is just another trick using a one-sided argument. We need to 'Go Compare'. We have already spent considerably more than this getting nowhere on Brexit. We spent £37 bn on fictional PPE from dodgy suppliers. £39 bn is not a small amount but it ignores what we get back for it and in the scheme of things it is not the largest sum of money we spend. For comparison, Brexit will have cost us £100 bn every year until 2030.

To those who want to bomb France. We were not at war with them last time I looked ...

Sovereignty

Typical complaints include :

"We cannot even decide on the shape of our bananas".

"I want my country back".

"I want a crown on my pint glass"

"I want an English lion on my egg"

Many but not all claims about sovereignty concern hypnotic inductions about Queen and country etc. These have been installed by our popular press over many decades. The fact that they are mostly untrue does not mean that, if you disprove them, your subject will repent. Some of these beliefs are hardwired into the subject's heart and soul, rather like the Pavlovian response to stand up when the national anthem is played.

Perhaps the best strategy is to use the meta model to unpick which parts of their country they want back, and perhaps to listen carefully to their 'story', getting them to highlight which aspects of the story are down to the EU, which our own government and which down to general changes. There is a great deal of nostalgia built into the collage of reasons why people wanted to Leave the EU.

The banana issue is a great opportunity to explain that they were lied to. If you get that far the next key move is to ask them hypnotically to wonder what other lies they have been told. Some will tell you that all politicians lie and almost suggest that it is an agreeable situation. Lots of open-ended questions can help and a desire to leave your subject with more questions than answers can be a good strategy. By the way, the eggs still have lions on them, but they are not English.

Democracy

On this thorny topic, Brexiteers typically say things like :

"We already had the final say in 2016".

"It's anti-democratic to keep repeating a vote".

"Are you against democracy?"

*"It was the only thing I've ever done where my voice counted.
And you want to take that away from me".*

Firstly, the referendum is commonly thought to be binding when it is not. It clearly stated that it was an advisory referendum. At the same time David Cameron said he would abide by the result, which is where the confusion arises.

Typically, referenda that are binding require a 2/3 majority and are often conducted in stages. An initial vote on principles and another on practices for example.

In any case, democracy is a continuing, process not a project with a single end point. If democracy were a project, women would not have a vote, hanging would still be legal, putting children down mines and up chimneys would be normal and homosexuality would be punished by chemical castration.

Our Prime Minister in waiting, immortalised by the genius that is Cold War Steve. In real life, Liz Truss thinks that the suffering of war is the ideal opportunity to get more selfies for her Instagram profile. Rishi Sunak is also using the moment to cast a shadow on Boris Johnson's premiership. By anyone's definition, these shallow actions would justify Angela Rayner's use of the term "Tory Scum".

The 51.9% vote to Leave comprised several major 'segments', only the last one of which addressed the 'exam question'. The vote conflated these major elements :

1. Those who wanted to 'stick it to Cameron'. Of course, David Cameron behaved atrociously, producing an appalling leaflet and campaign in general. Vote Leave's campaign was far superior in potency.

2. Those who were swayed by Nigel Farage's Nazi inspired 'Breaking Point' poster. This created the illusion of 'millions of immigrant invaders'. It was supported by a campaign of fake news through targeted Facebook ads about Turkey being a member of the EU etc.

3. People who thought we would be getting £350 million back every week for the NHS, from the advert on the side of a bus. Supported by a series of other trivial but potent lies such as Boris' bendy bananas etc. We never did get the £350 million back.

4. And a group who wanted to Leave the EU for a host of reasons, some imagined and others to do with perceived rule by a foreign entity and an unaccountable bureaucracy. No large institution is perfect and that is why we include a better Europe in our mission statement for Re-Boot Britain.

Mission creep / EU superstate

Typically, Brexiteers offer remarks like this :

> *"Germany and France run the EU, we don't have any say.*
> *It was supposed to be a trading arrangement only".*

> *"Don't know anything about that, it was all done for Germany*
> *and we spent Billions on them after the war".*

"It's our money, we give them money for nothing. It only helps Germany, out means out. We'll be alright. We survived the war, we can do it again! We must escape the Nazis".

"It started as a trading thing. Now they want to interfere in our daily lives".

All organisations have mission creep. Nokia started life making toilet roll. 3M began by mining and now do Post-It Notes and so on. My hunch is that the main issue here is that the EEC started as a trading bloc and has now extended beyond that purpose. The UK has generally approved of EU decisions. Some 97% of EU decisions are approved of or initiated by our own British MEPs. We have generally not agreed when it has not suited us and that's why we have the Pound, are not in Schengen and so on. As for the return on our investment, the best place to find out what the EU does for us is at www.myeu.uk

Oblivion / Self centeredness

Typically, Brexiteers say things like :

"It'll be alright, as I tell them I'll lose my home and job".

"We don't mean you. It's the other immigrants".

"I don't care about anyone else, my hoover is not powerful enough".

"All I care about is my health and social care".

One of the most difficult areas as you are trying to get your subject to care about things they clearly don't care about …

One strategy is to play the scenario forward, pointing out how the things they care about will be affected. Sadly, this is usually met with the response 'project fear'. They must find out for themselves. If you are feeling brave you can confront the selfishness, asking them if there was ever a time when they needed others and so on.

Since they are likely to have low awareness of others, there is little point in trying to change that. Any change must come from finding ways to make them selfishly want to Remain in the EU.

Taking someone on a visit to a care home is a salutary experience as they suddenly gain a preview of their future and the fact that very few Brits work in such places.

Immigration

"Immigrants are stealing all our jobs because they push wages down".

"If you love the EU so much, why don't you move there?"

"They're comin' over 'ere takin' are jobs".

Immigration is another one of the most difficult areas as you are often dealing with irrational beliefs about people who appear to be different than the people who fear them. The term immigration is also loaded with sub-plots so it is difficult to offer a serious of algorithms to deal with all known victims of 'Brexitosis'. With some of the statements it is possible to supply facts if your subject is listening. For example, the illusion of immigrants taking jobs can be challenged quite easily if your subject listens. There are some sectors in which the perception of Brexiteers is justified by their experience e.g. building, yet the numbers generally don't support the perception. As we know facts do not always convince.

I often point out that people do not leave their families to come to the UK. Many of them also do jobs that British people will not do for the wages on offer. In some cases, they do jobs that we are not capable of doing, yet this shines the light on your subject's inadequacies and makes the conversation difficult.

Immigrants do not push wages down. That comes down to our own government, unscrupulous employers and supply and demand factors. Go for the root cause.

Myths and legends

Typically, Brexiteers say things like :

"Get rid of unelected bureaucrats".

"Bring back King Arthur".

"We must take back control".

"I want sovereignty".

"Get on with it, we won".

"Trust me it's all fear mongering".

"You Remainers have no faith in the British people and think we are only great because of Germany and France".

"Bananas? We're going to grow our own".

"EU is collapsing".

"Oh, yeah ... how's that turning out for Greece?"

Other

"If there's another vote I'm never going to vote again".

"I feel really sorry for Boris Johnson".

"Oh yes and Poor TM It's not her fault she's doing her best".

"I actually don't understand any of it".

"You're all fear mongers".

"Brexit is an unmitigated disaster".

"Brexit – what's this?"

"Get over it Leave won".

"End off".

"The same essperts what couldn't predict 2008!!"

"Err many did... they just don't write in The Sun ... and no one listened. Oi wan' me sovrinty back!"

Well, I leave you to your own Brexorcisms from here on ...

Acknowledgements

I am grateful to the following people for helping to provide the questions : Sarah Yoga, Maria Luisa, Lee Alexander, Ulrike Behrendt, John Castle, Chris Gamble, Grazia Valentino-Boschi, Annelles Schouppe, Mary Miraglia, Dimitri Seirlis, Barry Morgan, Karen Windahl Finnigan, Pieter Feld, Jaqueline Bridgeman, Rachel Ashley, Udo Keller, Sian Davies, Teresa Burton-Brown, Cathy Pearcy, Gail Caroline, Guillaumme Gee, John Laforge, Cliff Chapman, Chris Eden-Green, Helen Glanville.

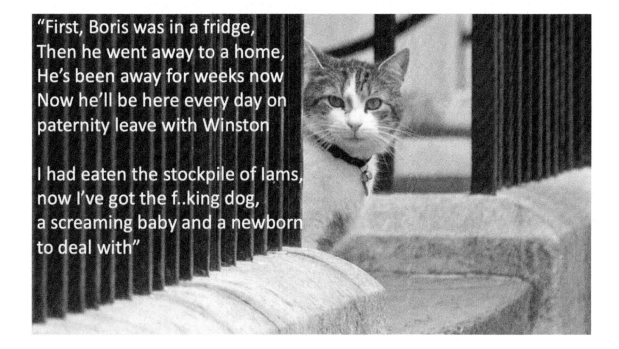

"First, Boris was in a fridge,
Then he went away to a home,
He's been away for weeks now
Now he'll be here every day on
paternity leave with Winston

I had eaten the stockpile of Iams,
now I've got the f..king dog,
a screaming baby and a newborn
to deal with"

Brexit doesn't pay

As part of our ongoing commitment to ensure that Brexit doesn't pay, we run weekly meetings at 8 pm on ZOOM to target MPs in vulnerable seats. Please join us via www.brexitrage.com/diary Here is a brief overview of our long-term project.

We wish to send a potent message to Brexit supporting MPs that Brexit doesn't pay. We will do this by damaging the majorities held by Brexit supporting MPs in Parliament by systematically engaging their constituents in conversation about their record nationally and locally, through information leaflets and on social media. We plan to do this as 'non-party campaigners' and will offer no guidance as to how people vote. We will just ask them not to vote Tory. By doing this we will leaven their majorities and allow other political parties to do their best. We have already achieved significant effects in Tunbridge-Wells and Chesham and Amersham.

See below the basic elements of a database that identifies a number of MPs who have:

- Slim majorities making their seat vulnerable.
- An association with the far-right side of the Conservative party.

We will include some target "Trophy Tories" who we would like to send a message of shock and awe to, to quote Dominic Cummings.

The first part of our plan is to identify some very special people who can lead local groups to campaign slowly but steadily to reach our goal. They will be skilled organisers, capable of leading teams and with good networks, working autonomously. Here are the areas in question:

COUNTY	Constituency	MP first name	MP surname
SOUTH			
Hertfordshire	Hitchin and Harpenden	Bim	Afolami
	Welwyn Hatfield	Grant	Shapps
	Stevenage	Stephen	McPartland
East Sussex	Lewes	Maria	Caulfield
Hampshire	Aldershot	Leo	Docherty
	Fareham	Suella	Braverman

	New Forest West	Desmond	Swayne
	North-East Hampshire	Ranil	Jayawardena
	North-West Hampshire	Kit	Malthouse
	Portsmouth North	Penny	Mordaunt
	Southampton, Itchen	Royston	Smith
Kent	Dartford	Gareth	Johnson
	Dover	Natalie	Elphicke
	Gravesham	Adam	Holloway
	Sittingbourne and Sheppey	Gordon	Henderson
	South Thanet	Craig	Mackinlay
Oxfordshire	Witney	Robert	Courts
Surrey	Carshalton and Wallington	Elliot	Colburn
	Epsom and Ewell	Chris	Grayling
	Reigate	Crispin	Blunt
	Esher and Walton	Dominic	Raab
	Surrey Heath	Michael	Gove
Berkshire	Wokingham	John	Redwood
Buckinghamshire	Wycombe	Steve	Baker
Isle of Wight	Isle Of Wight	Bob	Seely
West Sussex	Crawley	Henry	Smith
	East Worthing and Shoreham	Tim	Loughton
	Horsham	Jeremy	Quin
Bedfordshire	Mid Bedfordshire	Nadine	Dorries

WEST

Avon	North East Somerset	Jacob	Rees-Mogg
	North Somerset	Liam	Fox
	Weston-Super-Mare	John	Penrose
Cornwall	North Cornwall	Scott	Mann
	South-East Cornwall	Sheryll	Murray
	St Austell and Newquay	Steve	Double
Devon	Newton Abbot	Anne Marie	Morris
Dorset	Christchurch	Christopher	Chope
	Mid Dorset and North Poole	Michael	Tomlinson
Somerset	Somerton and Frome	David	Warburton

Re-Boot Britain by changing minds on Europe and Brexit

	Yeovil	Marcus	Fysh
NORTH			
Northumberland	Blyth Valley	Ian	Levy
	Berwick-Upon-Tweed	Anne-Marie	Trevelyan
Cheshire	Macclesfield	David	Rutley
Greater Manchester	Bolton West	Chris	Green
	Bury North	James	Daly
	Bury South	Christian	Wakeford
	Bolton North-East	Mark	Logan
	Heywood and Middleton	Chris	Clarkson
	Blackley and Broughton	Graham	Stringer
	Hazel Grove	William	Wragg
Humberside	Cleethorpes	Martin	Vickers
	Haltemprice and Howden	David	Davis
North Yorkshire	Thirsk and Malton	Kevin	Hollinrake
West Yorkshire	Morley and Outwood	Andrea	Jenkyns
	Shipley	Philip	Davies
South Yorkshire	Penistone and Stocksbridge	Miriam	Cates
SCOTLAND			
Scotland	Moray	Douglas	Ross
	West Aberdeenshire and Kincardine	Andrew	Bowie
LONDON			
Greater London	Chipping Barnet	Theresa	Villiers
	Kensington	Felicity	Buchan
	Islington North	Jeremy	Corbyn
	Hornchurch and Upminster	Julia	Lopez
	Uxbridge and South Ruislip	Boris	Johnson
	Sutton and Cheam	Paul	Scully
EAST			
Norfolk	Great Yarmouth	Brandon	Lewis
	South Norfolk	Richard	Bacon
Suffolk	Suffolk Coastal	Thérèse	Coffey

Re-Boot Britain by changing minds on Europe and Brexit

Cambridgeshire	Huntingdon	Jonathan	Djanogly
Essex	Braintree	James	Cleverly
	Epping Forest	Eleanor	Laing
	Harwich and North Essex	Bernard	Jenkin
	Maldon	John	Whittingdale
	Rayleigh and Wickford	Mark	Francois
	Rochford and Southend East	James	Duddridge
	Saffron Walden	Kemi	Badenoch
	Thurrock	Jacqueline	Doyle-Price
	Chingford and Woodford Green	Iain	Duncan Smith
	Witham	Priti	Patel

WALES / NORTH-WEST

Clwyd	Clwyd West	David	Jones
South Glamorgan	Vale of Glamorgan	Alun	Cairns
Mid Glamorgan	Bridgend	Jamie	Wallis
Lancashire	Fylde	Mark	Menzies
Merseyside	Southport	Damien	Moore

MIDLANDS

Derbyshire	High Peak	Robert	Largan
	Amber Valley	Nigel	Mills
	Mid Derbyshire	Pauline	Latham
Leicestershire	North-West Leicestershire	Andrew	Bridgen
Lincolnshire	Sleaford and North Hykeham	Caroline	Johnson
Northamptonshire	Corby	Tom	Pursglove
	Daventry	Chris	Heaton-Harris
	Northampton South	Andrew	Lewer
	South Northamptonshire	Andrea	Leadsom
	Wellingborough	Peter	Bone
	Mansfield	Ben	Bradley
Nottinghamshire	Gedling	Tom	Randall
Staffordshire	Lichfield	Michael	Fabricant
	South Staffordshire	Gavin	Williamson
	Stone	William	Cash
	Tamworth	Christopher	Pincher

	Stoke-On-Trent North	Jonathan	Gullis
Warwickshire	North Warwickshire	Craig	Tracey
West Midlands	Dudley South	Mike	Wood
	Halesowen and Rowley Regis	James	Morris
	Solihull	Julian	Knight
Hereford and Worcester	Bromsgrove	Sajid	Javid
	North Herefordshire	Bill	Wiggin
	Redditch	Rachel	Maclean
Shropshire	Shrewsbury and Atcham	Daniel	Kawczynski

NORTHERN IRELAND

In turn, we will supply support through bringing the team leaders together, designing and supplying leaflets at various points and providing training in the gentle art of Brexorcism.

Join us in this enterprise every Monday evening on ZOOM. To support the project please find us on Go Fund Me at www.gofundme.com/f/reboot-britain

EU freedoms

350 ++ reasons to join the EU anew

This is a splendid list from Paul Cawthorne.

EU AND BRITAIN'S GLOBAL ROLE

1. The EU has helped maintain peace in Europe for over 60 years.
2. The UK has greater global influence as a member of the EU.
3. Brexit diminishes the UK's global influence.
4. The EU provides a counterweight to the global power of the US, China and Russia.
5. The US administration values its 'special relationship' with the EU much more than with the UK.
6. The UK's closest natural allies are France, Germany and our other West European neighbours.
7. The UK's global role is best defined by its membership of the EU together with other international organisations including NATO, the UN Security Council, OECD, G7 and G20.
8. No prominent UK political leaders or parties are advocating leaving any of these other global institutions.
9. The UK worked together with other EU members in the Common Foreign and Security Policy (CFSP).
10. The EU has worked closely with NATO in enhancing European security.
11. EU members have collaborated to support the Iran nuclear deal.
12. EU members have imposed common sanctions on Russia since the annexation of the Crimea in 2014.
13. EU security cooperation to combat piracy off Somalia.

EU TRADE AND INVESTMENT

14. The EU is the world's largest trading bloc.
15. The EU has over 500 million consumers.
16. The EU represents 17% of global GDP.

17. The EU is the third largest economy in the world, just behind the US and China.
18. The EU accounts for 44% of all UK exports of goods and services.
19. The EU accounts for 53% of all UK imports of goods and services.
20. The UK enjoyed tariff-free trade within the EU.
21. The abolition of non-tariff barriers (quotas, subsidies, administrative rules etc.) among members.
22. The EU never has been a 'protectionist racket'.
23. The EU is a springboard for trade with the rest of the world through its global clout.
24. Participation in EU free trade agreement with Japan .
25. Participation in EU free trade agreement with and Canada.
26. Participation in EU free trade agreement with South Korea.
27. Participation in EU free trade agreement with Mexico.
28. Participation in EU free trade agreement with Chile.
29. Participation in multilateral trade negotiations through EU membership of the WTO.
30. Outside the EU the UK would has to renegotiate all its trade agreements.
31. On average a free trade agreement takes at least 7 years to negotiate.
32. As a member of the EU the UK maintains a say in the shaping of the rules governing its trade with its European partners.
33. Brexit leaves the UK still subject to EU trading rules but no longer with any say in shaping them.
34. UK trade with some countries in Europe increased by as much as 50% because of EU membership.
35. Cheaper food imports from continental Europe.
36. Cheaper alcohol imports from continental Europe.
37. All major non-European trading powers are giving priority to trade with the EU as a whole, not the UK on its own.
38. Potential future trade partners such as India and Turkey are likely to demand concessions on free movement in exchange for a trade deal.
39. The net benefit of EU membership is at least £60 billion per year (CBI estimate).
40. The EU has accounted for 47% of the UK's stock of inward Foreign Direct Investment (FDI), worth over $1.2 trillion.
41. The UK's net annual contribution to the EU budget was around €7.3bn, or 0.4% of GDP (less than an eighth of the UK's defence spending).
42. The City of London, as a global financial hub, has acted as a bridge between foreign business and the EU.

BENEFITS OF THE SINGLE MARKET

43. Investment flows across borders inside the EU have doubled since the introduction of the Single market in 1993.
44. The Single market underpins access to European supply chains.
45. Free movement of labour from the EU has overwhelmingly benefitted the UK economy.
46. Since leaving the Single market the UK experienced labour shortages in many sectors.
47. FDI into the UK has effectively doubled since the creation of the EU Single market.
48. Access to the EU Single market helped attract investment into the UK from outside the EU.
49. No paperwork or customs for goods throughout the Single market
50. Tory Brexiteers have conveniently forgotten that Margaret Thatcher was a leading architect and supporter of the Single market.
51. British banks have been able to operate freely across the EU.
52. British insurance companies have been able to operate freely across the EU.
53. Long delays at ports and airports have occurred since the UK left both the Single market and customs union.
54. The Single market has brought the best continental footballers to the Premier League.

BENEFITS OF THE SINGLE MARKET

55. No customs duties are paid moving between EU member states.
56. All member states apply a common customs tariff on goods imported from outside the EU.
57. Goods that have been legally imported can circulate throughout the EU with no further customs checks.
58. Membership of the Customs union is essential to maintaining a frictionless border in Northern Ireland.

HOW DOES THE UK BENEFIT FROM EU FUNDING?

59. 13% of EU budget earmarked for scientific research and innovation.
60. The UK received £730 million a year in EU funding for research.
61. EU funding for UK universities.
62. Potential damaging loss of Horizon 2020 research funding if the UK leaves the EU.
63. Cornwall received up to £750 million per year from the EU Social Fund (ESF).
64. £26m capital funding from the EU for the Eden project.
65. £25m funding from the EU for Blackpool's tourist infrastructure and improved sea defences.
66. £50 million EU funding towards the International Convention Centre and Symphony Hall in Birmingham.
67. £450 millions of EU funding destined to be spent on improving infrastructure on Merseyside in the period 2014 to 2020, including John Lennon airport and the cruise liner terminal.

68. The Scottish Highlands, East Wales and Tees Valley received EU funding of over €300 per person in the period 2014-2020.
69. 20,000 projects in the north of England received EU funding between 2007-2013 creating over 70,000 jobs.
70. EU funding for the regeneration of Redcar seafront.
71. EU funding for the Digital City in Middlesbrough.
72. Structural funding for areas of the UK hit by industrial decline (South Wales, Yorkshire).
73. Support for rural areas under the European Agricultural Fund for Regional Development (EAFRD).
74. £122 million EU funding for the "Midlands engine" project.
75. Financial support from the EU for over 3000 small and medium enterprises (SMEs) in the UK.
76. EU funding for British sport, including football apprenticeships, tennis and rugby league.
77. Access to the European Solidarity Fund in case of natural disasters.
78. From 1985 the UK received a budget rebate equivalent to 66% of its net contribution to the EU budget.
79. Leaving the EU has meant no more access to EU funding in many important areas.

EU AND CONSUMER RIGHTS

80. Europe-wide patent and copyright protection.
81. EU consumer protection laws concerning transparency and product guarantees of quality and safety.
82. Under EU law consumers can send back a product bought anywhere in the EU if it breaks down within two years of purchase.
83. EU law prohibits misleading advertising.
84. Improved food labelling.
85. A ban on growth hormones and other harmful food additives.
86. Cheaper air travel due to EU competition laws.
87. Common EU maritime passenger rights.
88. Common EU bus passenger rights.
89. Deregulation of the European energy market has increased consumer choice and lowered prices.
90. EU competition laws protect consumers by combatting monopolistic business practices.
91. Strict controls on the operations of Multinational Corporations (MNCs) in the EU.
92. Outside the EU there is no guarantee that a future UK government will maintain the current levels of consumer protection.

EU AND LABOUR RIGHTS

93. Minimum paid annual leave and time off work (Working Time Directive).
94. Equal pay between men and women enshrined in European law since 1957.
95. The right to work no more than 48 hours a week without paid overtime.
96. Minimum guaranteed maternity leave of 14 weeks for pregnant women.
97. Rights to a minimum 18 weeks of parental leave after childbirth.
98. EU anti-discrimination laws governing age, religion and sexual orientation.
99. EU rules governing health and safety at work.
100. The rights to collective bargaining and trade union membership are enshrined in EU employment law.
101. Outside the EU a UK government could lower labour protection standards.

EU AND EDUCATION

102. EU funding for UK universities.
103. 46,000 EU nationals work in UK universities.
104. The mutual recognition of professional qualifications has facilitated the free movement of engineers, teachers and doctors across the EU.
105. The mutual recognition of educational diplomas.
106. The Common European Framework of Reference for Languages (CEFR) has standardized assessment of language proficiency across the EU.
107. The freedom to study in 28 countries (many EU universities teach courses in English and charge lower fees than in the UK) .
108. The Erasmus programme of university exchanges (benefitting 16000 UK students a year).
109. Brexit is seriously compromising the rights and opportunities for the younger generation.
110. Brexit is overwhelmingly opposed by people under 30.
111. The Brexit referendum divided many families between pro-EU younger generations and pro-Brexit parents and grandparents.

EU AND THE ENVIRONMENT

112. The EU has played a leading role in combatting global warming (Copenhagen 2009, Paris 2015, 2020 targets).
113. Common EU greenhouse gas emissions targets (40% reduction by 2030).
114. Improvements in air quality (significant reductions in sulphur dioxide and nitrogen oxides) as a result of EU legislation.
115. Reductions in sewage emissions.
116. Improvements in the quality of beach water.
117. Improvements in the quality of bathing water.
118. EU standards on the quality of drinking water.
119. EU targets to reduce water pollution in Britain's rivers.
120. Restrictions on landfill dumping.
121. EU targets for recycling.
122. EU directive enforcing the use of unleaded petrol.
123. Common EU regulations on the transportation and disposal of toxic waste.
124. The implementation of EU policies to reduce noise pollution in urban areas.
125. EU policies have stimulated offshore wind farms.
126. EU support for solar energy.
127. EU award of €9.3 million to Queens University Belfast for research into tidal and wave energy.
128. EU promotion of the circular economy to enhance environmental sustainability.
129. Outside the EU the UK government is free to lower environmental standards.
130. Strict safety standards for cars, buses and trucks.
131. Protection of endangered species and habitats (EU Natura 2000 network).
132. Strict ban on animal testing in the cosmetics industry.

EU CITIZENS IN THE UK

133. More than 3 million citizens of the EU27 are legally resident in the UK.
134. EU citizens work, study and pay taxes, contributing greatly to the UK economy.
135. Over 200,000 EU citizens left the UK in 2020, contributing to labour shortages.
136. The UK never implemented the EU directive 2004/38/EC which allows EU member states to repatriate EU nationals after three months if they have not found the means to support themselves.
137. Free movement of labour in the EU helped UK firms plug skills gaps (translators, doctors, plumbers).

138.   10% of doctors in the NHS are EU nationals.

139.   7% of nurses in the NHS are EU nationals.

140.   Free movement of labour helped address shortages of unskilled workers (fruit picking, catering).

141.   28% of construction workers in London are from the EU.

142.   EU migrants make up 45 percent of the tourism and hospitality workforce.

143.   The retail industry has 170,000 people from the EU directly working for it, which accounts for 6% of the industry's UK workforce.

144.   The European Medical Agency (EMA) which employs 900 people has relocated to Amsterdam.

145.   The European Banking Authority (EBA) which employs 170 people has relocated to Paris.

146.   Uncertainty about Brexit caused great anxiety and insecurity among the over 3 million EU residents in the UK.

147.   Brexit has already provoked a brain drain of EU workers from the UK.

148.   There has been a rise in racial abuse and violent attacks since the 2016 referendum.

UK CITIZENS IN THE EU

149.   At least 1 million UK citizens live in the EU27.

150.   80% of these are below retirement age.

151.   Brexit has been overwhelmingly opposed by British citizens living in the EU.

152.   British businesses, workers, pensioners and students have enjoyed huge benefits from freedom of movement inside the EU's Single market over the last 30 years.

153.   The freedom to set up a business in 28 countries.

154.   The ability to retire in any member state.

155.   Pension transferability.

156.   The right to vote in local elections if resident in any member state.

157.   The right to vote in European Parliamentary elections if resident in any member state.

158.   Since Brexit UK residents in the EU have lost the right of freedom of movement across the EU.

159.   Brexit has caused great anxiety and insecurity among UK residents in the EU.

160.   Consular protection from any EU embassy outside the EU.

161.   The right to reside in any EU member state.

162.   The freedom to work in 28 countries without visa and immigration restrictions.

163.   The mutual recognition of professional qualifications has facilitated the free movement of engineers, teachers and doctors across the EU.

164.   The mutual recognition of educational diplomas.

BENEFITS FOR BRITISH TOURISTS IN THE EU

165. No time-consuming border checks for travellers (apart from in the UK).
166. EU competition laws have facilitated the use of EasyJet, Ryanair and other low-cost airlines.
167. The right to receive emergency healthcare in any member state (European Health Insurance Card).
168. EU laws making it easier for British people to buy second homes on the continent.
169. The enhancement of price transparency.
170. The removal of commissions on currency transactions across the Eurozone.
171. Mutual recognition of the common European driving license.
172. The introduction of the European pet passport.
173. The abolition of mobile telephone roaming charges.
174. Thanks to EU membership, Spain, Portugal and Greece have become major destinations for British tourists.
175. Since Brexit, British second homeowners can only stay in an EU country for a maximum continuous period of 90 days.

EU DICTATORSHIP MYTH

176. The notion of an 'EU dictatorship' is a commonly repeated Brexiter myth.
177. As a member of the EU the UK never ceased to be 'an independent sovereign nation.'
178. The UK never lost control of its 'borders, money and laws.'
179. The vast majority of the UK's laws have always been decided by the Westminster parliament.
180. The UK voluntarily agreed to share and pool sovereignty within the EU in many areas where collective action is more effective than decisions made at a national level (e.g. combatting climate change).
181. As a member of NATO the UK has surrendered partial sovereignty in the interests of collective defence. This has never been opposed by the leading Brexiteers.
182. The most powerful EU institution is the European Council which includes the elected heads of national governments.
183. The UK enjoyed veto power in many important EU policy areas.
184. The European Commission is fully accountable to the elected European Parliament.
185. The European Parliament is elected every 5 years.

186. The system of proportional representation for EP elections ensured a much broader and fairer representation than at Westminster (including Green and, ironically, UKIP/Brexit Party MEPs).

187. The EU has no more of a democratic deficit than the UK (unelected House of Lords) and the US (electoral college system).

188. The UK enjoyed an opt out from the single currency.

189. The UK maintained full control of its borders as an island nation and non-member of the Schengen area.

190. From 1985 the UK received a budget rebate equivalent to 66% of its net contribution to the EU budget.

191. Rejoining the EU would not prevent a future Labour government from nationalising the railways or other public services.

192. To become a member of the EU a candidate country must have "stable, functioning democratic institutions" (Copenhagen criteria).

193. The EU helped support and maintain democracy in Spain, Portugal and Greece from the 1970s.

194. The EU has helped support and maintain democracy in the ex-communist states of Eastern Europe since 1989.

195. The EU has strongly opposed actions by the Polish and Hungarian governments which undermine democracy and the rule of law.

196. The EU has strongly supported the democratic government of Ukraine in its resistance to the Russian invasion.

THERESA MAY AND HER BREXIT CABINET IN THEIR OWN WORDS

197. Former Prime Minister Theresa May has never believed in the wisdom of Brexit.

198. "I think being part of a 500m trading bloc is significant for us. I think one of the issues is a lot of people invest here in the UK because it's the UK in Europe". (Theresa May April 2016).

199. "It is not clear why other EU member states would give Britain a better deal than they themselves enjoy". (Theresa May April 2016).

200. "No country or empire in world history has ever been totally sovereign" (Theresa May April 2016).

201. "I do not want the people of Scotland to think that English Eurosceptics put their dislike of Brussels ahead of our bond with Edinburgh and Glasgow". (Theresa May, April 2016).

202. Outside the EU "London's position as the world's leading financial centre would be in danger". (Theresa May, April 2016).

203. "The only thing leaving the EU guarantees is a lost decade for British business)" (Sajid Javid, May 2016).

204. "None of our allies wants us to leave the EU – not Australia, not New Zealand, not Canada, not the US. In fact, the only country, if the truth is told, that would like us to leave the EU is Russia. That should probably tell us all we need to know". (Philip Hammond, March 2016).

205. "A strong NHS needs a strong economy – we should not put that at risk with Brexit". (Jeremy Hunt March 2016).

206. "The Single market is essential to this government's agenda for trade and competitiveness". (David Lidington, 2010).

207. "Conservative Members believe in the Single market because we believe profoundly in the importance of free trade and we want Europe to be at the centre of a free-trading world". (Liam Fox 2013).

BREXITERS IN THEIR OWN WORDS

208. Leading Brexiteers have conveniently forgotten what they once said about the EU, the Single market and the use of referendums.

209. "A democracy that cannot change its mind ceases to be a democracy". (David Davis, 2012).

210. "We should not ask people to vote on a blank sheet of paper and tell them to trust us to fill in the details afterwards". (David Davis, 2002).

211. "You could have two referendums. As it happens, it may make more sense to have the second referendum after the negotiation is completed". (J.R. Mogg, 2011).

212. "There will be no downsize to Brexit, only a considerable upside". (David Davis, October 2016).

213. "Getting out of the EU will be easy and quick – the UK holds most of the cards". (John Redwood, July 2016)

214. "The day after we leave, we hold all the cards and we can choose the path we want". (Michael Gove, April 2016).

215. "Conservative Members believe in the Single market because we believe profoundly in the importance of free trade and we want Europe to be at the centre of a free-trading world". (Liam Fox 2013).

216. "The free trade agreement that we will have to do with the European Union should be one of the easiest in human history". (Liam Fox, 2017).

217. "Brexit was never going to solve our domestic problems". (Nigel Farage, 2017).

218.   The decision to trigger Article 50 without a clear plan was like "putting a gun to your mouth and pulling the trigger". (Leave campaign director, Dominic Cummings, May 2018).

BORIS JOHNSON IN HIS OWN WORDS

219.   Boris Johnson never really believed in Brexit but saw it as an opportunity to realise his ambition to become Tory Prime Minister.

220.   "I'm in favour of the Single market. I want us to be able to trade freely with our European friends and partners". (Boris Johnson, 2013).

221.   "If we left the EU......we would have to recognise that most of our problems are not caused by 'Brussels', but by chronic British short-termism, inadequate management, sloth, low skills, a culture of easy gratification and underinvestment in both human and physical capital and infrastructure". (Boris Johnson 2013).

222.   "I can hardly condemn UKIP as a bunch of boss-eyed, foam-flecked Euro hysterics, when I have been sometimes not far short of boss-eyed, foam-flecked hysteria myself" (Boris Johnson 2015).

223.   "This is a market on our doorstep, ready for further exploitation by British firms. The membership fee seems rather small for all that access. Why are we so determined to turn our back on it?" (Boris Johnson, February 2016).

224.   Leaving the Single market would mean ".... diverting energy from the real problems of this country – low skills, social mobility, low investment...that have nothing to do with Europe". (Boris Johnson, Daily Telegraph, February 2016).

225.   We will "take back control of huge sums of money, 350 million pounds a week, and spend it on our priorities such as the NHS". (Boris Johnson June 2016).

226.   "My policy on cake is pro having it and pro eating it". (Boris Johnson, August 2016).

227.   "There is no plan for no deal because we are going to get a great deal". (Boris Johnson, July 2017).

228.   "Fuck Business". (Boris Johnson, June 2018).

LEAVE CAMPAIGN AND REFERENDUM

229.   The 2016 referendum was advisory and not legally binding.

230.   The 2016 referendum took place without any preparation of how to proceed in the case of a Leave victory.

231.   The 2016 referendum unfairly excluded two categories of people directly impacted by the result: EU citizens resident in the UK and long-term British residents abroad.

232. The referendum made no provision for a "super majority" which is normal international practice when constitutional change is involved.
233. The Leave EU campaign has been found to have violated electoral law.
234. The Leave campaign violated an agreement to suspend campaigning after the murder of Jo Cox.
235. The Leave campaign lied about £350 million a day becoming available for the NHS.
236. The Leave campaign grossly exaggerated the threat of mass immigration (45% of Leave Facebook ads were on immigration).
237. The Leave campaign blatantly exploited xenophobia and anti-immigrant sentiment.
238. The Leave campaign lied about Turkey joining the EU.
239. The Leave campaign lied about a free trade deal with the EU being "the easiest thing in human history".
240. The Leave campaign deliberately misled the public by repeatedly stating that Brexit would not threaten Britain's place in the Single market.
241. The Leave campaign misled the public about the ease of signing trade agreements with the Commonwealth countries and other non-European partners.
242. The referendum result was heavily influenced by a 20-year orchestrated anti-EU campaign led by pro-Brexit tabloid newspapers involving lies, xenophobic propaganda and smear tactics.
243. Leading Brexiteers Arron Banks and Andy Wigmore had a series of undisclosed meetings with Russian officials during the referendum campaign.
244. The UK government tried to block the release of an Intelligence and Security committee report about Russian influence in the Brexit referendum campaign.
245. At the time of the referendum the majority of the public had little or no understanding of the workings of EU institutions (Council, Commission, Parliament etc).
246. At the time of the referendum the majority of the public had little or no understanding of the functioning of the EU Single market.
247. At the time of the referendum the majority of the public had little or no understanding of the functioning of the EU Customs union.
248. At the time of the referendum the majority of the public had little or no understanding of the jurisdiction of the European Court of Justice.
249. At the time of the referendum the public were given little or no explanation of how the Article 50 procedure would work.
250. The referendum was never about ordinary citizens "taking back control". It was a cynical and failed attempt to make peace within the Conservative party,
251. The Leave campaign slogan "take back control" was invented by a hypnotist.

252.   There is now an overwhelming majority of the British public who believe it was a mistake to leave the EU.

WHO WOULD REALLY BENEFIT FROM BREXIT?

253.   Brexit has been driven by a radical right-wing agenda to create a deregulated economy with reduced labour, consumer and environmental protection.

254.   Brexit stops the UK from implementing the EU's tax avoidance directive from 2019.

255.   Brexit favours the economic interests of its super rich backers who keep the majority of their assets offshore.

256.   The Leave campaign was supported and financed by a group of offshore super rich Brexiteers who looked to profit from the outcome ('the bad boys of Brexit').

257.   Brexiter John Redwood has advised investors to take their money out of the UK.

258.   Brexiter Lord Ashcroft has advised UK businesses to set up in Malta.

259.   Brexiter and Britain's richest man Sir James Radcliffe has moved to Monaco to avoid up to £5 in tax.

260.   Radcliffe has added $14 billion to his fortune since 2016.

261.   Brexiter Sir James Dyson is moving his company's HQ to Singapore

262.   Dyson added over $6 billion to his fortune since 2016.

263.   Major Leave campaign donor and hedge fund manager, Crispin Odey, has advised clients to prepare for a recession and higher inflation since the referendum.

264.   US food corporations would stand to benefit from a post-Brexit trade deal by the abolition of EU food quality standards including the use of GMOs, nutritional labelling and chlorine treatment of poultry.

THE FINANCIAL COSTS OF LEAVING

265.   Leaving the EU involved paying a hefty divorce bill of £39 billion.

266.   The pound has lost 15% of its value since the Brexit referendum.

267.   A devalued pound has increased the price of continental holidays for British tourists.

268.   A further devaluation of the pound will cause rising food prices and higher inflation.

269.   The devaluation of the pound has increased the purchase price of second homes in the Eurozone.

270.   The devaluation of the pound has reduced the real value of pensions for UK residents in the EU27.

271.   The UK economy lost up to £35 billion in output in the two years after the referendum as many businesses relocated to the EU27.

272.   Real wages have been falling since the referendum.

273.   The government's own Brexit impact reports predicted a negative economic effect in the event of any Brexit scenario.

274.   The government has attempted to conceal the findings of its negative impact studies.

BREXIT AND JOB LOSSES

275.   3.1 million jobs in the UK are directly linked to exports to the EU.

276.   Over 70,000 retail jobs have disappeared since the referendum.

277.   Construction has also suffered, with 17,000 jobs disappearing in the year until March 2018.

278.   Potential for more manufacturing job losses if UK based firms feel the need to relocate to the EU27.

279.   Uncertainty provoked by Brexit has already caused loss of jobs in the UK car industry.

280.   Airbus, which employs 14,000 workers in the UK, has threatened to move production out of the country.

281.   BMW which employs 7,000 workers in the UK, has moved some of its production out of the country.

282.   Panasonic are moving their European headquarters from London to Amsterdam.

283.   The City of London is predicted to lose at least 5,000 jobs in the financial sector.

THE NEW WILL OF THE PEOPLE

284.   The electorate has changed since June 2016 with new young voters overwhelmingly opposed to Brexit.

285.   Future demographic trends will continue to augment support for EU membership.

286.   Opinion polls since the beginning of 2018 have consistently indicated that a majority of the public are now opposed to Brexit.

287.   Far more people now believe that Brexit was a mistake than those who believe it was a good idea.   The gap continues to grow.

288.   Fishermen and farmers, who voted overwhelmingly for Brexit in 2016, have now turned against it.

289.   The majority of voters in Wales would now support EU membership.

290.   Two thirds of Scottish voters (66%) now support EU membership, compared to 62% in June 2016.

291.   Refusing to recognise that the new 'will of the people' can reverse Brexit is a negation of democracy.

TAKING OUR COUNTRY BACK?

292. Support for Brexit has been based on a false nostalgia to 'take our country back' to a better world that never existed.
293. In the early 1970s before Britain joined the EC average life expectancy was 10 years lower than today.
294. Before the UK joined the EC 20% of children left school with no qualifications.
295. In 1973 only 15% of young people attended university.
296. In 1973 inflation was nearly 10%.
297. In 1973 the UK economy was considered the 'sick man of Europe with living standards 7% below the EC average.
298. Britain was definitely not a better place in the early 1970s before we joined the EU.
299. The supposed benefits of Brexit are based on wishful thinking, delusions of grandeur and a misrepresentation of history and economic reality.

THE EU AND NORTHERN IRELAND

300. The EU acts as a guarantor of the Irish Good Friday Agreement.
301. Northern Ireland has remained a member of both the Single market and the Customs union under the post-Brexit protocol.
302. Northern Ireland's economy has outperformed the rest of the UK since Brexit.
303. Since 1998 the EU has provided more than 1.5 billion euros in funding for Northern Ireland peace projects.
304. Membership of the EU Customs union guarantees a frictionless Irish border.
305. Leaving the EU could compromise peace in Northern Ireland.
306. Leaving the EU could hasten the break-up of the UK by stimulating support for a united Ireland.
307. 69% of the population of Northern Ireland now favour EU membership, compared to 56% in the 2016 referendum.

GIBRALTAR AND THE FALKLAND ISLANDS

308. The EU acts as a guarantor of the special status of Gibraltar.
309. 97% of Gibraltar's residents voted to remain in the EU.
310. Gibraltar has decided to join the EU's Schengen area.
311. Brexit could encourage Spain to press for a modification of Gibraltar's sovereign status.

312.   Leaving the Single market could seriously damage the economy of the British Falkland Islands (94% of fish exports go to the EU).

313.   Leaving the EU is likely to encourage Argentina to renew its claims over the Falkland Islands.

SCIENCE, HEALTH AND RESEARCH INSIDE THE EU

314.   13% of EU budget is earmarked for scientific research and innovation.

315.   The UK received £730 million a year in EU funding for research.

316.   EU funding for UK universities.

317.   Loss of Horizon Europe research funding after the UK left the EU.

318.   UK participation in the EU Galileo satellite system.

319.   UK participation in the EU's Copernicus programme, the world's largest single earth observation programme.

320.   Membership of the European Medicines Agency (EMA) which monitors the quality and safety of medicines.

321.   Cooperation in the peaceful use of nuclear energy as a member of Euratom.

POLICING AND SECURITY

322.   EU cross-country coordination in Europol offers greater protection from terrorists, paedophiles, people traffickers and cyber-crime.

323.   The European common arrest warrant.

324.   Britain loses influence on cross-border policing and security by leaving Europol after Brexit.

CULTURAL BENEFITS OF EU MEMBERSHIP

325.   EU membership helped facilitate intercultural dialogue.

326.   Membership of the EU helped revolutionise eating habits for many people in the UK.

327.   Minority languages such as Welsh and Irish are recognized and protected under EU law.

328.   EU funding for the British film industry.

329.   EU funding for British theatre, music and dance.

330.   Glasgow (1990) and Liverpool (2008) benefitted from being European capitals of culture, stimulating their local economies.

331.   UK membership of the EU promoted the use of the English language which has replaced French as the EU's lingua franca.

HUMAN RIGHTS IN THE EU

332.   Human Rights protected under the EU Charter of Fundamental Rights.

333.   The death penalty can never be reintroduced as it is incompatible with EU membership.

WHO THINKS BREXIT IS A GOOD IDEA?

334.   Brexit has been consistently opposed by the overwhelming majority of leading economists.

335.   Brexit has been consistently opposed by the overwhelming majority of leading environmentalists.

336.   Brexit has been consistently opposed by the overwhelming majority of leading scientists.

337.   Brexit has been opposed by the BMA and the overwhelming majority of NHS doctors.

338.   Brexit has been opposed by the Royal College of Nursing and the overwhelming majority of NHS nurses.

339.   Brexit has been opposed by the overwhelming majority of Britain's trade unions.

340.   None of the other EU member state are considering leaving the EU.

341.   Even Eurosceptic governments in Hungary and Poland support continued EU membership.

342.   No other EU member state is likely to leave the EU in the foreseeable future.

343.   Not a single democratically elected head of government, apart from Trump, has publicly expressed support for Brexit.

344.   In 2016 Brexit was supported by all the EU's extreme right wing xenophobic parties including the French National Front, Italian Lega and Dutch PVV.

345.   Ukraine, Georgia and Moldova now wish to apply for membership.

346.   Only three European countries wish to remain outside the EU Single market: Russia, Belarus and the UK.

347.   Brexit is "the stupidest thing any country has ever done" (Michael Bloomberg, October 2017).

BREXIT WON'T FIX

348.   BREXIT WON'T make the economy grow faster.

349.   BREXIT WON'T help reduce unemployment.

350.   BREXIT WON'T protect our manufacturing base.

351.   BREXIT WON'T protect our financial services industry.

352. BREXIT WON'T lead to better trade deals than we have now.
353. BREXIT WON'T make our firms more globally competitive.
354. BREXIT WON'T reduce poverty.
355. BREXIT WON'T reduce teenage pregnancies.
356. BREXIT WON'T reduce child obesity.
357. BREXIT WON'T help combat drug abuse.
358. BREXIT WON'T lead to a fairer and more equal society.
359. BREXIT WON'T lead to a better funded NHS.
360. BREXIT WON'T improve educational standards.
361. BREXIT WON'T help maintain workers' rights.
362. BREXIT WON'T make the United Kingdom more united.
363. BREXIT WON'T dampen demands for Scottish independence.
364. BREXIT WON'T facilitate peace and harmony in Northern Ireland.
365. BREXIT WON'T help protect the status of Gibraltar.
366. BREXIT WON'T reduce violent crime.
367. BREXIT WON'T reduce tax evasion.
368. BREXIT WON'T help us combat terrorism.
369. BREXIT WON'T reduce net immigration.
370. BREXIT WON'T help us combat global warming.
371. BREXIT WON'T make our beaches cleaner.
372. BREXIT WON'T improve the quality of the air we breathe.
373. BREXIT WON'T enhance consumer protection.
374. BREXIT WON'T improve the quality of our food.
375. BREXIT WON'T enhance data protection.
376. BREXIT WON'T lead to better funded universities.
377. BREXIT WON'T facilitate scientific research.
378. BREXIT WON'T increase Britain's global standing and influence.
379. BREXIT WON'T help us combat Russian military expansion and cyberwarfare.
380. BREXIT WON'T restore our lost imperial greatness.
381. BREXIT WON'T reduce xenophobia and racism.
382. BREXIT WON'T enhance gender equality.
383. BREXIT WON'T help combat homophobia.
384. BREXIT WON'T protect and enhance the rights of UK citizens living in the EU, nor those of EU citizens living in the UK.
385. BREXIT WON'T strengthen our democracy.
386. BREXIT WON'T bring back our lost sovereignty (we never lost it in the first place).

387.   BREXIT WON'T give us more control of our borders (we have never been part of the Schengen area).

388.   BREXIT WON'T give more opportunities to the younger generation.

389.   BREXIT WON'T improve the lives of older people (who voted overwhelmingly to leave the EU).

390.   BREXIT WON'T silence patriotic Rejoiners who are convinced of the overwhelming benefits of EU membership for the people of the UK.

WE JUST DIDN'T NEED TO LEAVE!

391.   The EU will still allow us to drive on the left.

392.   We can still have our road signs in miles and yards.

393.   We can still give baby weights in pounds and ounces.

394.   We can still measure our heights in feet and inches.

395.   We can still weigh ourselves in stones and pounds.

396.   We can still quote temperatures in Fahrenheit.

397.   We can still drink beer in pint measures.

398.   We can still have blue passports and stay in the EU (like Croatia).

399.   Nobody is going to force us to fly EU flags on public buildings

400.   The EU has always allowed our bananas to remain curved!

BREXIT WONT FIX IT!

401.   Leaving the EU is not the solution to any of Britain's social and economic problems.

402.   Leaving the EU will not reduce poverty in the UK.

403.   Leaving the EU is not the solution to growing inequality.

404.   Leaving the EU will not help reduce violent crime.

405.   Leaving the EU will not enhance environmental protection.

406.   Leaving the EU will not protect us from the impact of climate change.

407.   Leaving the EU will not improve the provision of healthcare in the NHS.

408.   Leaving the EU will not help solve the housing crisis.

409.   Leaving the EU will not help raise educational standards.

410.   By pursuing Brexit the government has been paralyzed and has not unable to address any of these other issues.

411.   Leading Brexiteers have stopped arguing that Brexit will bring economic benefits and grudgingly accept the inevitably of short-term collateral damage.

412.   Jacob Rees-Mogg has accepted that Brexit may not bring any tangible benefits for 50 years.

About the person who wrote EU freedoms

Paul Cawthorne graduated from the London School of Economics in 1982. In 1989 he left Thatcherland to become a poll tax exile. Over the last 30 years he has worked as a teacher of history, geography, economics and business management in national and international schools in France, Italy and Switzerland. He is currently living and working near Varese in the north of Italy and impatiently waiting to become an Italian (and EU) citizen.

Paul is married with two children.

Brexit freedoms

Jacob Rees-Moog has given up on his new job on day one. Instead of coming up with Brexit freedoms, he chose to ask Sun readers what they might be. This is both a complete abdication of duty and a clever trick so that he can blame the people for the fact that there are no Brexit freedoms further down the road. Not wishing to be outdone, we decided to write to Jacob to offer some assistance. Please write your own Moggmentum letter to Jake at **jacob.reesmogg.mp@parliament.uk** or **Jacob Rees-Mogg, House of Commons, London SW1A 0AA**. Here is our list of suggestions to help you on your way.

Dear Jake you ask me for laws we can get bak now Brexit is done cos that eu cant stop us well I think there are loads

1. Return football to 4 4 2 format we won the cup
2. Get rid of sweepers
3. Reinstate Bobbi charlton as England captin
4. Freedom to use asbestos in school an hospitals
5. Alf ramsey back in goalfor England
6. War with Russia
7. Ban transfers from forin clubs
8. Install bollards in town tostop those yobs on lectric bikes
9. Jail Johnson no need fer that EU cort of justise
10. The sublimation of women
11. Ban tennis and other poncy games done by thewokeist lefty loosers
12. Bring back syphilis to stop wimmin shaggin around so much in my area
13. Ban forin beer in my local watneys redbarell in all pubs
14. Ban all thoise drinks for the toffs campari perno pimms keep it reel
15. End votes for women youknow that they canntthink look at that Truss
16. Reinstate tortose shell earings forthe missus she likes em
17. Bring back smoking
18. Ban lefty loosers from going on questun time billy bragg blair lammy all that lot
19. Bring back booze cruises
20. Rebuild pebble mill bbc studio
21. 20 benson and hedges a day made compulsory
22. Jail Johnson and Dick

23. Rerun crossroads miss diane as news presenter
24. extended work hours but no more pay
25. Bring back R-Whites lemonade
26. SOVRINTY, SOVRINTY
27. Ban the metre and 564 ml in pubs an clubs
28. Make all single alcohol measures doubles forthesame prize
29. Coal mines re-opened and age of employment reduced to five years
30. Imp all in favour of drinking my pints by the gallon then paying for them in pre 1971 prices of £.S.D.
31. Misogyny to be properly rebranded as a crime aginst MEN as Dominic Raab defined it
32. Sterilise lesbos and gays the only bent thing in brexitbritain should be bananas see also banana
33. Keep killing the illegals on the boats harpoon them if necessary
34. freeports we always ad em of course but now we can say it was that eu lot that stopped us avin em
35. End vacinnation and 5G masks
36. Sack P&O staff with immunity
37. Shit in our rivers
38. Louder vacuum cleaners
39. Incandessent light bulbs and incandessent voters
40. Valerie Anne Brown writes in to say stop the channel crossings Jacob! Take us out of the ECHR or whatever it's called !!
41. Jacob to avoid that nasty tax by the EU
42. Dogs off the leash in parks ban cats
43. More K-TEL albums. Ban byonce adele sheeran and all those woke claptrap poncy screechers an crooners bing crosby and perry homo
44. Reform The Slade cockney rejects and Sham 69 hurry up harry
45. short bak & sides 4 evry1
46. Bare bating as olympik sport
47. Bring bak dog license
48. Woolworths to return and k-tel records on the shelfs
49. The catholic church is the only true faith lets burn any heretics to be decided by the local planning committee this will make things very simple in Englund
50. Evryone to wear size 7 shoes
51. Make trainers £7 a pair
52. Make all the food free for Brexit votersas you promised not calamari tho i dont like it
53. Recalibrate dart boards to use imperial measures

54. Buy British cars
55. World war III putin bankrolled Brexit to destabilise the west now he can walk into eastern Europe to take back control
56. Get rid of mobile phone regs higher prices for all
57. Get rid of citizens rites
58. Get rid of eu driving lisences are lisence is the best one for driving in Europe
59. Shut that french tunnel and the frogs
60. Ban seat belts they are inconvenient whilstwatching videos in the car
61. longer lorries on are roads
62. Bring back the burch
63. Love thy neghbour on prime time TV with Nigel farridge
64. Ssgregate the blacks and chinkeys
65. Get rid of Scotland nothin but trubble
66. feet and inches guineas
67. Stop wimmins sports xept mud resling in bikinis
68. Watrebording for traffic offenders
69. Keg bitter back on menus babysham for the missus
70. Welsh lamb replaced by imports
71. Hormone filled beef to make us beefier
72. Get rid of eu flight compesantion directive
73. Scampi in the basket back in berni inns
74. Bring back hanging for asbos
75. Jail Johnson for shagging that bird
76. Give are Queen life peeridge hang that nonce andrew
77. A banon garlic sauce in restorants
78. Get rid of that Saddam Kahn and the mossies
79. Evryone toget degrees when they leave sckool ban universitys and books
80. Free food gas and electrisity
81. Ban tampons from EU they dont stoptheflow
82. Gypsy camps moved to Guantanamore bay
83. Scrap NHS itonly encourages sick people
84. Ban abortons to cuntrol populashun
85. Woolworths back in towncenters
86. More british kidneys in fraybentos pies rename fraybentos as fraybilston build the factory inthe black cuntry
87. Ban euros in shops

88. Musicians to write more patriotic songs scrap radiohead pink floyd tracy chatman and all that lot
89. Prawn cocktail back
90. Stop porn being shown in muslim churches
91. Bingo halls inevry town bingo
92. Railway time brought bak
93. Ban sesame seeds on burger buns astheyget in my teeth
94. Introduce a rule to stopimports of bentbananas see bananas
95. Ban forin dentists one had a go at my mum aboutnot cleening teeth
96. Chips to be fried in lard
97. Potato famine for irish they eat two much anyway
98. British bangers for British gammon no richmond irish sausages
99. Nigel farridge for chanceseller
100. Strippers in all restaurants ITS NOT SEXIST Jake !!!
101. Sort out endangered species whatever
102. GB News to be national channel
103. english channel, to be guarded by alsations
104. Salute are Queen evry morning
105. Sun university to start the peoples degrees
106. Run are own Eurovision song contest we don't need romaniuns
107. Bring back traditional British diseases consumption lasser fever typhoid polio
108. Speak in propper English like an eastender
109. Ban the word NO better be brexit optimists
110. Boris to replace prince charles
111. Traffic police to carry guns
112. The right to restart the troubles in northern ireland
113. Bring back hangin for sum lefty loosers
114. No more french sticks just hovis
115. Benefit scroungers to work on farms
116. get rid of cycle lanes they clog up towns make, it danger for drivers
117. OAPs to work inprisons they are takers not givers Jake
118. Priti patel torun a restaurant shes no good at the illegals
119. Pitta bread and Chibatter banned innit
120. Unlimited fishing
121. Somerset brie cornish gouda deptford champagne
122. You are English if ur ancestry goes back to 1066 anyone who cant prove residence from that date must leave

123. GMT brought back all over the world
124. Guardian to be closed and all journos locked up
125. Ban the dutch cap french letter and spanish fly
126. Freedom to use leaded petrol
127. ban olives they make me shit green
128. King arthur to come back with the round table best king we ever had
129. Cuntry Manor to be the national wine at £1.29 a quart
130. Let me knockdown my wall inthe consrevation area topark my car
131. Let my husbandget loadsa gov contractcts without having tofill in stipid forms
132. Wars with india china russia africa borneo take bak are cuntries
133. Jail Johnson and Dorries shes aving im ain't she?
134. Pole dancing on ice sat at 7 o clock on the BBC
135. Stop the 24 hour clock cos its confusing
136. england flags on all dwellings
137. Bakelite plugs and round pins
138. Tank tops compulsory
139. Bring page 3 back
140. Women to only be allowed to order cocktales when the. football is on in the pub takes too long
141. Vegans locked up
142. Mines in the channel, stop them dingies gettin to England
143. Fracking
144. Halal meat and veg banned
145. Freedom to grow are own pineapples for english gammon
146. Restart Laker Airways so me and the missus can use my uncles appartmint in Benidorm
147. Green Shield stamps whenever I has to use a bus go shopping or sups a half downa local
148. snickers to be renamed marathon
149. Freedom to leave fish to rot on, the dock of the bay
150. Dyson motors to be as big as we like
151. BSA norton bikes back no yamaha
152. Bring back coal mining
153. 179 000 unnecessary COVID deaths to mask Brexit by BOJO
154. Scampi fries to be made of real scampi
155. Mark francois to be made a lord for services to women
156. Contraception banned for Brits we need more of us to take on the wokeists
157. Bring back wrestling on a Saturday afternoon Boris johnson v big daddy
158. The biggest oneof all sovrinty priceless

159. The blue passport shood onlybe valid for England
160. New austin allegro model and ford anglia
161. Freedom to construct buildings of whatever materials we want to use
162. No right of entry to England for France Holland Germany Italy that will keep them out
163. Public floggings to be reinstated on sunday afternoons
164. Call it the tory brexit berlin wall across the channel are boys are cuntry
165. I can work in kent essex but not normandy dont care whatever
166. Ramsgate to build new martello towers
167. capitol punishment brought back for women who lead men into crime
168. Cheryl Lewin writes in from British Life on facebook saying "Yes he's better than the nobs that r in votes would b better if they got ride of all labour the r scum bags trying t destroy our country"
169. Prince Andrew to come bak
170. Are queen to recover from Euro Covid
171. Bonsai plants to be banned too small oaks better
172. Ian duncan smith can pick his nose in public he used to have to do it in the toilets before brexit

You are the man you can get it done Jake !! take us bak ome tell that Euro lot they can go fcukthemselves

You have six kids as well a man aftermy own hart keep spreading the British seed

Kep the Moggmentum up !!

Pete

Private Eyelines

Whilst we advocate increasing our footprint in mainstream media through articles, letters and comments, another way to deal with fake news is to beat them at their own game. Find our parodies of The Sun, Mail and Express at www.brexitrage.com/gutterpress

So successful have these been that some people think they are written by Private Eye. The editor of Byline Times, Louise Houghton, recommended the approach as a writing style for their authors, having told me and other professional journalists that we could not write properly!

As mentioned previously, satire reaches the parts of us that spreadsheets, facts and data do not. I report anecdotally that our Private Eye pages are read by Leave Voters more that Remainers / Rejoiners, which demonstrates that they reach outside the bubble.

A book of these pages is planned in a short while, so I will not spoil the moment. Each page is supplied with a fact and fiction checker, as people seem to have trouble telling the difference these days in the post-Brexit world!

Andrew under fire from the Palace
essential comment and analysis

 Gove Dick The Truss Patel Smith Windsor

The Telegraph
Gammon's Go To Newspaper

Record drowning of migrants in 2021

Priti Patel celebrated record deaths by drowning at an illegal rave at Downing Street recently.

"Leg irons are ineffective and expensive, so we choose death by drowning as the most effective way to take back control of our borders"

Pretty Patel

Border Force

Anus Horribilis

HRH Queen Elizabeth sent a message of hope :

"2021 was another Brexitus Anus Horribilis. In 2022, I will be jailing Andrew in along with Johnson and the other criminals. Fuck Brexit."

500 NHS Hospitals erected

Miraculous progress by Johnson, who single-handedly erected 200 "Nightingale Hospitals" last night to continue the war on COVID

"The hospitals are to be staffed by fictional children's entertainers. Peppa Pig inspired me to erect the tents"

Sajid Jabbed

Commentary

Boris Johnson is still a fu...king c...nt

NEWS BRIEFING.

Puzzles	20
Obituaries	29
TV listings	31
Weather	32

Book review

Cricket, Racism and me

Geoff Boycott

Lion eats Truss

Lenny the Lion is deported after eating Liz Truss. Truss had declared Lenny to be an "illegal", due to his African heritage

Brexit Buggers Britain

Page 3

Corona Crisis + Brexit Disaster = Britastrophe

THE NORTHERN Farmer

CUMMINGS
OPTICIANS
Barnard Castle 01833 638 094

Fucking Farmers since 24 June 2016   February 2021

IN THIS ISSUE

Britain's sexiest farmer awards

Francois : How to deal with sex pests

Liz Truss : My life with hormone fed beef

Cheese special

Hens and pork, from farm to fork

Looking after pigs and poultry: P32-35

"I fucked a pig as a dare when I was at Eton. Since that time my ambitions have grown exponentially like COVID. now I just fuck the taxpayers by fixing dodgy deals"

Cameron

"It's a shame that the Scots, Welsh and Irish farmers will lose from Brexit but it does not matter that much as I gain so, overall it's a win for me"

Dave

FIRST PRIZE

A year's supply of corn-fed gammon

I want my blue passport!

NEW : The Angus Young Steak Pie

EXTRA BEEF hormones !!!

SECOND PRIZE

Bag O' Sovrinty to compensate for loss of farmers' livelihoods

FURY OVER BREXIT WAR

Transform your life with Gove – Page 7

Even CATS hate you BOJO

DON'T CRY FOR ME, I'M MATT HANCOCK

Brexit microwave failure – Siemens called – Page 3

Have I got POO for EU

Operation Pisspot

Kent County Council to export KENTISH POO to FRANCE, to pay them out for our VOTE to leave

BREXIT CODSUP – ENGLISH cod protest at No 10, crying *"STOP FRYING"* and *"NET ZERO"*. Billy the bass has been interrogated by MI5 for perching in front of No 10. A **BREXITEER** cried *"Don't tell 'em Pike"*.

BE THE BASS – The Royal Navy have rounded up some rogue Sturgeon near Scotch Egg Corner, baiting Boris with faggots launched from catapults, carping *"Och Aye The EU"*.

IRISH POTATO FAMINE II – Priti Patel threatens to re-enact the 1845 Irish Potato Famine. *"Starvin is the new thrivin. I ain't talkin spuds, I'm talkin famin u like"*

LITTLE AND LARGE – Johnson goes to **CURVISSA** to source lounge suit for dinner with Ursula Von der Leyen. *"Sadly we were unable to find his size"* – Carrie, clothing consultant.

Hancock to receive anal probe for prioritising vaccine when Dom wanted to kill OAPs.

Michel Barnier

I bought a copy of My Secret Brexit Diary, an astonishing tale of open-ness, decency and collaboration in decision-making and negotiation by Michel Barnier. His revelations stand in stark contrast to the approach taken by the British government during five years of Brexit negotiations and some comparisons are useful.

The very first act that Michel undertakes is to establish unity of the 27 nations and to assess any important red lines that would destroy unity. In Barnier's words:

"The mission of this small 'commando' unit is to travel through the 27 countries of the union over a period of few weeks establishing personal contacts with ministers and prime ministers so as to find out where each of them draws their red lines and, in broad terms to construct our own line of negotiation on the basis of four first principles that I will, from now on, recite to each of my interlocutors.

First, there can be no negotiations until we receive notification from the British government. In the Council, the 27 member states have been very clear on this point.

Second, we will only succeed in this negotiation by building and maintaining very strong unity between the 27 member states.

Third, no EU country should find itself in a position where it has less say than a country outside the Union.

And finally, no country outside the Union should be given a veto on, or even the right to intervene in, the decision-making process of the 27.

These are the key points to which we will hold fast throughout our work, and which are the conditions for its success."

In stark contrast, the very first act of the British government is for Dr Liam Fox to tell a lie, by suggesting that the European Commission was responsible for David Cameron's loss of the referendum. Michel Barnier reflects:

"Fox says 'Our enemy is the Commission, which wants to be forgiven for making Cameron lose. Many of the 27 need us'.

I am told that these remarks which have been reported to me, were made yesterday in private before a group of businessmen in London by UK Trade Minister Liam Fox. This Scottish MP, a former defence minister for David Cameron and a former candidate for the conservative leadership, losing to Theresa May, is obviously at the forefront when it comes to imagining the future of trade relations between the UK and the EU. But first of all, Brexit must be achieved, and he is in favour of a fast-track agenda. That, however, is no reason to propagate such untruths.

So it was the Commission that lost David Cameron the election? This is to pass over in silence, just a little too quickly, the 'new settlement' agreed with him at the European Council on 18 - 19 February 2016, in the midst of the migrant crisis – a settlement that further strengthened the UK's special status within the Union. In the end it wasn't enough to prevent Brexit, but not for the lack of trying ...

It is also to forget that, if all European leaders voluntarily kept silent throughout the referendum campaign, they did so at the express request of the British Prime Minister. According to him, any intervention by 'Brussels technocrats' or foreign leaders would have been immediately exploited by the Brexiteers ...

In any case, Liam Fox's statement only strengthens my determination: we must secure and consolidate the unity of the 27 as rapidly as possible."

I sense a twinge of regret in Barnier's penultimate statement, that the European Union maintain silence during our referendum process when it may have been wiser to speak out and promote the benefits of the union. We are currently beginning to find out just what these were, somewhat too late to do anything about it in the short term. We must remove the Brexit culture carriers from government and Re-Boot Britain, with the eventual ambition of applying to join anew.

"This book pulls no punches. The path is clear.
We have to be brave enough to take it."
Sir Terry Leahy, CEO of Tesco (1997–2011)

BRITANNIA UNHINGED

GLOBAL LESSONS FOR GROWTH AND PROSPERITY

KWASI KWARTENG MP | PRITI PATEL MP
| DOMINIC RAAB MP |
CHRIS SKIDMORE MP | ELIZABETH TRUSS MP

Useful links

Re-Boot Britain / Rage Against The Brexit Machine (RATBM)

Website :   www.brexitrage.com

Facebook :   www.facebook.com/brexitrage
                        www.facebook.com/groups/RATBM

EU Tube :   www.youtube.com/academyofrock Find the EU Tube playlist

Go Fund Me :   www.gofundme.com/f/reboot-britain

Patreon :   www.patreon.com/rebootbritain

Twitter :   @brexitrage @academyofrock @Rebootkent

RATBM music on Bandcamp: www.academy-of-rock.bandcamp.com/

RATBM music on Apple Music / iTunes / Amazon / Spotify : Search on Google with the terms Rage Against The Brexit Machine iTunes etc.

True and Fair Party : Gina Miller's new party www.trueandfair.co.uk

The Good Law Project : Conducts legal actions against illegal acts by HM government www.goodlawproject.org

Professor A C Grayling : Philosopher and consistent anti Brexit thinker www.acgrayling.com

The Rejoin Party : A political party with one vision www.therejoineuparty.com

A different bias : Phil Moorhouse's personal video blog on You Tube

Poems Against the Brexit Machine : A collective book of poetry to reach people's hearts www.brexitrage.com

Voices for Europe : A pan Remain group aimed at bringing together the disparate Remain groups www.voicesforEurope.com

EU Flag Mafia : A grass roots enterprise that systematically surprises our government with unusual stunts that punch well above their weight www.euflagmafia.com

Professor Chris Grey : Well respected academic www.chrisgreybrexitblog.blogspot.com

By Donkeys : Large scale video displays and billboard adverts that reach people's heads and hearts – very focused and effective www.ledbydonkeys.org

Prof Michael Dougan : Broadcaster and writer on a range of topics relating to Brexit www.liverpool.ac.uk/law/staff/michael-dougan

The Federal Trust : Long term organisation devoted to education and research on a federal Europe www.fedtrust.co.uk

The Tony Blair Institute – Do remember to listen without prejudice as George Michael pointed out https://institute.global

Graham Bishop : Graham is a finance professional who writes on European Affairs and Brexit impacts www.grahambishop.com

James O'Brien : LBC Radio Host and author of several books on Brexit www.penguin.co.uk/authors/1083269/james-o-brien.html

Maximillien Robespierre : Personal video blog on You Tube

Bremain in Spain : Led by Sue Wilson OBE www.bremaininspain.com

The Rejoin Register : Network organisation run by Gareth Steele and Alex Gunter of UKPEN www.rejoinregister.org/

Scientists for EU : The brainchild of Dr Mike Galsworthy https://www.scientistsforeu.uk

Best for Britain : Campaigning group https://www.bestforbritain.org

Brexit Carnage : Daily news run by journalist Phil Waller www.brexitcarnage.org

Stay European : Grassroots campaigning organisation. Stay European have a book called Routes to Rejoin www.stayeuropean.org

My EU : Find out what the EU has done in your area www.myeu.uk

Be properly dressed : EU style and fashion items www.ihearteu.co.uk

Cold War Steve : Brilliant satirical artworks www.coldwarsteve.com

A Better Britain in a Better Europe for a Better World

www.brexitrage.com

Index

Printed in Great Britain
by Amazon

78588915R00201